FRANCISCO ROMERO was Professor of Philosophy and Metaphysics at the University of La Plata and at the University of Buenos Aires. In keeping with his humanist views, he resigned his professorship in protest against the Perón regime in 1946; he resumed the post in 1955, and remained active as a teacher and writer until his death in 1962. *Teoría del hombre* was originally published in 1952. Before his death Romero prepared the Prologue for the present English edition.

His work shows the influence of Husserl, Hartmann, and Dilthey. His chief concern was to develop a philosophical position which would provide a context for the interpretation of man in his cultural situation. Neither the positivistic or reductive naturalistic systems, he believed, could provide a satisfactory basis for humanism. His own thought was aimed at providing such a basis without depending upon "mere abstractions or other-worldly concerns."

The present volume was translated, largely in Romero's own library, by William F. Cooper, Assistant Professor of Philosophy, Lycoming College, who has also done research on Romero's work in general and has lived in Argentina for extended periods. The Foreword, by Professor William J. Kilgore of Baylor University, provides an introduction to Romero's work and assesses his place in twentieth-century philosophy.

Francisco Romero (1891-1962) was probably the most influential of Latin-American philosophers. This volume is a translation of the central work in his fifteen published books, and serves as the best introduction to his thought.

Romero sought to develop a "philosophical anthropology" which would provide a rigorous approach to the great philosophical questions about man. He analyzes the intentional or objectifying consciousness which, he maintains, distinguishes man from the animals. In doing so he draws a strict distinction between the merely intentional attitude, which is fundamentally egotistic because it is concerned with the subject's own interest, and the spiritual attitude, which is oriented purely and disinterestedly toward objects, in cognition as well as in the religious, ethical, or aesthetic sense.

The basic duality and tension between these two modes confer a special quality on human life. The final part of the book deals with aspects of such phenomena as masking, justification, self-consciousness, sociability, historicity, and meaning. A novel theory of value is also proposed.

THEORY OF
MAN

—

THEORY
MOFAN
BY
FRANCISCO ROMERO

Translated by
WILLIAM F. COOPER, with an Introduction by
WILLIAM J. KILGORE

UNIVERSITY OF CALIFORNIA PRESS
BERKELEY AND LOS ANGELES · 1964

UNIVERSITY OF CALIFORNIA PRESS
BERKELEY AND LOS ANGELES
CALIFORNIA

CAMBRIDGE UNIVERSITY PRESS
LONDON
ENGLAND

Published with the assistance of a grant
from The Rockefeller Foundation

Library of Congress Catalog Card Number: 64-22285
Designed by William Snyder
Printed in the United States of America

To Anneliese

Translator's
Acknowledgment

The English version of *Teoría del hombre*, Francisco Romero's major work, was begun and largely completed through the initiative and support of Professors David Bidney and Newton P. Stallknecht of Indiana University. In addition to this encouragement, they provided valuable editorial suggestions, as did Professors Henry B. Veatch and Harvey L. Johnson, also of Indiana University, and Professor W. J. Kilgore, of Baylor University. I am indeed grateful to each of them for their contributions to this edition.

Much of the preliminary editing was done by Mrs. Lorna Morey, Mrs. Nancy Gaines, and Mr. Dale M. Blount. The preparation of the manuscript in its final typewritten form was the task of Mrs. Mary Fiscus and Mr. John D. Sowell. I deeply appreciate the long hours each of them gave to the translation. The index was prepared with assistance from the Department of Philosophy of Lycoming College.

Both Mr. Juan Carlos Torchia Estrada of Washington, D. C., and Mr. Max E. Knight of the Editorial Department of the University of California Press have edited the entire manuscript, a very tedious job yet one that has improved the quality of the translation immeasurably. To them is due a very special word of thanks.

To Professor D. J. Bowden of the Indiana School of Religion I am indebted for generously providing the study space in which my own work was done.

My wife has been very kind to me and extremely patient with the circumstances related to the translating task. Her support and encouragement have been unfailing. These words could never be more than mere tokens of my gratitude to her.

William F. Cooper
Lycoming College

CONTENTS

An Introduction to the Philosophy of Francisco Romero

Francisco Romero had attained a generally recognized stature as the dean of Ibero-American philosophers at the time of his death in 1962. Although he was self-taught in philosophy, he demonstrates superior competence as a professional philosopher in dealing critically with philosophical problems in the general tradition of Husserl, Max Scheler, and Nicolai Hartmann. He formulated his philosophical position with the purpose of providing a theoretical background for the development of creativity, freedom, and responsibility in man's cultural and social activities. Although he sought to develop a position consistent with the intellectual achievements of contemporary scientific investigation, he opposed "scientism" with its "deterministic, atomistic, and mechanistic views" of man's highest moral, aesthetic, mental, and spiritual achievements. With his strong emphasis upon freedom, he vigorously combatted, through philosophical discussion as well as personal participation, fascistic and totalitarian tendencies in dictatorial political regimes.

Romero sought to develop a philosophy that had both theoretical rigor and practical relevance. Although philosophical inquiry and criticism was to be pursued for its own sake and not as a prop for value preferences, it also was to provide a context and a means for evaluating and resolving problems in the social matrix in which it participated. He has developed a critical and reasonably consistent philosophical position through written dialogue related to some of the basic issues of contemporary philosophical discussion, particularly those concerned with philosophical anthropology and the philosophy of culture.

The development of philosophical ideas in Latin America has tended to reflect and reinterpret some of the major philosophical currents in Europe. During the colonial period philosophical scholasticism predominated, oriented toward such writers as Thomas Aquinas, Duns Scotus, and Francisco Suarez. These traditions have continued in some circles until the present. During the period of the revolutions against Spain, beginning about 1810, the writers of the Enlightenment Rousseau, Locke, Voltaire, and Condillac exerted a noticeable influence. In the second quarter of the nineteenth century, Saint-Simon, Condorcet, the French Ideologues including Cabanis and Destutt de Tracy, and, to a lesser degree, Bentham and Thomas Reid were major influences on Latin American philosophical development. About the middle of the nineteenth century, the eclecticism of Cousin was widely accepted. During the last quarter of the nineteenth century and extending beyond the first decade in the twentieth century, the Positivism of Comte and the naturalism of Spencer (also called Positivism in Latin America) exercised a wide influence in philosophic, educational, and other circles. In the second decade of the twentieth century, a strong reaction arose throughout Latin America against Positivism and the deterministic, atomistic, and mechanistic views associated with it. The philosophy of Bergson was used widely as a base for criticizing the Positivism of the intellectuals who frequently were identified with the established political and social order. More recently the influence of a number of other European philosophers has been evident. As for philosophical thought in the United States, little of it influenced Latin America before 1950, except for William James, and to a more limited extent Dewey, Brightman, and Whitehead.

Francisco Romero was born in Seville, Spain, in 1891, and immigrated to Argentina in 1904. He began a military career with the Argentine army in 1910 and retired with the rank of major in 1931. During the period of his secondary education and in the Military College of Buenos Aires, he showed an active interest and ability in writing. He began to publish articles in literary criticism in 1916. A close friendship with the Argentine philosopher

Alejandro Korn began in 1923. The two had many cultural attitudes and intellectual interests in common. Throughout, their writings emphasize freedom, creativity, and human dignity. Upon his retirement from military service in 1931 Romero succeeded Korn in his professorships at the universities of La Plata and Buenos Aires. During the remaining thirty-one years of his professional activity, Romero published numerous articles and books. He also was editor of the philosophical publications of the publisher Losada, and was in charge of the Alejandro Korn Chair in the Colegio Libre de Estudios Superiores. He received major literary honors and professional recognition both in Argentina and abroad. In 1946 he resigned his university positions as a result of strong political differences with the Peronist government. He resumed his university affiliations in 1955 and remained active as a teacher and writer until his death in 1962.

Through the influence of his writing, his teaching, and his editorial work he encouraged the development of original work in philosophy, the study of the history of the development of philosophical ideas in Latin-America, and the analysis and criticism of problems related to the philosophy of culture. His earlier writings in philosophy were primarily critical essays on the works of contemporaries, his later writings developed more his own position. His *Teoría del hombre* [1] is the most thorough and systematic presentation of his treatment of problems in philosophy. Before and even after the publication of this work some critics of his writings claimed that his specialization in the development of European philosophy since Kant was somewhat at the cost of a thorough grounding in Greek, medieval, and early modern philosophy, that his writings were essays on the philosophical ideas of other men in which he was more successful in setting forth unresolved problems in their approach than in pointing to a satisfactory resolution of such problems, that he had not developed a systematic approach of his own philosophical position, and that his writings were an expression of an intellectual restlessness struggling without complete satisfaction to find an adequate interpretation of the cultural situation of his day.

[1] Francisco Romero, *Teoría del hombre* (Buenos Aires: Editorial Losada, 1952).

For Romero philosophical inquiry is an expression of the cultural activity of man. The view that the task of the philosopher is merely to investigate ultimate and theoretical questions artificially proposed by philosophical technicians fails to relate philosophical activity to its cultural matrix. In some senses the problems studied by philosophers are probing questions related to the theoretical foundations of value judgments, knowledge claims, and the structure and interrelatedness of experience. There is need to recognize, as Dilthey and others point out, the cultural context in which such problems arise and the life situations in which they participate.[2] Philosophical activity represents a movement within cultural activity in which critical inquiry is focused on the cultural activity itself "in order to understand and to evaluate it, to discover its sources, clarify its goals, and to stimulate its meaning."[3] It is to clarify, criticize, and evaluate cultural processes exemplified in science, technology, literature, art, customs, religion, government, and other social institutions. It is directed toward the critical appraisal of the grounds for belief in supporting such activities, of the goals or objectives of such activities, and of the adequacy or consistency of means as these relate foundational beliefs to goal-directed activity.

For Romero philosophical activity frequently takes the form of a dialogue in a cultural situation in which a philosopher evaluates and criticizes the ideas of others, and proposes his own critical views which in turn are appraised by others. Philosophers are not expected to be in complete agreement; and their philosophical positions should be set forth in a critical and consistent manner. Both Romero and Korn insist that the right to doubt is a basic privilege of the philosopher. For such an interchange of ideas to be significant, an open and corrigible position is prerequisite. Dogmatism, closed positions, and claims to certainty where one is limited to probabilities are vices which a philosopher is to avoid. Philosophical activity can be carried out satisfactorily only in a climate of freedom of inquiry, of interpretation, and of expression. Any ideological restraints imposed upon a philosopher's search for an adequate interpretation of his culture not only distorts his expres-

---

[2] Francisco Romero, *Filósofos y problemas* (Buenos Aires: Editorial Losada, 1947), pp. 146–150.
[3] *Ibid.*

sion of his own critical evaluations but jeopardizes the acceptance of his sound judgments by the threat of their failure to be authentic. Philosophical activity is not only a consequence of cultural freedom but its authentic development supports and enhances the further development of freedom.

At the same time Romero insisted that the content of a philosophical work should be stated in objective terms with the conclusions supported and justified by public evidence and sound arguments.[4]

Romero shared the view with many other Latin American philosophers that a philosophical vocation should not be limited to an ivory tower, but rather the value judgments commended in his philosophic activity should be expressed and tested in the wider cultural participation by the philosopher himself. A philosophical position not only should be supported by evidence that is critical, public, and objective but it also should be experiential, personal, and authentic. Romero, through his influence and actions, sought actively to support those cultural forces and movements which he believed to be structured to further the development of human creativity and freedom. His opposition to the application of positivistic theories of education with their "deterministic and mechanistic" interpretations of human behavior was a result of his strong support for the study of liberal-arts types of programs in the Argentine universities and for the furtherance of democratically oriented institutions. He was a leader among Argentine professors who resisted totalitarian tendencies as expressed in Peronism. He regarded such tendencies as threats to the attainment of the fullest expressions of life on its highest level.

Romero proposes to develop a humanistic philosophy concerned with the maximum realization of commendable human values. The basic structure and categories of his philosophical system provide a theoretical context adaptable to the achievement of this type of "sound humanism." Both positivistic and reductive naturalistic systems impoverish the "higher meanings and possibilities of the human spirit" and thereby fail to provide a satisfactory basis for humanism. He also rejects humanistic approaches that depend

---

[4] Francisco Romero, "Confesiones filosóficas" in *Estudio de historia de las ideas* (Buenos Aires: Editorial Losada, 1953) , p. 164.

upon "mere abstractions or other worldly concerns." Any humanism acceptable to him will be consistent with the kinds of values
supported by the Renaissance and by the spiritual aspirations of
man.

Romero's humanism is directed toward the fullest qualitative
realization of the possibilities of human life on the level of spirit.
The distinguishing predicates of this level of being are universality
and disinterestedness as these are exemplified in perceiving, conceiving, or acting. The culminating activities of this level are
found in man's active search for satisfying answers to the questions
of what he ought to be and what he ought to appreciate or value.
Human activity on this level expresses a moral attitude in which
both particularism is renounced and a radical objectivism is expressed through altruistic behavior.

Romero provides philosophical justification for his conclusions
by building upon foundations suggested by Edmund Husserl,
Wilhelm Dilthey, Henri Bergson, Nicolai Hartmann, Martin
Heidegger, Max Scheler, Alejandro Korn, and Ortega y Gasset. By
following a phenomenological method, suggested in part by Husserl, Romero examines the contents of experience, interpreted
broadly as the content of consciousness, and discovers, like Nicolai
Hartmann, four identifiable structures or levels.[5] Hartmann's
divisions include a spatial outer world, differentiated into the
inanimate and animate levels; and a nonspatial world, differentiated into the psychic and spiritual. Romero distinguishes a
spatio-temporal order comprising the inorganic and organic structures and a temporal order comprising the intentional and spiritual structures. Another division proposes a naturalistic order
which includes the inorganic, organic, and intentional levels; and
a spiritual order.

In the interpretation of these structures of reality, several predicates apply to relations both within and among these levels. Reality
for Romero signifies the continuing interrelated unity actively
binding together the objects within and among these structural
levels. Transcendence also is a relation applicable both within and
among the different levels. It refers to the emergence of qualitative

[5] Francisco Romero, *Papeles para una filosofía* (Buenos Aires: Editorial
Losada, 1945), p. 29.

distinctions within the natural and spiritual orders; these distinctions transcend the original conditions from which they develop by the emergence of something new requiring new predicates not applicable to the objects lower in the scale. Romero emphasizes that temporality is applicable to all levels of transcendence including the level of the spirit. An object transcends itself for Romero by its capacity to "radiate its action" and to exercise "influence beyond itself." Some of his critics have not been satisfied with his use of this notion of transcendence. The notion is basic throughout Romero's thought, making possible the differentiations within and among different levels of reality. Although the level of spirit attains to complete transcendence, a consistent application of the notion of transcendence appears to imply some level that would transcend the level of spirit with the possible introduction of an infinite regress. However, Romero proposes to avoid this difficulty by characterizing the level of the spirit as *absolute* transcendence, thereby eliminating in his system further possibilities of transcendence.

Romero, similar to Bergson and Korn, emphasizes the dynamic character of experience. Movement, becoming, impetus, characterizes all four structures of reality.[6] The impetus toward transcendence increases in intensity, and its possible multiple forms of expression from the lower to the higher levels culminate in the structure of spirit. There also is operative a restraint toward immanence, which is a tendency toward regression to lower levels. Pure immanence would be a mere abstraction in his views, because it lacks an impetus for transcendence, which is characteristic of all four structures of reality, it would be analogous to a corpse or skeleton. Immanence can be viewed not only as a stricture limiting transcendence but also as a focal point from which transcendence breaks forth (p. 180) . In this regard immanence also may be compared partly to the notion of potentiality in Aristotelianism representing a capacity for development that has not yet occurred.

The notion of structure is fundamental in the metaphysical position of Romero. Structure is contrasted with a mere aggregate of parts.[7] Structure has its base in the parts composing it, but the

[6] *Ibid.,* p. 28.
[7] *Papeles,* p. 11.

emergence of structure presents a novel factor irreducible to the activity of the parts from which it arose. The appearance of new structure is an instance of transcendence in which the parts function in a new relationship to create something novel. Romero uses this organic notion of structure not only to interpret transcendence but also to criticize metaphysical positions characterized as "atomistic" or "mechanistic."

In his notion of "colonization" Romero refers to the use by higher structures of lesser structures to develop more complex functions. The emerging structures add to the elements and organization of the existing structures in constituting a structure transcending the original materials. The function of the colonizing emergent structure is irreducible to the colonized structures from which it emerges. Rather its norms and ends are imposed on the colonized structures "enslaving and governing" these more elementary forms which function as its matrix and from which it continues to receive nourishment. Thus, the organic level subjects the inorganic level to its own functions using the inorganic structures to promote the continuation of life according to the norms found in the organic level (p. 67). The new colonizing forms continuously depend upon the forms colonized throughout the different levels of reality. The organic is dependent upon the inorganic, the intentional upon the organic, and the spiritual upon the intentional.

Each level has properties appropriate to its functions. The inorganic level is characterized particularly by gravitational force, by a limited amount of transcendent activity tending to be limited to the acting source, and by a stability and regularity tending themselves to be interpreted through rigorously formulated physical laws. The organic level is characterized by preintentional and nonconscious psychic and graded activities that serve as instruments of regulation and adaptation for the individual organism. Rapid acceleration of colonizing activities characterize this level. Romero, following Karl Sapper and Wilhelm Roux, finds additional activities of this level to be incorporation (of foreign materials), assimilation, nutrition, elimination, continuing identity, growth, spontaneous movements, reproduction, hereditary transmission, self-regulation, and individuality of members (p. 64).

On the merely animalistic level the psychic is a vital and instrumental function serving the needs of the organism. In human behavior this psychic activity becomes more complex and signifies the emergence of the level of consciousness, which, as in Brentano and Husserl, involves a subject's consciousness of an object. The psychic states of the organic level become objects of consciousness on the intentional level. The self emerges on this level through the appearance of a subject conscious of an object, and of an object intended by a subject. A subject is conscious of an object only as he knows, wills, or feels the object. The subject and object relationships emerge together and create this new structure on the intentional level (p. 10). The subject grows through new experience which consists in the enlargement and sharper differentiation of objects in the environment. Through the formation of terminology involving classes of objects the self is increasingly able to apprehend and to conceptualize its world and to exercise a degree of control over it through emotional and voluntary acts.[8]

In the development of the intentional level, the cognitive function takes precedence over the will and feeling in consciousness. The preintentional emotional and impulsive states evolve into intentional acts on the level of consciousness through the cognition of objects toward which the conative and affective activities of the subject are directed or projected (p. 23). On the organic level a state is merely lived or endured, but on the intentional level it becomes an object of consciousness and is characterized in certain ways by an act of judgment. Individuality is developed most completely on the intentional level. Whereas the identifying characteristics of individuality or separateness, unity, continuity, and partial autonomy are found to some degree on lower levels, individuality is developed more completely on the intentional level, emerging with more complete and conscious expression and the greater coördination of parts and "centers of fuller harmony and more complete unification of functions (p. 79)."

The self achieves its identity as a center which controls acts. Its confrontation with an objective order to be acted upon both presupposes the development of language and intelligence and

[8] Francisco Romero, *Ortega y Gasset y el problema de la jefatura espiritual* (Buenos Aires: Editorial Losada, 1960), p. 91.

motivates their development. The intelligence analyzes, organizes, and synthesizes its cognitive, affective, and conative materials with a freedom of movement and capacity for innovation.[9] As a subject of intentional acts, the self is a psychic-physical being taking its place alongside other natural objects and is describable by the characteristics appropriate to this order.

As an intentional being man creates his culture and is created by it (p. 117). The whole of what man objectively creates is culture. This includes his language, instruments, law, government, technology, science, literature, art, and other economic and social institutions. These aspects of culture vary in their degree of dominance in different periods and places so that in a particular context one type of cultural activity, such as religion or technology, may take precedence over the others and make them subservient to it.

Although "mere intentionality" is on the plane of the natural and is unique to man, it is the bridge to the spiritual. As the subject of acts on the intentional level, the self logically precedes the higher feelings of man or his ability to act voluntarily and freely. His higher feelings and his freedom are possible only because he is a self or a subject. The possibility of exemplifying an attitude on the spiritual level is dependent upon the ability of the self both to actualize and to sublimate itself.[10] An adequate appraisal of man's activities as a person or spiritual being require a different set of categories from those applicable to the naturalistic level. Whereas his spiritual activities have the intentional level as a basis for their development, the understanding of the distinctively human requires the spiritual level with its own set of interpretive terms to account for the distinctively personal. As an intentional being, man, as an individual, confronts the world as something given to him, as an object to dominate, control, and exploit for its material benefits. As a spiritual being, man, as a person, accepts his responsibility for his ordering the world according to the ends he believes to be worthy of achievement. This capacity for both levels, the natural and the spiritual, accounts for the duality of man. Historical development exemplifies the increasing control over the

[9] *Ibid.*
[10] *Ibid.*, p. 92.

natural in the actualization of man's spiritual capacities. In this sense, history is for Romero, as it is for Korn, a continuing and sometimes successful struggle for freedom against the coercive domination of man by external forces in his environment and by internal forces based on ignorance, violence, and egoism. Romero also is in fundamental agreement with other recent Latin American philosophers like Deustua, Korn, Vaz Ferreira, Caso, and Vasconcelos in emphasizing that the attainment of man's unique possibilities as a person is possible only by the growth of freedom through conflict, in which the control over the natural world and the order in the political and social world have as their goals man's development, refinement, and creative expression of his unique spiritual capacities.

Although the level of the activity of spirit is basically characterized by the "projection of a subject toward its object," it also has distinguishable but not separable expressions of its activities. Absolute objectivity is concerned with the object for its own sake without regard to the subjective interests of the subject. Universality is the overcoming of particularity through projection toward the object for its own sake and through striving for completeness in cognitive, moral, aesthetic, and social activities (p. 164) . Freedom is the activity both of avoiding the particularity and constriction of the natural order and of achieving the autonomy of the spiritual level in its conflict with the intentional level. Unity on the spiritual level is the bond shared by spiritual subjects directed toward universalized interests in intellectual, moral, aesthetic, and social activities. The historicity of spirit consists in its originating, developing, and flourishing within a historical process. Objective interest and respect for all that is characterize the spiritual level through the concern to understand objects for what they are, in their capacity to serve as instruments to be manipulated in the satisfaction of individual desires. Spiritual responsibility is the carrying out by a spiritual subject of the obligations he feels toward himself and toward other persons in the development of the complete expression of the spiritual level of existence. Self-consciousness on the spiritual level differs from self-consciousness on the intentional level by its activity in becoming a center and agent for the realization of the colonization of other levels of existence in the achievement of the fullest expression of the level of the spiritual. Absolute transcendence consists in a spiritual subject directing his activities toward the development of objects so that they render their most complete function in the attainment of the fullest expression of the spiritual level. "Absolute transcendence and full objectivity become the same thing" (p. 172).

The movement toward transcendence culminates in the human person who not only possesses meaning for himself but also constructs meaning for the cosmos, both by his efforts, shared publicly in a community, to attain a spiritual order in the cosmos and by his discovery in the cosmos of a continuous process which culminates on the spiritual plane.[11] This ideal of the human person seeks to achieve the higher spiritual meanings of personality not as something that mechanically works itself out in the natural order but rather as a goal toward which to struggle is a continuing and unfinished task.

The person, for Romero, "is pure activity," the unity of the spiritual acts of a subject. The manifestation of the person consists both in a particular "complex of spiritual attitudes" and as an "ideal center from which these attitudes radiate." [12] He accepts the thesis of Ortega y Gasset that human activity is essentially purposive and, through decision, is directed toward the creation of a future state of affairs. He commends Fichte's notion that the self is "pure action, pure freedom; it is not substance nor the support of the acts, rather it is the naked act." [13] While purposive activity is possible on both levels, the intentional and spiritual, the former is characterized by the changeableness and variation of passing interests whereas the latter is characterized by the long-range planning, resoluteness in carrying forward such plans "against wind and sea," and the formulation of ample and extended goals of endeavor for an entire lifetime.[14] In his spiritual activity the person colonizes the structures created on the intentional level to achieve transcendence by "radiating his actions" and "extending his influence" to

[11] *Ibid.*, p. 95.
[12] Francisco Romero, *Filosofía de la persona* (Buenos Aires: Editorial Losada, 1944), p. 11.
[13] Francisco Romero, *Ideas y figuras* (Buenos Aires: Editorial Losada, 1949), p. 55.
[14] *Filosofía de la persona*, p. 24.

attain an active community that struggles to bring to the spiritual level the total activities of the human community in the moral, religious, aesthetic, and legal spheres. Romero does not want to insist that each individual human being in each historical period participated in this spiritual level of experience, but he does insist that this capacity in man has been active from the beginning of human history (pp. 207–208).

Romero's interpretation of the spiritual represents both a development and a criticism of Max Scheler's position. Romero considered Max Scheler's work, *Man's Place in Nature,* as "the most convincing doctrine of man and of the spiritual that I know." [15] Scheler characterizes the spiritual as objectivity, freedom, self-consciousness, and insubstantiality. Romero characterizes the spiritual as absolute objectivity, freedom, self-consciousness, insubstantiality, universality, activity, distinterestedness, responsibility, historicity, and transcendence. The activity of spirit is grounded in impulse for Scheler and intentionality for Romero. In Scheler it is life that realizes the spirit, whereas in Romero the spirit as order and harmony subjects life and intentionality to its own procedures. In Scheler there is a realization in man of the spiritual principle in the universe, man being a partial center of its impulses and spirituality. As man becomes conscious of the activity of spirit in him, the primordial being becomes conscious of himself in man. The meaning of life for man is to be found in this developing awareness of the nontemporal spirit in him. Romero has no deity or all-pervasive spirit in the universe. Spirit emerges from lower levels deriving its structure from the intentional level but transcending this through its quality and range of activity. Meaning in life is expressed through acceptance of responsibility in the maximum use of all levels of reality for the highest possible attainment of spiritual activity, which always is characterized by temporality.

Romero's and Hartmann's interpretations of levels of reality disclose significant contrasts as well as similarities. Both thinkers propose four different structures of reality with the succeeding or higher levels dependent upon the lower levels, which also exercise a limited determinism upon the higher levels. They recognize

[15] *Papeles,* p. 13.

degrees of autonomy or independence in the higher levels insisting that an adequate interpretation of the functions of the higher levels requires new concepts and categories inexplicable by or irreducible to the concepts or categories employed in the explanation and interpretation of the lower levels of reality. Romero grants a larger degree of independence to the higher levels and insists more on the legitimacy of the interpretation of the activities of the higher level in terms applicable primarily to its own structure. Romero acknowledges with Hartmann the dependence of the higher levels upon the lower but places greater emphasis on autonomy by granting the spiritual subject absolute transcendence in the completion of its activities. The level of the spirit becomes stronger for Romero than for Hartmann. For Romero the impetus active throughout the levels of reality is toward transcendence so that in conflicts between the lower and higher levels the short-term advantage in a particular conflict rests with the lower levels but the long-term advantage with the higher levels.

Value for Romero is the measure of transcendence of an entity or activity. The greater the transcendence the higher the value and the reality. He rejects the views that values are either subjective attitudes, whether of an individual or of a culture, or a quality imposed upon acts or entities. There are both spiritual and non-spiritual values, the former being absolute and the latter relative. Relative value involves limited transcendence, absolute value complete transcendence. For example, truth as a value is relative on the intentional level and absolute on the spiritual level. On the intentional level truth is sought for its use as an instrument in the realization of other ends whereas on the spiritual level it is sought purely for its own sake (p. 191). Likewise, on the intentional level there are moral obligations which are to be directed toward the attainment of the greater transcendent possibilities both on the intentional and lesser levels of reality. On the level of spirit, moral obligations are absolute and are directed to achieving, through acts, the maximum transcendence of spiritual subjects.

Romero sought persistently to develop a philosophy of culture. Culture is a creation of the intentional level of human behavior. Descriptive, analytic, and explanatory concepts common to the social sciences and to positivistic approaches are applicable to it. The spiritual activity of man is to be directed toward the realization of the transcendent possibilities not only in persons but also in the cultures in which they participate. If there is conflict in the dual nature of man between the intentional and spiritual levels of his existence, there likewise is a conflict between the intentional and spiritual expressions of culture. Any community comprises a society of individuals and a society of persons. As a society of individuals the community is in continuous conflict of material interests. As a society of persons the community represents a unity of ideal interests. The goal of social organizations, such as the state, is the creation of those conditions which support a propitious environment for the development of a society of persons through the protection and furtherance of human freedom.[16] Totalitarian political regimes are not only brutal but prevent even the minimum conditions for the attainment of human dignity. "They cure the disease by killing the patient." [17] The enjoyment of the personal right to political freedom is the base from which other freedoms develop as a society of persons struggles to forge from the intentional expressions of culture a more adequate attainment of universalism, responsibility, altruism, creativity in the arts and sciences, and concern for human dignity in political, economic, and other social institutions.

A detailed internal evaluation of Romero's philosophy would require a lengthy treatment. But there are several topics on which attention can be focused in a summary treatment of continuing problems in his philosophy. These include lack of precision in his terminology, the manner of his resolving some basic philosophic problems by stipulation of meanings rather than by presentation of evidence and argument, incompleteness of his system, architechtonic arbitrariness, inadequacy in treatment of problems, and limitations in his methodological procedures.

The lack of clarity and precision in some of Romero's basic terms is evident in such concepts as "transcendence," "value," "determinism," and "absolute." An activity is transcendent when its action "goes beyond" the object or structure from which it arises. The criteria for identifying "going beyond" are not always clear, particularly in crucial instances where it would be necessary

[16] *Filosofía de la persona,* p. 40.
[17] *Ideas y figuras,* p. 128.

to determine whether this activity was an instance of "going beyond" or "going back." "To be valuable" means, for Romero, "to be transcendent." Is it not conceivable for an emergent structure to be "less valuable" than a structure from which the emergent arose? Romero would classify such an instance as a "return to immanence," but that instance would seem to make transcendence dependent upon value in spite of his view that value is determined by transcendence. Romero's view of determinism presents a comparable problem. He states that determinism is characteristic of the natural order and at the same time that the greater the transcendence in the natural order, the greater the possibility is for nondeterministic activity. However, it is not made clear how this decrease of deterministic activity occurs nor how it is identified. Romero's use of the word "absolute" as applicable to "transcendence," "objectivity," and "values," on the spiritual level of activity also lacks clarity. Apparently it is used as a teleological concept signifying the attainment of the maximum possible development or complete realization of its nature. If such is its meaning, then it is difficult to see how growth on the spiritual level is a continuing possibility and how comparative evaluations may be made on the spiritual level.

Romero's attempt to resolve some basic problems in philosophy through his manner of constructing his basic categories rather than through an examination of evidence and presentation of argument is apparent in his treatment of problems like determinism, freedom, and value. By definition any activity on the natural order is determined because this is a proper characteristic applicable to any activity on this order. Likewise, if an activity is on the spiritual level, it is characterized by freedom, because, by definition, this is characteristic of any activity on this level. One activity is more valuable than another if it has greater transcendence because, "to have greater transcendence" also means "to be more valuable."

The incompleteness of Romero's presentation is illustrated by his failure to develop an explanatory principle to account for the activities of transcendence or of regression into immanence. This process of the emergence of higher levels of activity from lower levels is basic in his system. The organic develops from the inorganic, the conscious from the nonconscious, purpose from the mechanistic order. Qualitative differences arise from new quantitative differences through the emergence of new structures. The spiritual emerges from the natural and is both dependent upon it and in conflict with it. This tendency for transcendence occurring within and among the inorganic, organic, and intentional structures is attributable to impulsive, continuing, pulsating activity which is not an adequate explanatory principle within a deterministic framework characteristic of these structures. Regressions must occur in Romero's system through some privation of impetus that also would need to be determined. The inadequacy of this notion of impetus as an explanatory principle is evident through the failure to provide criteria for predicting specific kinds of instances of transcendence or of regression before the occurrence of such events. Romero's notion of impetus does not appear to explain transcendence as it tends to obscure the need for such an explanatory principle. Likewise, the impetus continues on the spiritual level, but it no longer is mechanistic; nor is it possible to achieve further development on the spiritual structure because absolute transcendence already is attained once this level is reached.

That the organization of his system is forced or somewhat artificial in some instances is evident in his interpretation of culture on the level of intentional activity. Three fundamental expressions of culture are the development of cognitive, moral, and aesthetic capacities. It is difficult to determine how the scientific knowledge that he proposes to have developed on this level is possible if this level of activity is limited to particularity and if scientific knowledge requires the development of generalizations based on laws that propose to be universally applicable. If the intentional level of activity is always characterized by an interest in objects on the basis of their usefulness in advancing the particular interests of the subject, then moral behavior would be possible without "other regarding" virtues or actions. Neither would aesthetic experience require an interest in an aesthetic object for its own sake. Furthermore, since acts on the intentional level are interpretable through deterministic categories of the natural order, praiseworthy moral acts or creative artistic expression would need to be satisfactorily explicable in a deterministic framework.

The inadequacy of his treatment of some of the problems discussed in his philosophy is evident in a consideration of his ethics. By making value the measure of transcendence of an entity or activity, Romero encounters some difficulties inherent in traditional self-realization theories of ethics. If all transcendent values are absolute, then the realization of any one of them would appear equally obligatory to any other. However, the possible resultant complex of values realizable on the transcendent level are varied, and he does not take sufficiently into account the difficulty that in acting on his proposed transcendent level the attainment of some states of affairs might be more praiseworthy than others. Likewise, he does not recognize that according to his views a person might be confronted with exclusive but obligatory ways of acting since the attainment of some transcendent values in a situation might also preclude the possibility of attaining other transcendent values. The maximization of transcendent values and the attainment of autonomy in moral decisions may be highly praiseworthy objectives in his position, yet the problem arises in particular instances of the criteria for identifying the course of action that would maximize such value or be the adequate expression of autonomy.

Romero does not provide an adequate justification for his method of establishing his conclusions. He rejects, like Nicolai Hartmann, the "rationalist assumption" that complete agreement prevails between the categories of reason and the structures of reality. Although such a view might be held as a possibility, it is difficult to determine how it is possible to know this. Rather the problem might suggest the inadequacy of the categorical scheme that was used to interpret the "structures of reality" by the "categories of reason." It also is difficult to see how it is possible to hold that the structures of the real are ordered (nonchaotic) and yet incapable of being structured fully into a rational (ordered) system of relations. It would be highly unfair and contrary to his whole philosophical attitude to hold that Romero's philosophy develops into irrationalism, but his failure to clarify his statement that there is an element of reality not accessible to rational analysis might provide some basis for such an opinion.

In a further development of his method Romero accepts the empiricist approach that all knowledge has an empirical basis and is subject to being controlled and limited by the data that are known. However, he includes within an acceptable empirical approach knowledge that is a part of the intuitive content of consciousness and without immediate support of sense data but fails to resolve the problems relating to the cognitive status of illusions and dreams.[18] His views are offered as hypotheses based on

[18] *Papeles*, p. 109.

experience interpreted in its widest meaning. The resolution of differences of cognitive claims between persons would appear to require ultimately that he accept a similar structure of thought. He does not propose that the acceptance of a similar structure of thought would be always commendable because this would tend to lead to dogmatism. Correction of cognitive claims is possible within his system by providing instances of additional experience for which his views cannot account. Philosophical views, for him, are probable rather than certain, but they should represent the most adequate possible interpretation of experience through rigorous criticism and comparison with the cognitive claims of other competent investigators. Similar to Korn, Romero holds that there is both: continuing belief that truth can be attained and doubt that any given presentation is to be accepted as the truth. Many aspects of this methodological approach have merit, but the manner of resolving differences in conflicting cognitive claims in specific situations is not satisfactorily clarified.

Romero's philosophical anthropology focuses on the attainment of the fullest development and appreciation of intellectual, moral, aesthetic, and social values. His humanism is grounded in a naturalistic foundation which projects into a spiritual level that never loses its temporality or historicity. Romero is concerned with proposing a critical basis for determining what goals are worthy of man's efforts and what values are worthy of man's appreciation. He prizes an open society in which political freedom is enjoyed as a fundamental right of all men and contributes to the flowering of the highest creative expression of man's other freedoms in his unending quest for knowledge, wisdom, truth, beauty, autonomy, and justice. Critical insight, continuing struggle, altruistic concern, and dedication to the life of the spirit are goals worthy of unceasing endeavors.

William J. Kilgore

Baylor University,
March, 1964

SELECTED BIBLIOGRAPHY
OF WORKS BY FRANCISCO ROMERO

Lógica (Buenos Aires: Espasa-Calpe, 1938) . The first seventeen editions of this work were published in collaboration with Professor E. Pucciarelli. The eighteenth (1962) and subsequent editions are by Romero alone.

Alejandro Korn (in collaboration with A. Vassallo and L. Aznar), (Buenos Aires: Losada, 1940)

Sobre la historia de la filosofía (Tucumán: Universidad Nacional de Tucumán, 1943)

Papeles para una filosofía (Buenos Aires: Losada, 1945)

Ideas y figuras (Buenos Aires: Losada, 1949)

El hombre y la cultura (Buenos Aires: Espasa-Calpe, 1950)

Sobre la filosofía en América (Buenos Aires: Raigal, 1952)

Estudios de historia de las ideas (Buenos Aires: Losada, 1953)

Filosofía de la persona (Buenos Aires: Losada, 1951) 2d ed.

Filosofía contemporánea (Buenos Aires: Losada, 1953) 3d ed.

Filósofos y problemas (Buenos Aires: Losada, 1957) 2d ed.

Qué es la filosofía (Buenos Aires: Columba, 1957) 3d ed.

Alejandro Korn, filósofo de la libertad (Buenos Aires: Reconstruir, 1956)

Ubicación del hombre (Buenos Aires: Columba, 1957) 2d ed.

Teoría del hombre (Buenos Aires: Losada, 1958) 2d ed.

Relaciones de la filosofía (Buenos Aires: Perrot, 1959)

Ortega y Gasset y la jefatura espiritual (Buenos Aires: Losada, 1960)

Filosofía de ayer y de hoy (Madrid: Aguilar, 1960) , 2d ed.

Historia de la filosofía moderna (Mexico: Fondo de Cultura Economica, 1959)

For a complete bibliography of Romero's works see *Homenaje a Francisco Romero* (Universidad de Buenos Aires: Facultad de Filosofía y Letras, 1964) , pp. 221–322.

Author's prologue to
this edition

As the title indicates, this work is an exposition of a systematic theory of the being of man. It may be well to emphasize from the beginning the principal traits of this doctrine, which, perhaps through deficiencies in the exposition or for other reasons, have not always been understood in keeping with the purposes of the author.

The theses upheld are as follows. Man, in the proper sense, appears when the intentional or objectifying consciousness emerges. Before this, there exists only a confused consciousness of "states," as in the animals, which under normal conditions does not objectify although it is capable of discontinuous objectifications in exceptional cases. Intentionality or objectification is the foundation of intelligence, which, as a normal function, is found exclusively in man. The primary or fundamental intentionality is cognitive. Regardless of the importance attributed to the behavior of the emotions, feelings, and will, their properly human quality is based on their projection toward objectified entities or situations which can only be established through cognition. Because man—and man alone—is an intentional consciousness, a focus of objectifying acts, he is a subject who perceives and thinks objects (beings, things, situations, relations, and so on) and who turns toward them in emotional and volitional attitudes. To perceive objects is to attribute autonomy and consistency to them, to recognize that they are and that they enjoy certain properties. This is equivalent to exercising with respect to them a kind of implicit judgment, which can be referred to as "a judgment of presence." Given these considerations, man is seen to be, simultaneously, the being who is a subject, who perceives objects, and who judges. What is fundamental in man, therefore, is to be found in his condition as a subject, in his capacity to apprehend objects, and in his gift of judging—three aspects of the same thing.

The specifically human elements of society and culture are explained on the basis of the objectifying attitude. Human society and culture are consequences of the intentional or objectifying posture and, in their turn, they corroborate and strengthen that posture in the individual.

The main part of this investigation is concerned with the spirit. A strict distinction is made between the merely intentional attitude and the spiritual attitude. The merely intentional attitude, though projected toward objects, is not spiritual because it presupposes a "subjective regress," a concern for the objects on the basis of the interest of the subject himself, which is an egoistic concern. Yet in that intentional attitude the spirit is latent, for the spirit appears when the interest in the objects themselves is fortified and they are dealt with in a "disinterested" manner, without subordinating them to the actual interests of the subject. In a rather loose fashion, common sense has constantly identified the "spiritual" with the "disinterested." The nature of the spiritual is rigorously defined, in the present work, as the condition of those intentional acts lacking the "subjective return," that is, it is "disinterestedly" oriented toward objects, in the cognitive attitudes as well as in the religious, ethical, aesthetic, and other attitudes.

The merely intentional and the spiritual attitudes live together in man. The former, in and of itself, defines him as man and separates him from the animals. A full humanity, however, is achieved with the appearance of the spirit, though not only through the incorporation of this superior principle—the highest in all reality—but also through the tensions which it establishes with nonspiritual intentionality. These confer a special quality to human life. These tensions, this duality, constitute what is most characteristic in the whole, complete man, and they are studied in the final part of this work under the general aspects of duality—acts of masking, justification, and self-consciousness as well as the phenomena of sociability, historicity, and meaning.

The author intends the *Theory of Man* to be an investigation in philosophical anthropology, limited to give an account of what is essentially human yet resting on its own philosophical-anthropological foundation. However, a theme such as man—and perhaps any theme that is confronted philosophically—cannot be completely isolated. Many studies concerning man [1]—as indicated in their titles—purport to inquire also into his place within the whole of reality; for, actually, it does not seem to be possible to engage in philosophical discourse about man without assigning a place to him or searching for his meaning in the complex of what exists. The author has sought to satisfy the dual demand of setting forth a theory of man which rests on its own foundations and is sufficient to itself, as well as to formulate a hypothesis concerning the situation and the significance of man in reality in keeping with his theses of an anthropological scope, which completes these theses yet is at the same time separable from them. This hypothesis differs from the rest of the investigation in its decidedly metaphysical character; it draws together the points of view the author has set forth previously in other contexts and is the sketch of a metaphysics on which he has been working for some time.

Something along this same line should be said with regard to the suggestions of a theory of values set forth in summary fashion in the text. In the theories about value there is one traditional concept which links value and being, and another very generalized concept in contemporary philosophy which isolates value and considers it to be self-subsistent. It even comes to conceive of being and value as two distinct realms. In the view of the author, the supreme principle or being in reality is "transcendence," and value in each entity or situation is the measure of transcendence which it embodies. Thus, between being and value there is a fundamental connection, a thesis which, in a way, implies a return to the traditional concept. The nature of the connection, however, permits the use of all the rigorous, subtle distinctions obtained in the profound analyses of recent axiology in the determination of the essence and the modes of values.

Since man occupies a central and privileged position in the

[1] See Francisco Romero, *Ubicación del hombre* (Buenos Aires: Editorial Columba, 1961) 3d ed., chap. 1.

complex of existence, theories concerning his essence are necessarily and at the very root linked with a multitude of problems which, in one way or another, are related to what is human. Some of these problems have been a continuous concern of the author and will be examined by him later, either as special studies (theory of knowledge, theory of values, theory of culture, ethics, philosophy of history, problems pertaining to our contemporary situation and humanism, as well as others) or as clarifications and supplements to this work.

Francisco Romero

Martínez (Buenos Aires) , 1961

PART ONE: INTENTIONALITY

INTENTIONAL CONSCIOUSNESS

PREINTENTIONAL PSYCHISM AND INTENTIONAL CONSCIOUSNESS

It is best to conceive of psychism [1] in its earliest stages as an undivided succession of states, a kind of psychical repercussion of life. No distinction between subject and object exists in such psychism, nor can one properly speak of it as consciousness. Life is recorded psychically; it resounds and multiplies in a clouded psyche. This psychism is, so to speak, inherent in life from its beginning, being a direct echo of life and the instrument of the living entity to be used for its internal coördination and external conduct. The superior or intentional psyche is based on this foundation, and its distinguishing characteristic consists in the objective direction of its acts. Also resting on this foundation, though in less direct fashion, is the spirit, the principle whereby man passes beyond the natural realm.

Our sole concern at this point is to make clear the nonintentional character of animal psychism, yet, at the same time, conceding to some species of animals a vague rudiment of intentionality that is limited and detained in its first stages. As a normal function,

[1] [Romero uses the word 'psychism' and its adjectival form 'psychical' with a meaning similar to that developed by Brentano. Husserl's discussion on pp. 249–250 of his *Ideas* (New York: Macmillan, 1931), clarifies the use of this terminology.—Trans.]

true and complete intentionality carries with it, of necessity, both nomination and objective communication, in preparation, as we shall see, for that inversion of interest of which the spirit consists. If intentional consciousness actually operated in animals, it would manifest itself in a language of objective content; it would give rise to the beginning of self-consciousness, and that being would not then be an animal, but the sketch of a man. Provisionally, we accept Max Scheler's conclusions concerning the psychism of animals as it pertains to affective impulses (which would seem to be apparent in plants), instinct, and associative memory. We do not share his opinion concerning what he calls practical intelligence. We disagree with his supposition that practical intelligence is similar in animals and in man—that there is only a difference of degree between a chimpanzee and an Edison (as inventors of technical artifacts). We believe that the difference—or the primary difference—between man and the animals must be sought in this aspect, yet without denying the statement that it is the spirit that completes and perfects human nature. Undoubtedly, Köhler's well-known experiments make evident a practical intelligence in chimpanzees, but it is greatly limited in its field of action; it is nascent and uncertain. Aside from constituting an exception among the animals, whose superior limit they represent, the problem in these anthropoids is that of a psychical function lacking the elements and resources that characterize human intelligence. In man, the intentional or objective capacity is seen as a continuous and normal activity. It is accompanied by nomination, which makes possible the fixation of these objectifications in consciousness and their transmission to other consciences. Human intelligence is founded on intentional or objective consciousness, and it is inherent for this consciousness to name and transmit its contents. This transmission constitutes the intentional community, the realm where each particular consciousness resides as in its own natural environment, where it finds acceptance, support, and reinforcement. Between the first thrusts of intelligence, such as appear in the chimpanzee, and human intelligence, there is a separation that cannot be reduced legitimately to a mere difference of degree. On the one hand, we find in animals those initial and discontinuous instances of what is undoubtedly the root and origin of all intelligent behavior—but no more than this. On the other hand, these same principles are at work in man, though they are not bound to the limitation and failure which is evident in the animals. They function in a normal and continuous fashion, cultivating the whole potential implicit in them. This development does not evolve in a mere linear progression, but is the result of the appearance and consolidation of structures and resources without which the normal, ample functioning of intelligence would be inconceivable. The typically human intelligence depends on a complex in which are found the acts of objectification, these being normal in man. Seemingly, apart from him, these acts are found only in animals belonging to superior species and, even in them, rather sporadically. Along with these acts are other specifically human elements of the intelligence, such as nomination and explicit judgment, the communication of what is objectified, and the transfer of each one's experiences to others through signs. This makes it possible for psychical activity to become public property, and each individual is or may become heir to and beneficiary of the achievements of the group.

"In general, how does the superior animal see his surroundings?" asks a contemporary psychologist.[2] His answer is as follows:

> Certainly it does not see persons, trees, houses, rocks, and so forth, for in such perception there is, as we know, a precipitate of knowledge that animals do not possess. The animal sees only complexes of color qualities. Yet—and this is the unique feature—the animal does not experience these complexes as objects that, as such and along with others, are spatially related in its surroundings. Perhaps it is permissible to describe the animal's manner of seeing as follows: there are certain modern paintings, that, when one stands immediately before them, present no more than a conglomeration of color qualities; objects and a spatial order can be seen only from a certain distance. Perhaps the animal sees its surroundings as we see such a painting at close range— as a totality of color qualities, which quite naturally are extended. Only when the animal moves does an object stand out from the complex as something with form and separateness.

[2] Aloys Müller, *Psychologie* (Berlin and Bonn: 1927). Spanish trans. by José Gaos (Buenos Aires: Espasa-Calpe Argentina, 1940).

The observations of Katz, who summarized many of the findings of the more recent studies in animal psychology, are more to the point. We will review his contributions because of the support they provide for our position.[3] The things of which an animal is aware are enclosed in rigid contexts or "models" of an emotional nature—models of which the animal itself is an inseparable part. "The work of Lorenz," Katz says, "is an inexhaustible source of evidence that a bird relates to its companions, whether of the same species or a human being, in a way that is entirely dependent on the 'model of action' of which the companion forms a part." After an examination of coinciding events, he adds, "How can we interpret these unforeseen changes in the behavior of animals with respect to the aimated objects in the examples described? These objects are structured into 'models of action' that already exist and that are strongly colored with emotion, and, when the total situation changes, these objects exercise an entirely different function." As Thorndike has insisted for years in his studies in animal psychology, animals react to "total" situations. The significance that a companion has for an animal depends completely on the situation in which the companion is "enclosed." The same holds for the behavior related to inanimate things.

> The experiences of those working with animals in a rural setting with regard to the sequence of "models" in the animal's perception of things have been confirmed by laboratory experiments that refer to less emotional aspects of perception. There is, first of all, the experiment of Bierens de Haan in which an octopus failed to recognize a crab as a possible prey when the crab churned about, suspended on the end of a string instead of crawling along the surface. Why? For an octopus, evidently, a crab that moves normally is first and foremost, optically speaking, a form-of-movement-in-space-and-in-time.

It is proper for man to perceive objects, to recognize reality as a conglomeration of separate entities endowed with existence and

---

[3] David Katz, *Animales y hombres: Estudios de psicología comparada* (Madrid: Espasa-Calpe, 1942). Spanish trans. by José Germain and Antonio Melian, pp. 234 ff. The entire section "Realizaciones sensoriales en el hombre y en los animales" is most instructive.

consistency. Man is, in the first place, an intentional consciousness —without it he is not man. What is characteristic of intentional consciousness consists in a cluster of intentions or acts projected toward objects in the function of cognitive, emotional, or volitional apprehension. "States" or psychical acts without intentional character, that is without objective direction, occur in man as in animals, but it is man's prerogative that many of his states lose their condition as such by becoming the content of intentional acts. Of these, the cognitive acts enjoy an undoubted priority and preëminence in the shaping of human nature, for they are what establishes intentional consciousness. Simultaneously these acts create or distinguish the object and present it to us as perceivable, for they have the concealed ability to give objective form to sensible material and the evident capacity to present this outcome to us as objects existent in themselves. The common observations concerning the priority or superior strength of the emotions or the will with respect to the intellect do not succeed in invalidating the former assertion, as will be seen later.

Intentional activity transforms the states into objects. The exploration and description of the mechanism and function that produce that transmutation are the concern of the theory of knowledge. We use the word "object" in its most inclusive sense— it takes in everything that comes into the cognitive glance, everything that is apprehended by the subject. Objects, in this widest sense, include the bodies distributed in space, their parts taken separately, psychical acts, souls, the creations of fiction, the ideal entities of mathematics (numbers, figures), relations, qualities, properties, modes, and so forth. Object, in this general sense, is anything to which one turns his attention, whether presented in perception or in intellectual insight, whether the result of one's own imagination or that of another, of a conjecture or a conclusion of any kind. From this point of view, which presupposes the profile and existence of the subject, an object is anything that testifies to its presence before a subject. Regarding this point, one should be aware that the levels of objects are many and diverse. The qualities of objectivity are very different in visible and tangible bodies, their parts, properties, situations, and states; in the psychical events that we apprehend in ourselves through intimate experience and those we assume in others; in the nontemporal entities of mathematics, grasped either through intellectual intuition or by conclusion, and also in relations; in the characters and circumstances of poetic fiction and myth; the meanings of words, norms, and precepts. If it is "something" for a subject, it is an object in the sense of general objectivity, of intentionality. The task of exhaustively characterizing and classifying the various kinds of objects is recent, for only of late has philosophical thought begun to set forth a theory of objects.

From the cognitive point of view, presence is the most general characteristic of objectivity. An object is what presents itself before a subject. It is anything to which a subject may refer because it is placed before him. The presence testifies to a "something," whose makeup depends on its own special type of objectivity. States must be differentiated from objects, a state being understood as the changes within the subject that are lived but are not cognitively perceived by him. So far as he lives his state, the subject does not exercise his specific function toward it, this function being to observe objects or turn his attention to them. Pure states include and cover the psychical field. If we wish to speak of the subject of a state, we must keep in mind that so far as he spontaneously lives his state, psychically speaking, the subject is that state, because the distance between the subjective and the objective poles has not been opened up. This separation is indispensable, not only for the subject to perform his function but for him to be a subject in the proper sense. When we are overcome by intense physical pain, our consciousness or subjective field coincides with that state and all else disappears. Psychically, we are our pain. We revert to being a subject when, in addition to suffering, we turn our attention to the pain and perceive it. At this point we can see that the relation between state and object is of three kinds. In the first place, the state may be foreign to any objectification; it is merely lived, as when we suffer intense pain or vaguely live our kinesthetic states without cognitively turning toward them. In the second place, we may render the state iself, *as a state,* into an object, as we observe it, as we take notice of it and distinguish it as something in our perceptive awareness. Finally, the state (though normally a complex of states) may come to be the content of an intentional act, disappear as a state, and, thanks to the molding of the categories, acquire an objective character completely different from its original condition. This happens with normal perceptions in which the states that make up the sensations are changed into representations.

As has been stated, the detailed examination of cognitive objectification is a concern of the theory of knowledge. However, interesting and valuable as the inquiries in this field may be, the conclusions of the theory of knowledge may not all be taken as final and definitive. Furthermore, the area taken as a whole lies beyond the scope of this study, although two or three general points are relevant to our purpose. These will be taken into consideration when the development of the exposition so warrants.

A lived state constitutes a single, undivided situation in consciousness. There is neither object nor, strictly speaking, a subject. When the objectification occurs, subject and object are born simultaneously, separated by an interval or distance that makes possible the specific function of each. Let it be said in passing and without insistence that in objectification two elements are to be distinguished: the transcendental, in which the object is constituted, and the perceptive, in which the constituted object is given to the subject. Much uncertainty in the theory of knowledge stems from not distinguishing transcendental and perceptive activity in the subject. Perception—in the broad sense that covers any kind of presence, including, for example, that of a conclusion—is always the attribution of objectivity, since there is no perception unless it is of something. However, the special structure of the objects is imposed beforehand by the hidden transcendental activity. The primitive content of all psychical life is the flux of lived states, the continuous flow of psychical activity that changes in keeping with the internal circumstances of the individual and the external stimuli coming to him, all of which is organized according to categorical limits and functions. As the first categorical structure, perhaps one should consider the subject-object polarity that is the basic framework of intentional consciousness. One of the most important and surprising events in the history of the cosmos occurs with the transformation of the undivided, vital, psychical flux into intentional consciousness. A totally new form of reality appears; it cannot be compared with preceding realities because of its initial difference from them and what it carries within as germ or latency. According to our interpretation, this aspect of reality is foreign to the vital level but not to the natural order, which is surpassed only when the spirit becomes present. Intentionality and consciousness are the same, though one can at least argue that intentionality necessarily presupposes self-consciousness in every case.

One cannot properly speak of consciousness when there are only lived states. Consciousness is inevitably consciousness of something. The realm of states is, in a certain sense, a confused mixture of the subjective and objective without the emergence as yet of either subject or object. The subject and the object emerge simultaneously, and, with their simultaneous appearance, the intentional consciousness, which they constitute, is founded. To be an object means to be given to a subject. To be a subject (in the cognitive aspect, the only aspect of interest at present) is equivalent to apprehending objects. The object stems from the objectification of the states. The subject emerges as a focus capable of observing the objective, allowing, however, that this observing already attributes objectivity as it extracts the state from its condition as a lived process in order to convert it into something noticed or known. The reiteration of subjective acts, the consolidation of the subject, and becoming accustomed to being a subject, make of the subject a "self." At the same time, his organization of his objectifications raises these to the category of "world." What is proper to man, as stated above, is to perceive objects, to objectify; we see now that it is equally legitimate to say that man is characterized by being a subject, though, to be sure, this addition introduces not a new fact but an aspect consubstantial with what was previously stated. Thus, by way of an inclusive summary statement and in keeping with what has been asserted, one can maintain that man is characterized by being a self and having a world.

It is neither possible to conceive the existence of an object (as given) without a subject, nor that of a subject without an object. States are transformed into objects when their presence is acknowledged, when there is the awareness that 'that is.' [4] The subject, for

---

[4] [To distinguish quotation marks used by Romero and those used, in addition, by the translator, original quotation marks are rendered as double quotes, added ones as single quotes.—Trans.]

its part, first appears as the ability to acknowledge the presence of states, either as mere states or as objects in which the states are thoroughly elaborated in terms of objectivity. The awareness of presence is always an imputation of existence. Though totally different from the sphere of states and from the vague preconsciousness that is a flux of lived and purely functional psychism, the intentional consciousness emerges as a reinforcement and a specialization from the midst of that preconsciousness. In it appears a center or focus that is intentionally directed toward the states and, by merely acknowledging them, detaches and provides them with a special embossment, so that to their original condition of merely being is added that of being for something else, that of referring them to a subject as its perceptions. With the appearance of this form of reality, which we refer to as intentional consciousness, an innovation comes about that consists in the duplication of reality through its objectification by this intentional consciousness. Though in fact reality is left intact and permitted to continue to be what it had been up to that point, intentional consciousness grasps it in terms of knowledge and establishes in the subject that version or reflection of reality whereby the subject is enriched, acquires depth, and constructs its own world. With the arrival of intentional consciousness, therefore, reality is not merely augmented with a new kind of partial and computable existence such as appeared previously. It is as if the whole of reality had grown, each entity being not only what it had been, but having in addition its own reflection or duplicate within the subject. And since each intentional consciousness, in its turn, is objectifiable by the others, it is as if an amazing array of mirrors were at work. Here things take on a new and complex life in an unending play of reflections and repercussions; until now they were merely existent and bound to blind physical and biological activity. Man's condition of being the focus from which awareness is projected into reality bestows on him from the beginning—in his being defined by intentionality— his prerogative as a universal being. It is a characteristic best understood in its first phases as a possibility or even a calling. Later it will be a distinctive task of the spirit to perfect and consecrate this destiny for universality, which is latent in the essence of man from the first intentional thrusts.

Cognitive intentionality—the foundation of what is human in our view—consists in a certain relation between the subject and the object. Though this phase of the discussion does not provide the opportunity to investigate this relation at length, it is well to keep in mind that it presupposes a functional heterogeneity between subject and object. Each has its own distinctive profile; there is a separation or interval between them. In the preconsciousness of states, unity prevails, since there is no duality of a subjective center and an object. Intentionality—and man, if our thesis is true— appears with the simultaneous emergence of subject and object, related in such a manner as to include a contraposition, a face-to-face relationship. This separation is indispensable if intentionality is to be, allowing the subject and object to fulfill their functions. It is maintained inexorably in every case—in the apprehension of so-called external objects, ideal entities, and even the inner experiences of the perceiving subject. Aside from being an indispensable element of intentionality, the face-to-face relationship is like an ever-continuing exercise which limbers and strengthens the subject, confirming it as a center or focus of consciousness and preventing it from relapsing into the preintentional situation and being overcome in the chaos of states. This word "chaos" brings us to recognize that the transition from the preconsciousness of states to intentional consciousness, as regards psychical order, is the transition from a chaos to a cosmos, from a confused mixture of elements to a structure that is rigorous, harmonious, and differentiated.

All apprehension, all cognitive movement, is intuitive. This is true of knowledge erroneously referred to as sensible, as well as of rational knowledge, and of any other possible kind.[5] Discursive operations, whose difference from the intuitive has as a rule been misunderstood, are reduced to sequences of intuitions in which the character and value of their nexuses are also apprehended intuitively. Intuitions of cognitive import are always intentional, that is, they are intuitive apprehensions of an object by a subject that keeps its distance with regard to the object. It is not our concern at this point to confront the difficult problem of the nature and validity of the other kinds of intuition, real or imaginary, that may

[5] On this point, see Romero, "Intuición y discurso" in *Papeles para una filosofía* (Buenos Aires: Editorial Losada, 1945).

be described as mystical, penetrative, or identifying. These are well known in Oriental thought and not unknown in the West. Such intuitions presuppose the dissolution of the face-to-face relation, an emptying of the subject into the object, a compenetration or assimilation of each into the other that supresses the functional peculiarity of each element. In these intuitions the destruction of the subject during the intuitive trance is inevitable, and we do not see how it is possible to speak of knowledge if the subject, the one who knows, is effaced. Not only is knowledge unimaginable when the heterogeneity of the knowing and the known is suppressed, but the resulting situation is suspiciously akin to the preconsciousness of states. The usual qualification that one is here concerned with states of exceptional content and quality introduces a modification of little importance. If we still wish to extract knowledge at any price, we should have to accept that such identifying intuitions, though not perceptive in themselves, may come to be so later and in a roundabout manner, when these states of which the intuition consists are objectified and the subject, no longer in the unifying trance, observes them intentionally. We would not know, therefore, through these intuitions; only as we returned from them would we know, just as one who lays hold of a great treasure under the cover of darkness, taking time only to gather it up, waits until morning and the light of day to examine and appraise it. Intentional structure is absolutely necessary for man, lest he cease to be man. And if among these modes of intuitions there are some that actually involve an identification with the mystical essence of the universe or with the divine, then, perhaps, during this unifying experience there is a participation of some kind in the cosmic being or the divine essence. However, this participation will be without knowledge in the proper sense, and so long as the experience lasts one gives up his being as a subject, indeed, as a man. In order to know, the subject must be recuperated and must contemplate the identification in terms of objectivity and thereby abolish the identification as a living actuality and a passive renunciation. In our opinion, even in these extreme—and questionable —cases, man fulfills his destiny through maintaining his intentional character, which, to the extent that it records the passage of infinite presences, confirms the being of the subject and gives added depth to his understanding of himself.

THE PRECEDENCE OF COGNITION

The thesis concerning human nature, which we have begun to set forth in the preceding pages, is in opposition, as may have been noticed, to several interpretations of the origin and being of man. These interpretations, however, are supported by authoritative expositors and claim widespread acceptance.

Of these interpretations, we shall refer to the following: the position that sees the spirit as that which is unique and differentiating in man; the view that maintains that man lacks a fixed nature and that he is to be understood in terms of his becoming, in terms of his history; the proposition that the practical or manual experience with things is fundamental as well as being the principal condition for the appearance of the conception of an objective world; the thesis concerning the priority of the emotions and the will over the intellect; and the views that give the dominant role to certain organic or impulsive tendencies, such as the sex or power instincts.

It is not our intention to engage in a detailed refutation of these concepts. Lacking any affinity for debate, not only by temperament but also perhaps by distrust in its efficacy, we shall be content to outline the principal reasons that separate us from them. Thus, through contrast, the profile of our position will be more clearly delineated and in this way will confront the reader with its own claim for acceptance. We feel that nearly all positions we oppose have good supporting arguments, at least so far as they emphasize important aspects of human nature, otherwise they would not have found such well-qualified champions nor such a large number of supporters. Nevertheless, we maintain they are insufficient to account for what is essentially human. In our comments the positions of particular authors are not of primary interest; rather, we turn our attention to the over-all meaning of these views and to the general form they have assumed in becoming common property.

Our thesis may be described as intellectualistic because it stands on the affirmation that intentional structure is man's founding characteristic and that this structure appears with the simultaneous emergence of the subject and the object in a relation that is primarily cognitive apprehension, the subject apprehending the object. The intentional structure functions in emotional and volitional attitudes that are equally intentional, but the intentionality of the emotions and the will, so far as they are a specifically human function, require that the world of objects be cognitively given. In describing this position as intellectualistic, and in order to avoid any unjustified and negative overtones that the word may carry, two important points should be considered. In the first place, there is a tendency to think of intellectualism as the impassive manipulation of things considered as present and given of themselves in a series of acts, thus ignoring the warm and intimate dimensions of the mind, although accepting the world as existent. Our intellectualism takes another path. It is founded on something often overlooked—that for man the existence of the world is an intellectual creation; it is the product of intentional capacities and must be included in the intellectual sphere. For, as we shall see, all subsequent intellectual activity is derived from and is the extension and intertwining of that attitude which creates for man a world of objectivities. Therefore, the activities commonly held to be nonintellectualistic, if indeed they are human, presuppose a basic intellectualism, since they presuppose a subject and a world. In the second place, we do not exclude an initial movement which is of the will or at least akin to it, an active impulse that we might refer to as the "will to be a subject" or the "will to have a world," a blind thrust—the incarnation of universal transcendence—that would heighten the constitutive elements of intentionality in the preintentional psyche. Yet this admission is made with the explicit reservation not to consider that thrust as the constitutive element of man, this being reserved for the intentional structure that results from it.

In order to maintain that man is defined by spirituality, one needs to decide beforehand what is to be understood by spirit. If spirit is conceived in a broad sense, saying, as some do, that it is the totality of human psychic activity, what is confusedly affirmed is that man is characterized by being what he is. Such a concept of spirit, however, is far from being admissible. There are many elements and attitudes in man that belong to him exclusively, yet when taken as given these cannot be referred to as spiritual, lenient as we may wish to be. Even in the every-day use of language and without any attempt to establish set criteria for delineating the realm of the spirit, it is common to distinguish between spiritual acts and those that contradict the spirit or are indifferent to it. Therefore, the description as spiritual must be limited to certain kinds of acts. As for our own point of view, we adhere to a limitation that accords fundamentally with common sense yet goes on to make it more explicit. Spiritual acts are absolutely 'disinterested' acts, of clear objective direction, in which the subject transcends himself and severs all connections between his own concrete subjective interest and the fulfillment of the act. Depicting man as a purely spiritual being on the basis of this position leaves out much that is human. On the other hand, our reasoning shows that intentional structure, even though deprived of spiritual projection, is sufficiently characteristic of and exclusive to man to define him as an entity essentially different from everything else. No exception is made here of those beings closely related to him, which present some intentional efforts but in which intentionality is not constituted as a permanent function.

Although the historicity of man is examined at length elsewhere, a word needs to be said before proceeding. If man were pure becoming, that becoming would either recognize certain norms and tendencies or it would be without them. If they were present, even as mere guidelines of a dynamic process, they would be the essence of man; and were they absent, the becoming itself would be inconceivable because of its confusion and arbitrariness. We adhere to the historicity of man, yet consider it subordinate to the norms and tendencies that the specifically human context prescribes; that is to say, historicity is subordinate to intentional structure. Such historicity, therefore, is not indefinable, not without law or essence, but it is the historicity of a subject whose environment appears to him as a reality of objectifications, who reckons with himself and that environment in different ways, who objectifies space and time, and assumes before them the few possible positions at his disposal. Spiritual projection, latent in intentionality, prescribes to human historicity a course whose general direction depends in each case on the proportion in which the spiritual and nonspiritual elements are at work. At this point, it is well to remember that these two elements impose a duality on the complete or normal man that, in its variations and alternatives, is basic to man's movement in history. These fundamental conditions are not the only elements in this movement, for they are augmented by others that stem from them and that also give evidence of a remarkable consistency. From a certain point of view, the more extreme opinions concerning man's historicity do not stem solely from a reaction against prior notions of exaggerated constancy and rigidity but are also expressions of the pessimism regarding man that has replaced the confident optimism of another day. This optimistic concept of man, which included a purpose and destiny, is opposed to the pessimistic concept, which tends to interpret him as pure chance, as a living coincidence. One should be aware that, beneath the explicit letter of some of these concepts, presumptions and motives are found, which attenuate their radical departure or correct it in some other way.

Still others, in ascertaining the foundation of humanity, attribute an exceptional role to the actual intercourse with reality, its practical handling, that would provide the occasion for revealing the makeup and consistency of things. But, the being capable of taking advantage of this kind of experience cannot be imagined except as a subject, and, in turn, a subject is inconceivable except in relation to a perceived object. In addition, one would need to explain why animals, who have before them the same things which man has, do not succeed in using them for the same practical transactions. If man is the one who takes advantage of his mechanical relation with things, one must accept that he was human already and that something characterized him as such. If, however, he was not human before and became human through his practical intercourse with things, there was something in his prehuman state that predisposed or stimulated him to that kind of practical interaction capable of discovering the world for him, something, therefore, that was granted to him alone among all living things. The whole zoölogical spectrum testifies that the mere manipulation of things does not usher in humanity. And even if this practical handling were an antecedent, what is basic would not be the handling itself but its consequences, in the sense that it would strengthen objective perception and the constitution of a subjective center—events without which humanity is inconceivable. Thus the practical handling would not be the foundation but, rather, a process that precedes and assists in the true foundation.

The successful handling of things presupposes the capacity for objectification. To manipulate things to the degree necessary to derive knowledge from their handling presupposes the possibility of discerning them as things, of being aware of their relations, modes, and properties. Actually, any knowledge that would seem to be derived from a blind handling, from mere manipulation, stems from the opportunities that handling affords to the intentional apprehension. It is obvious that this practical interaction favors knowledge and in many instances may be indispensable. Science penetrates reality by submitting it to the process of experimentation, and any practical knowledge stems from the empirical interaction with a sector of reality. But it is not the hands that know—it is the mind. Manual activity is converted to experience because the mind fixes its attention on what is handled, because, through concrete use some aspects and inner phases previously imperceptible are made accessible to perception. Even in the most favorable instances, when handling occurs prior to intentionality it can only assist in the emergence of intentionality, and when handling occurs simultaneously with intentionality it is limited to offering favorable circumstances so that intentionality may be exercised with greater extension and depth.

Within the theoretical field some traces and aspects of manual activity should not be forgotten. In the development of modern science, the role of the experimental handling of objects for the strict purpose of knowledge is rather important. We have already been reminded that experimentation in general requires manual operation. Furthermore, Bacon's enterprise comes as a great condemnation of purely speculative procedures in which the hands remain inactive and only the mind is at work. His enterprise seeks to replace such a method by one in which the hands may not remain idle. The advance of modern science has been and is inseparable from the activist tendency—both intellectual and physical—which is proper to Western man. With natural knowledge defined, in one of its aspects, as the search for ultimate elements, things and organisms are submitted to an implacable dissection in which manipulation has no substitute, even to the extent that many of the important results stem from the discovery of new means of extending and refining manual activity.

Connected with all of this is a tacit principle or requirement of reason, which, so far as it is a faculty, would isolate basic elements or "simple natures," to use Cartesian terminology, in order to understand reality fully. The principle might be formulated as follows: One knows only what one analyzes, only what is reduced to its ultimate components. At the other extreme is the voice of Vico, alone in its day, proclaiming a principle at the opposite pole: One knows only what one makes.[6] The ultimate elements of the analytical reduction, according to this new approach, continue to be unknown, and it is a vain pretension to seek to establish any kind of knowledge upon them. That they have been isolated into their ultimate components does not make them known because they still remain unknown and strange. We know only those things in whose inner recesses we are able to penetrate, through creation, through action which itself adheres to each element. The subsequent problem of "comprehension," with the link or interpenetration between being and knowing, is thus set before us. This is not the occasion for examining, in all its aspects and implications, the serious opposition between "One can know only what one takes apart" and "One can know only what one puts together." Such theses are inseparable from important presuppositions regarding the nature of reality, even in its most significant metaphysical aspects. For our own purposes it is sufficient to show that with each alternative—provisionally accepting both as valid and justified— the primary element is knowledge itself. The knowledge stems neither from analyzing the object nor from living intimately with it and creating it, but from being aware of the objectivity of the knowledge, no matter what its source. In what pertains to knowledge, both analytical rationalism and synthetic creationism presuppose the subject, who cannot be separated, in his origin, from his power of objective perception or from his intentionality, for he is none other than the focus of actual and possible intentional movements. The subject, therefore, is such so far as objective presences are before him, so far as his apprehensions are fulfilled in terms of knowledge, for his existence is the primary condition of any activity worthy of being called human. Any instance of manual activity or even of creativity on the cognitive plane is subordinate

[6] See the essay "Reflexiones sobre la gnoseología de Vico" in Romero, *Filosofía de ayer y de hoy* (Buenos Aires: Editorial Argos, 1947) .

to the intentional structure, as in spontaneous or practical manual activity.

We insist that the act of objectification, to which we assign the primary and decisive role in the formation of the human, belongs to the realm of cognition. Perceptive activity, which constitutes the primary cognitive moment, is already of an intellectual type and, as we shall see, involves an implicit judgment. In recent psychology it has been customary to attribute a greater significance to affective and volitional phenomena than to intellectual activity, from whence would derive their priority and greater importance in the formation of human reality. Then again, the man in the street believes that he is continuously finding evidence that man is governed not so much by intelligence as by motives that stem from the emotional level such as desire, fear, love, and hate. Let us examine these assertions.

In the states taken as a whole, in the dark procession of preintentional psychism, it is probable that there are some vaguely cognitive, emotional, and volitional, or better said impulsive, elements. They are found in a rather confused mixture. It is also probable that, because of their intensity and abundance, the last two kinds of elements may prevail over the first and impress their seal upon it. But it must be conceded that these affective and impulsive movements, regardless of how much they may be improved or transformed, are insufficient to explain the appearance of human consciousness, to give an account of the transition from the nebulous psychism of the animal to the psychism of man. We do not completely negate the role of the affections and impulses in the formation of intentional consciousness. The psyche is always a whole, and no section ever functions without the direct assistance of the backing of the others. The subject is activity, and its emergence, as has been stated, is witness to an impulse that lifts and sustains it above the level of the states; this is an impetus that is renewed with each one of its acts. Subjective activity ought to produce a given affective quality, a special emotional emphasis that underlines each objectifying movement, each cognitive appropriation. Aristotle was quite aware of the pleasure that stems from all knowing. Even though one may attempt to assign a special role or a powerful influence to these or other modes of affective-impulsive activity, the situation would remain as we have sketched it: (1)

Basic in it is the appearance of intentional structure, the birth of a subject for whom there are objects; (2) viewing the situation from the opposite pole, the objects are embossed for a subject who perceives them and attributes being or existence to them. The structure thus established tends to consolidate and grow as the result of a necessity inherent in it (its essential historicity consists in this) and it exhaustively defines man, in his being as well as in his becoming.

The elements of the preintentional psyche are without doubt the disarrayed material of which objectifying consciousness is constructed. The emotive-impulsive elements may have a role of varying importance in the constitution of that consciousness, but they do not shape it. The fundamental event—new and incomparable—is the actual appearance of this type of consciousness, through which a type of reality heretofore unknown arises in the cosmos. And if the affective-impulsive element is not clearly determinative for the cognitive-intentional element, *the latter, in turn, is hereafter determinative for the former.* Although part of the affective-impulsive sphere may remain in man in its original condition, as states, as preintentional mass, another large part is implanted within the intentional structure; that is, it comes to be an attribution or activity of a subject who is also inclined toward objects. This is proper and exclusive to man—*that* in him which humanly defines the area of feelings and impulses, with the added reservation that the latter can be taken as acts of the will only when they are acts of a subject surrounded by objects. The nonintentionalized portion of emotive-impulsive elements remains outside the boundary of the specifically human, as does all that is strictly organic and further removed, yet, all that is a mere physical condition, such as taking up space, lengthening one's existence in a given part of general cosmic time, and finding oneself subject to gravity. Just as the physical entity is characterized by physical attributes and conditions, and the organic entity by the complex of phenomena we refer to as life, without thereby denying to it the physical elements inherent in it, so the human entity is characterized by intentionality though in no way is there any intention to ignore or forget what is nonintentional in man. Let it be said in passing that intentionality is decisive for understanding man in general, but that for understanding certain phases it is necessary to recur to other aspects including some other than the organic. For example, in human individuation, the references to temporal and physical location of each human unit are important even though they are mere physical data.

Human emotion and will, therefore, are intentional. It should be noted that to say "human will" is redundant, for there is no will without intentionality, that is, without humanity, and by the same token it is equally redundant to say that 'human will is intentional.' For the sake of clarity, however, the exposition seems to demand these and other terminological nuances, which may be easily overcome. Intentionality is what raises human emotion and will above the subhuman level of the psychism of states. The mere reference to this intentionality, however, does not exhaust what there is to be said, for one could have in mind a special kind of emotive-volitional intentionality, which would be autonomous and self-subsistent, independent and separate from perceptive intentionality. And our thesis implies, together with the assertion that the essence of man is his intentionality, that the basic intentional structure is the objectifying structure; as a result, the intentional acts of the emotions and the will presuppose cognitive intentionality. Every intentional act stems from a subject and directs itself toward an object. Without a subject from which to depart and without a receiving object, there can be neither emotional nor volitional intentionality, for neither the emotions nor the will, by the very nature of their function, have the prerogative to create a subject or present objects to it. As is well known, Brentano refers expressly to the priority of objective intentionality when he says: "We may consider as unquestionably correct the definition of psychical phenomena which states that they are either representations or are grounded in representations which function as their foundation." The totality of the cognitive intentional structure—subject, object, and the distance or functional heterogeneity between them—is indispensable for and precedes affective and volitional intentionality. If these intentionalities did not stem from a subject and project toward an object, they would be states and not intentionalities. And since, by their nature, affective and volitional intentionality are incapable of creating or distinguishing the subject and the object, the subject must exist beforehand and the object must be previously given, with the distance or interval between them maintained, for without it the act could not proceed from one to the other. The functioning of a basic cognitive intentionality is noticeable above all in the will—that energy which is often creative and tends to infuse a powerful life to expressions of human desire. However, it never works alone, but on plans and sketches of an intellectual type, on anticipations or tentative projects without which the impulse would be blind, without purpose, and inevitably frustrated. All this is apart from the fact that the will is not able to do without the knowledge of the given situation, which its purpose would modify or on which it would seek to be established. It is not difficult to understand, on the other hand, that, when lifted above the level of the purely lived, affective movements not only generally require objective presences toward which they would move, but they need to be instructed or enlightened concerning the particular nature of the objects in strictly perceptive terms or through some kind of specifying or individuating presentation. This intrinsic nature of objects, so far as it is given or represented, is one of the determining factors of each manifestation of emotion or feeling. A mathematical entity, a physical complex or event, a plant, an animal, a man are each quite different as objects so far as they are actual or possible recipients, occasions, or terminals of the emotional act. Such a difference, as well as individual differences specified for each one of them, are certainly not constituted by emotion itself, although one may assert that to emotion alone corresponds the grasping of values residing in the objectivities apprehended. In general, it seems necessary that each situation be cognitively established before evaluational awareness, of an intentional nature, can occur. Epistemological value rests on the degree of correspondence between knowledge and its object. The beauty of a landscape is grasped when the aggregate of those things that make up the landscape is perceived. The evaluative emotional reaction to the just and the unjust in certain attitudes or acts presupposes a knowledge of these events and situations. And once error in any of these perceptions is recognized, we immediately consider the corresponding emotional reaction to be erroneous and without validity. All of this is as relevant for mere intentionality—of a "subjective" or concretely individual foundation—as it is for spiritual or universal intentionality, in keeping with the distinction that we shall make with more precision later. These analyses, of course, are incomplete, but they sufficiently clarify what is our sole interest at present—the priority of the cognitive intentional structure in everything specifically human and its function as the common foundation on which all the rest is implanted.

With the attribution of precedence and primacy to cognitive intentionality, we are only maintaining that this is the basic structure and that all else is constituted on it. It would be rather abusive and even absurd to interpret what has been said in the sense that man governs his conduct solely and constantly in the light of his objective apprehensions or that these apprehensions are never distorted by the pressure of the emotions or the will. It is well known that one's affections and desires give rise to figments of the imagination that are taken as true perceptions, that they falsify real situations through the color and emphasis placed on each of the elements, and that they often channel the development of thought into the direction that pleases or toward what one desires. In a certain sense, however, all this occurs as objectivity authorizes or permits it, either by defect in the evidence or because of cracks or breaks through which affective or impulsive elements may be introduced. If cognition is frequently supplanted by the emotions and the will, it is because a large part of the activity of the intelligence [7] occurs in chains of images or thoughts whose connections are not critically examined. This is true primarily in the common use of the intelligence, which is foreign to deliberate discipline. This permits the intrusion of the emotions, so that these conclusions, which for the most part are barely supposed, either are derived apart from any logical sequence or are diverted from their original meaning. In spite of all this, however, the number of instances in which we are governed by the established constants is greater than those in which the emotions predominate. Many times, however, the latter seem to make up the larger part, because of their implications and consequences and, as a rule, because they reveal their error sooner or later. One in love may fancy he sees the

---

[7] Romero recognizes this novel use of the word "intelligence"—the same usage occurs in Spanish—and goes into some detail in clarifying the meaning he gives to it. Cf. pp. 58–59.

semblance of his beloved in a woman who passes at a distance. Those fearful by nature may imagine any number of dangers on a dark night. The miser may figure he already has in hand a sum he has yet to gain. No one, however, would pretend that, under the influence of great passion, the lover, waiting in broad daylight, would confuse the corner policeman with his beloved when he is only four feet away. Nor would the confirmed coward mistake a little child, playing in his yard with a toy pistol, to be a dangerous thief armed with a .45 automatic. Nor would the most miserly shopkeeper, moved by his desire for profit, unconsciously add five zeroes to the total of his sales for the day. None of that. Desires and impulses retreat before the perceived evidence. They are restrained, though perhaps crouched ready to leap when circumstances permit it, and these favorable circumstances are always weaknesses or fissures in the intellectual framework. Clear, decisive perceptions, conclusions that are precise and immediate, and forecasts on the basis of incontrovertible data assert themselves regardless of any deforming influence, except, of course, if a person is mentally deranged. With indecisive perceptions, those with respect to which a critical and serene mind would abstain from deciding to which object they belong in the hope of further evidence—here without doubt, love, hate, hope, and fear find room to weave in embellishments at their pleasure. Many distortions are found in conclusions, forecasts, and extended intellectual operations; here many elements are introduced, few of these of obvious certainty and most of them of a doubtful or problematic nature, making a correct evaluation difficult. To this interference of the emotions is added another interesting factor—the necessity to affirm, an urgency to get out of the discomfort of insecurity, waiting, and doubting. The requirements of our existence continuously demand that we make decisions, even though we may not have sufficient information to know which alternative is best. Life does not wait; situations make their demands and, as Pascal said in another regard, "il faut parier." Suppose we add this practical motive, and the mental attitude which derives from it, to the discomfort and even the torment that the intelligence undergoes when a situation varies and is inconclusive, unassisted by the balance afforded by a firm and unequivocal decision. Then would we understand how powerfully the will to affirm—similar to the will to believe—influences intellectual activity and how often it is capable of deviating the intelligence from its original intention. Without doubt this is one of the principal aspects of the intervention of the will in the use of the intelligence. But let us not forget the contrary effect—the indecision and delay in reaching conclusions because of the lack of energy of will, even when sufficient evidence is at hand to reach a justified conclusion. Yet through all of this the intellectual function has remained established as fundamental and as of most constant use in spite of myriad parasitic intrusions, in spite of the many disturbances that it undergoes as it functions.

Now just a few words to place our position in relation to two points of view that have enjoyed widespread acclaim and recognition in recent times. Pan-sexualism makes no provision for what is peculiarly human, which is the central problem in any theorizing about man. If sex is taken as the primary vital act, as the universal mover of life, then one must explain how the entity we refer to as man comes to be, since undoubtedly he cannot be qualified merely by the fact that he is one of the many beings in whom that impulse works. Rather, he must be identified by certain features that distinguish and separate him from the rest and, among these, a feature of exceptional importance for that position, namely the special forms, restrictions, sublimations, and interpretations imposed on sexual desires. The primary factor, then, would not be universal sexuality, but the appearance of a structure that molds it into typical and varying forms.

The will to power, for its part, is observed in many animals and is not in itself a distinguishing human characteristic. For the sake of convenience, let us again take advantage of Katz's observations, which summarize many interesting conclusions. The following quotation from Katz (*op. cit.*, p. 216) is sufficient.

> The investigations by Schjelderup-Ebbe concerning social rank and despotism among birds and mammals are among those studies in animal psychology that have exercised the greatest influence in the field of human sociology. His observations refer principally to the societies of *gallus domesticus,* yet his conclusions have been proved to apply to such a large number of birds that we may presume they are applicable to all those species which live in a social context. . . . Two hens

never live together in a hen house without deciding
which of them is to dominate.

Those who maintain that human society must be rigidly stratified
according to power relationships may be a little surprised when
they realize that their ideal has already been fulfilled in any
chicken yard. The blind exercise of power is no more than a
primitive form of individual self-assertion. What would be important for man, therefore, would not be the act, which is common
enough, but those forms it takes in man, which are insolubly
linked to his condition of being a conscious subject and having
before him, as a field ready for his conquest, a world of objectifications, extended in space and time. But if the act of domination,
beginning with the extreme and elementary form of absolute
despotism, is undeniable in man, one must also recognize that the
ancient and uninterrupted struggle against domination is also
consubstantial with him, and this is something completely foreign
to animal society. This struggle against domination begins with
the first ethical formulations and continues accumulating strength
in legislation, in customs, and in the growing consciousness of
equal right for all men. As a natural affirmation of individuality,
the instinct for power finds its most forceful replica in the
spiritual attitude. This attitude is peculiar and exclusive to man
and through it the primordial particularism, on which domination
is based, is gradually replaced by a universal domain where all
actual domination of one's fellow creatures is excluded, placing in
its stead a domination of reality by the spirit which is quite
contrary to that primitive impulse. To attribute the instinct for
power to man as his dominant characteristic is one of the crudest
and coarsest forms of a naturalism, long since discarded, not only
in the light of the pressure of ideal demands, but also because of
what the most dispassionate interpretation of historical experience
teaches us. That history—the unfolding of human nature down
through the ages—is the history of liberty, fortunately, has begun to
be a well-confirmed truth, almost a commonplace.

INTENTIONALITY AND JUDGMENT

In these initial pages we have asserted that objectification is the
foundation of what is human, that is to say, man is the being for

whom objective realities exist. It has also been indicated that objectification, and the constituting of the subject as such, are simultaneous, mutually supporting acts. Therefore, to say that man is the being for whom there are objects or who grasps a reality composed of objects is to say that he is a being who is fundamentally a subject. Perceiving objects and being a subject are both attributes exclusive to man, and they define man, though not in his fullness and perfection. We might say that they define a *minimum* of humanity in man.

As seen from the outside, objectification is the perception of something as an object or, strictly speaking, merely "perception," for there is no real perception without the recognition of the objectivity perceived. It is well to remember the broad meaning we have adopted for the word 'object': Object is everything to which presence before a subject may be assigned; it is everything that comes before a subject, regardless of the level in which it may be found. Objects, then, are the things and the beings of the external world, the ideal entities of mathematics, relations, concepts, conclusions of a reasoning process, the typical representations of myth, and all kinds of cultural objects, even the images of phantasy itself. By the same token, the very states of a subject become objects when he becomes cognitively aware of them—and this certainly is one of the most interesting examples of objectification. In other instances, the lived state is annulled when it yields its content to objectification, whereas here, its original condition as a state is retained in spite of the objectification. That is, the subject appropriates his own state (a kinesthetic experience, for example) as an object, recognizing its condition as a state and leaving it intact within himself. In conclusion, the subject also objectifies himself, and this objectification is the motive or occasion for much activity whose careful examination is indispensable for the understanding of man.

As seen from within, in the process of its formation, objectification consists in the activity that transforms a complex of states into an object. This complex of states is lived in such a way that, properly speaking, there is neither perception nor any particular aspect that could be referred to as a subject. Within the realm of the psyche, which heretofore was undivided, the object stands out on the one hand and the subject on the other. A polarization has occurred in what was a relatively uniform mass, creating differences and outlining in it a center or focus and certain elements on which objectivity is conferred. From this center stem the objectifying or intentional glances. We might liken what occurs here to what happens when we open our eyes and begin to recognize the objects that surround us.

The most general characteristic of being an object is presence— either actual presence or a possible presence, as when the subject retains experiences from previous objectifications. It should be kept in mind that we do not refer to the object itself, but the object so far as it is given to a subject or objectified by him. From this point of view, all objectivity is presentness. For a subject, its objects are present or they are not objects. Presentness may be complete, or partial, or, in a certain sense, even potential, but it is inevitable that it occur in some fashion so that the object will exist for the subject. The subject may not perceive an actual object (thing, being, ideality, a state of his own, his own reality) , yet he nevertheless takes it into account in some way or refers to it vaguely, as for example, when he remembers in a confused way that he has to do something or when he tries to relive some vague event of the past. Such instances involve the objectification of something that is little more than an almost empty profile, yet the objectification possesses a certain character, which, through persistence, tends to yield to the presentation of the full object. We do not believe that there are intermediary stages between the condition as a state and perception. These stages would merely be objectifications of a certain kind—the undistinguishing awareness of presences.

In distinguishing between preintentional and intentional psychism, we have found in the first place a difference in structure. In the one there is a continuous flux of states, in the other a structure defined by a subjective center that points or directs itself toward objects. These two psychical realities are diverse in nature and function. In addition to this basic difference is a difference in intensity or activity. It would not be accurate to say that the psychism of states is inactive, for in that case we would erroneously describe it as absolute rest, when actually, within its sphere, it is extremely active. To the extent that it regulates the work on the vital level, it contains and governs the complicated functioning of the instincts, it receives impressions and sends out impulses, it carries out all processes involved in associative memory, and, on occasion, it gives rise to a flow of passion that may reach violent proportions. Regarding this point, let us touch in passing on a question that is probably clothed with great metaphysical importance—the question of animal emotion, the source from which, undoubtedly, all human emotional activity flows. In the obscure form in which this emotion exists in animals, it would seem to be the equivalent in the vital order to the great forces or unifying tendencies that we perceive in physical nature. Indeed, it is because of these forces that this sector of reality is a structural and functional unit and not a scattered plurality. If this equivalence holds, then animal emotion would reach out even to the most remote foundations of the cosmos. Intense though it may be, preintentional psychic life unfolds in a kind of stupor or dream in an aggregate of operations that are relatively passive for the individual. Compared with this, intentionality is an exceedingly active functioning, in each of its moments, in its actuality, as well as in the vast accumulations to which it gives rise—accumulations that are incomparable in quantity and quality to the limited and elemental impressions that are the lot of the animals. One might say that the psychism of states develops on a plain. With intentionality something is erected on that plain—the subject— and thereby the uninhabited plain is transformed into a landscape contemplated by a spectator. The transition from animal to man is often portrayed by comparing the horizontal position of the animal body—except for anthropoids who only discontinuously and with great effort manage to raise themselves—to the vertical position of the human body. We can transfer this comparison to the realm of the psyche and conceive of the psychism in animal life as a purely horizontal plain. In the anthropoids that psyche sluggishly strives for an erect position but is unable to achieve it, whereas in man there is a psychical element—the subject—which stands erect with decision and definiteness. Regardless of the point of view, the vertical position is man's chief prerogative and one which he does not lay aside except when he temporarily diminishes his humanity, resting from it, as in sleep, and when, in death, his humanity comes to an end.

Prior to the birth of the subject there were only states. The individual psychical unity was merely the outgrowth of the natural continuity and interweaving of the states. For intentionality, however, the subject is an essential factor of the psychical structure. This has been denied more than once, since it was imagined that the subject could be explained as a mere complication of psychical phenomena. This conclusion stems both from an excess of scientific rigor and from an attempt to avoid making the soul a substance, as in spiritualist metaphysics. Similar motives—the purpose of adhering to a strict description and the zeal to avoid the dangers of the metaphysical transposition of the subject as occurred in German idealism—moved Husserl in the first instance to dispense with the subject as a special and distinct entity. In studying consciousness in the *Logical Investigations*,[8] he denies the existence of a pure self different from the total complex of lived experiences. These lived experiences, as is well known, are the actual events in consciousness so far as they are phenomena of consciousness, not so far as they are objects foreign to it, since they occur in immanent or lived time. In this first interpretation, consciousness consists only of the flux of the lived experiences in inner time.

> If we distinguish between the body of the self and the empirical self and restrict the psychical self to its phenomenological content, the pure self is reduced to the unity of consciousness—that is to say, to the real constitution of the lived experiences, a constitution which we (that is, each one for himself) find, on one hand, as existing on the basis of evidence within ourselves, and on the other, complementary hand, we accept it with good reason.

Phenomenological reduction trims off all transcending elements, which always have been a source of difficulty, in order to leave clearly defined the pure immanence, which is the field of absolute evidence, of unquestionable certainty. Husserl thought that once

---

[8] *Logische Untersuchungen* (Halle a. d. S.: M. Niemeyer, 3d ed., 1922), II:1, 353–363. At this point I am using parts of Romero, "Pérdida y recuperación del sujeto en Husserl" in *Filosofía contemporánea* (2d ed. Buenos Aires: Editorial Losada, 1944) .

this procedure had been carried out, the self would not be resistant to it, that it would vanish without leaving a trace. "Phenomenologically reduced, the self is not something distinct that floats above the multiple lived states; it is simply identical with the synthetic unity which is proper to them." In the nature of lived experiences, in the various real elements that make up the consciousness, there is such an interlocking, blending, and intertwining that the resultant unit constitutes the phenomenological self—the ultimate reality of the self—and it is not necessary to refer to any element foreign to this experiential connection in order to conceive of the self. This interpretation is corrected in the work in which Husserl began the task of developing the central core of his philosophy, a task left unfinished. The change in the concept of the self is fundamental. Whereas before it was nothing in particular, only the mere unity of the phenomena of consciousness, now it is something, and something exceedingly important, though it is difficult to imagine the how of this something. Once the phenomenological reduction has been carried out and all has been rendered pure immanence, it is discovered that the explicit form "I think of" remains undisturbed, with one of the arms of its bipolar structure pointing toward the subject. This pure subject is neither just one more lived experience among the others, nor is it a fragment or a real part of the lived experiences, one which appears and disappears with them, but rather something that is strictly *sui generis*. It appears to us as identical, as constant, and even as necessarily constant, its "look" is projected toward the objectivities through each intentional act.[9] This second interpretation, which assumes the self is an indescribable and bodyless something, a mere center point, is corrected in its turn. It is not conceived, now, as an active, yet empty, pole of identity, but as something that lives and is modified through living, as an essentially historical being.

> With every act it carries out and which has a *new* objective meaning, the self . . . acquires a *permanently new characteristic*. If I decide, for example, *for the first time* in an act of judgment regarding the existence of

[9] *Ideen zu einer reinen Phänomenologie und phänomenologischen Philosophie* (Halle a. d. S.: M. Neimeyer, 1913), sections 57 and 80.

some being and for some given determination of that being, the act passes on, but I *am* and hereafter *remain a self that has decided in thus and such a manner.*[10]

The self, therefore, is a concrete reality that lives and develops historically.

We believe that Husserl's third interpretation is the correct one, and we adhere to it. Let us clarify the nature of the subject's acts through which he transforms his states into objects. The state, as such, is lived and not perceived. It comes to be perceived and thereby objectified when one comes to realize that it exists, that it is there. To objectify is to be aware of a presence, to accept it and recognize it, realizing that to be aware of a presence and to create it as such are one single thing. This would not be possible if there were not something capable of such acceptance or recognition. The primary function of the pure self, of the subject, is to direct its glance toward the states and bring them out of their condition as states, elevating them to objective dignity through the mere act of being aware of them. We call this function primary because when the subject functions as an agent of intentional acts in the realm of the emotions or the will, it must have previously exercised cognitive objectifications since the intentional or, specifically, the human acts of emotion and will are such only when projected toward objectifications. At its root, therefore, the subject is an objectifying principle. And it is on this basis that the subject structures diffuse preintentional feelings, impulses, and tendencies; and with this core, molded by the subject and reconstructed in accord with his nature in light of the objective horizon that opens up before him, the subject produces the intentional acts which are not cognitive.

We are able to conceive the attribution of objectivity only as an act similar to judgment. The state is merely lived, endured. It is neither accepted nor rejected; it is not apprehended and, properly speaking, there is no consciousness of it. When one turns toward a state, it automatically becomes an object, and the 'turning toward' is a becoming aware that the state is there, that it is, and subsequently that it is of this or that form. To perceive, to apprehend something, is to attribute being and consistency to what is appre-

[10] *Méditations cartésiennes* (Paris: Colin, 1931), pp. 56–57.

hended. The subject, therefore, is born as the ability to assign presence to states, to judge that they are. This objectifying judgment, however, is not conscious, formulated, and explicit, since we are not conscious of it. Yet this judgment provides us with the consciousness of objects. Further, the lack of consciousness of this act of judgment does not argue against it, because, even in the ordinary activity of the intelligence, we are not conscious of the major part of our judgments.

The objectifying judgment is similar to the existential judgment dealt with in logic, and though this similarity has been noted more than once before, there is considerable difference between the two. One must keep in mind that for both the characteristic of judgment is assertion and not the attribution of predicates. Yet we do not become trapped in insurmountable difficulties if we insist—contrary to the opinion of Meinong and others—in maintaining predication as a *sine qua non* of judgment, since what constitutes the object may be thought of as the predication of existence, or, as we prefer to state it, of presence. The objectifying act may be conceived according to the formula "that is an existent" or "that is present," whereby one expresses that "that" (which was a state until the intentional glance fell on it) is an existent or something of the class of that which is placed before a subject. Let us consider a difficulty that does not invalidate this thesis because it can be clarified through a brief discussion. If objectification is the attribution of existence or presence, it would already seem to presuppose an objective element, an object already defined to which something is attributed. The difficulty is obvious and depends on what is thought of judgments in the realm of logic, which are characterized by being judgments that presuppose and work with elements that are already objectified. The objectifying judgment is identical with logical judgments in what is basic—assertion—but different in that it occurs on the transcendental level, in the foundry where objects are forged. Although the mechanism is the same, the material with which each class of judgments works is different. The judgment we call logical has a subject that is already an object. The objectifying judgment has a subject of a quite distinct kind because it is a state which in that instant ceases to be such, since it is precisely in its change from a state to an object that it becomes the subject of the objectifying judgment. It is at this point—when the state is seen—that its quality as existent or present is recognized. This condition of existence or presence is identical with the situation in which the state is objectified because it consists of the very thing that gives shape to the object, namely, the awareness that the intentional glance has landed on a target. The "it is" or "it is present" of the objectifying judgment is the same thing as the intentional act. We find the judgment, therefore, resting on the foundation most basic to man, or better said, it is this foundation itself, which we shall again encounter in everything specifically human in the life of man, so that whenever he ceases to judge, in a limited sense he renounces his character as man. As has been previously stated, man is the being for whom there are (or who perceives) objects, and he is the being who is a subject. Let us now add with equally strong emphasis that man is the being who judges. For, as we have seen, the subject unfolds as the being capable of judging, of attributing objectivity to states. In fact, we might say that this capacity to judge becomes substance or is structured into an entity. The subject is the judging entity, but he himself seems to appear in order to embody the judging attitude, as though awakened or called up by an obscure power in the preintentional psyche which would assert itself and thereby rise to the level of consciousness—the level it achieves as soon as it forges an adequate instrument.

To dwell on problems limited to the sphere of knowledge would lead us astray from our primary aim—the elucidation of the idea of man—so we will add only those comments that seem indispensable to our purpose. For us, as has been firmly asserted, the essential activity of the subject is judgment. This is not the only function in which the subject is engaged, yet it is the function which, so far as he is a subject, bestows being on him, and which through reiteration confirms him as a subjective entity and increases his stature as such. The cognitive operations of the subject occur on two levels: the transcendental, on which the object is constituted; and the logical, on which the object, already constituted, is handled according to the procedures and rules that are the concern of logic. The subject is of necessity unconscious of his activities on the transcendental level, though he is conscious (or possibly so) of the activity on the logical level. It could not be otherwise, since the transcendental task is to constitute the object and, by the same token, consciousness, which is always consciousness of an object or the very 'giving' of the object. This, of course, is simultaneous with the presentation of the object. On the other hand, the handling of the object, which we have referred to as logical, presupposes both the object and consciousness.

From one point of view, these two levels are essentially different, but from another, they are seen as unified and continuous. The difference has been noted above. Their unity and continuity, however, stem from the identity of the principle that governs them both—the judgment. The frequently censured Kantian derivation of the categories from the forms of judgment has to do with this unity. The derivation is an implicit recognition of this unity, although it would have been helpful to distinguish between the process of the investigation itself—which had to be as Kant carried it out, from the judgments to the categories, from the obvious to the hidden—and the real situation, which is the subordination of the forms of judgment to the categories. We do not hereby adhere to the Kantian solution of the transcendental problem—a matter which we cannot discuss at present—but rather mention it in order to indicate the wisdom of presupposing an intimate correlation between the two levels. The judging principle assumes different roles in each level, according to the nature of each, yet with important similarities. The basic judgment—which objectifies— corresponds to the existential judgment of logic and has even been referred to as such by Hans Cornelius, among others. One must keep in mind, however, what has already been shown, that the logical existential judgment explicitly assigns existence to an object that already enjoyed implicit existence, whereas the objectifying judgment constitutes the object through the procedure of discovering and testifying to the existence or presence which were unrecognized up to that point. The process, as can be seen, is the same, though it is subject to the respective conditions of each level. The acts of objectification that constitute the objects, not in the sense of general objectivity or presence, but as belonging to the large groups or classes of objects (material things, psychical acts, ideas) , are correlated with the logical judgments of determination. The determinative role fulfilled by the categorical elements in the acts of objectification is entrusted to the concepts used for predication in the judgments of determination. The recognition that an object, for example, is a material thing, is seen at its root to be a process similar to that of recognizing that this material object is, let us say, a block of wood. But the former occurs in the transcendental realm and the latter in the realm we designate as logical. In this light, knowing is revealed to us as a continuing process, although the continuity may, at a certain point, need to ignore the boundary that separates the two levels. This process may be seen as a progressive specification and recognition, beginning with a minimum specification—to be an object—and proceeding to the maximum—the exhaustive determination of the object which occurs in the defining judgments. This permanent intrusion of the judgment exposes the error of the expression "knowledge of the senses." Knowledge, even that which includes the mere presence of objects, is inevitably an intellectual act, regardless of the many sensible elements it may encompass. Husserl says as much, when he states emphatically that there is an ideal element in the *noema,* and when he speaks of the universality of the logical.

In the light of the place that judgment occupies in our interpretation of man, it is proper to recall that the presence of this judging element in perception has been upheld many times. Perhaps the most general recognition is afforded by the German word for perception: *Wahrnehmung.* Limited to its components, the verbal form, *wahrnehmen,* to perceive, literally means to take something as true, and this 'taking' is not conceivable apart from judgment. In many philosophers and psychologists the role of judgment is explicitly admitted, even though it is variously understood. Among those who have conceived it with greater depth we find Bolzano. "In my opinion," he states, "one cannot say that he perceives something or is aware of it, that he is conscious of it, understands it, or knows it, if there is no judgment." Immediately following this statement, he clearly establishes the difference between this judging and what has not yet been objectified, which is objectified through this very judging, and common judgments, whose subject is already an object.[11]

Witasek presents the problem as follows:

> Perhaps many will be surprised that we should discuss perception at this point [12] since our opinion regarding

[11] Bernard Bolzano, *Wissenschaftslehre* (Leipzig: F. Meiner, 1929–31), section 35, 5 and 6.

[12] In the section on thought.

perception—that it is a psychic complex which also contains as an essential part an act of judgment—is not very widespread at present. The general rule is that one accepts perception as given with perceptive representation, that is to say, with the representation of the sensation organized into a whole. But when this is closely examined, it is seen that it cannot correspond to the facts because perception contains not only the qualities of color, sound, and so on, but also the elements of belief and conviction. Whoever perceives something experiences immediately, and within the act, the faith in the existence of what is perceived—that is to say, he thinks of the object of the perceptive representation as something existent. Whoever sees (perceives) fog or snow believes implicitly that it is there. We can say, then, that perception consists in a perceptive representation and a judgment that includes it—the judgment of perception. The representation and the judgment refer, of course, to the same object.[13]

Even before Witasek and Bolzano, Reid had expressed a similar opinion, though this does not mean he was the first to hold such a position.

Each operation of the senses contains a judgment or a belief as well as a simple apprehension. When I perceive a tree, my faculty of seeing does not give only a notion of a simple apprehension of that tree, but it makes me believe in its existence, its form, distance, and height. And this judgment is not the result of a comparison of ideas, but it is implied in the perception itself. These natural and primitive judgments form a part of the basic elements with which nature has endowed human understanding, and they are a gift of the divine in the same sense that notions or mere apprehensions are.[14]

Some have gone even further, expanding the intrusion of the judging element in perception, maintaining that an articulation of judgments, a reasoning, functions secretly in perception. Spencer commits himself to this interpretation. His thesis is that uncon-

[13] Stephan Witasek, *Grundlinien der Psychologie* (2d ed., Berlin: Meiner, 1923) , p. 288.

[14] Thomas Reid, *Ouevres complètes,* trans. by Jouffroy (Paris: 1828) , II, 385–386.

scious or automatic reasoning constitutes the dominant element in ordinary perception. The things that surround us are known through acts of classification and recognition. The perception of each external object includes its identification as a particular thing as well as its classification among other things or its own species. A special perception is possible only through the intuition of the similarity or dissimilarity of certain attributes and relations present in that perception with reference to certain attributes and relations previously perceived. The established divisions between the different orders of cognitive psychical processes are superficial. We must admit that the distinction between reasoning and perception is relative and not absolute and that perception borders sensation on the one hand and reasoning on the other.[15]

Though this opinion is not as widespread as that which limits itself to recognizing the presence of judgment in perception, it has nevertheless had authoritative supporters. Among its most decided adherents is Binet, who studied the problem closely. But let us examine first some passages from another work of his in which he emphasizes the participation of judgment.

> Memory is not in any sense, as generally conceived, a reproduced sensation. On the one hand, one must realize that sensation, understood as the direct effect of an exterior stimulation on our senses, is a psychological entity that is not real. The sensation is always associated with other images which surround it and determine its nature, which clarify its meaning. In order that it may be better understood, there is a reaction of the spirit to the sensation and it is to this group of phenomena that the name perception is given. Memory, therefore, is not the reproduction of a sensation, but the reproduction of a complex group of states of consciousness directed toward knowing an external object. In addition, judgment intervenes in memory, and it is through judgment that we are aware of the process of a recall and that we correct the errors, the lacunae, and the thinning out of the recall so as to make it concur with reality.[16]

[15] Herbert Spencer, *Principles of Psychology* (2d ed., New York: D. Appleton, 1889), especially sections 314–316.

[16] Alfred Binet, *Introducción a la psicología experimental* (Madrid: Jorro, 1906), pp. 94–95.

We have presupposed the subject as passively receiving the sensation and turning his whole attention
toward understanding what is happening in him. This
mental state is not constant. Ordinarily, a conscious
impression stimulates a reaction on the part of the
subject, which is not only a motor reaction, but an
intellectual one as well. Attention is fixed on the
sensation, judgment comes in to classify or define its
characteristics, and the whole is accompanied by an
emotional state. In any perception studied in its natural
and concrete form, these diverse elements are to be
found. When anyone who finds himself in the circumstances previously described wants to localize a sensation
of contact, he begins by concentrating his attention, this
concentration being manifest in the nimble movements
which the hand tends to execute and which are halted
even as they are begun. As we have said, the very process
of the localization is an act of judgment that includes the
recall of some known point of reference, the estimate of
the distance between the point touched and that referred to, etc.[17]

As can be seen in these two passages, Binet recognizes the
presence of judgments in perceptions or, better said, that perceptions are constituted through judgments. In his book *The Psychology of Reasoning* his position is somewhat different; the thesis
he adheres to is more extreme and presupposes the similarity
between reasoning and perception. In all perception there are
sensations and something in addition which the spirit adds to
sensations. The additional element consists in representations and
images, and its role is extremely important. Sometimes it almost
erases the consciousness of sensations, and this has permitted
Helmoltz to compare the perception of external objects to the
interpretation of signs. These signs would be our sensations, to
which our spirit would only concede attention sufficient to grasp
their meaning. External perception is a synthetic process because
the data actually submitted through the senses are united to those
provided by previous experiences; that is, a combination of the
past and the present is produced. But, in addition, perception is an

---

[17] *Ibid.*, p. 64.

unconscious reasoning; the essential elements of reasoning are appropriately found in external perception, so that these two acts, apparently so different, actually have an identical internal structure. Perception and reasoning have these three elements in common: (1) they are mediate or indirect ways of knowing; (2) they demand the intrusion of previously acquired elements (memories, acts of experience, premises); and (3) they presuppose a similarity between the act which is affirmed and the previous statement on which it rests. The conjunction of these elements shows that perception can be compared to the conclusion of a logical syllogism. Binet compares the perception of an orange to the classical example of the syllogism: "All men are mortal; Socrates is a man; therefore Socrates is mortal." Simplifying his discussion, the implicit reasoning in perception would be: "All complexes of these particular sensations (in this example those that actually and normally are given in oranges) are oranges; this object gives us these particular sensations; therefore, this object is an orange." [18]

Occasionally Binet cites Helmholtz in support of his thesis, but, actually, Helmholtz had already clearly formulated this thesis in terms not very different from those of Binet. For Helmholtz, perception is an unconscious syllogism in which the major premise is composed of a series of earlier experiences and the minor premise by the present experience. Later, without modifying his position and insisting that the perceptive process is founded on what is referred to as thought, Helmholtz avoided the expression "unconscious syllogism" in order to avoid confusion of his thesis with that of Schopenhauer and his followers, who also maintained that perception is an unconscious reasoning, but of another kind— a causal reasoning that advances from the sensations to the presumed object, as well as from the effect to the cause. Helmholtz maintained that this interpretation was obscure and unjustified.[19]

Wundt has also turned his attention to the role of judgment in the phenomena of perception. After referring to simple recogni-

---

[18] Binet, *La Psychologie du raisonnement* (Paris: F. Alcan, 1886).

[19] The ideas of Helmholtz on this problem were discussed more than once by him and may be seen in his "Die Thatsachen in der Wahrnehmung" (1878) contained in his work *Vorträge und Reden* (5th ed., Braunschweig: F. Vieweg, 1903), II, 233. The ideas of Schopenhauer are developed at length in chapter iv of *Ueber die vierfache Wurzel des Satzes vom zureichnenden Grunde* in *Sämtliche Werke* (Wiesbaden: E. Brockhaus, 1946–1950), Vol. VII.

tion, which occurs when we find ourselves before an object previously perceived, he says:

> In general, the process of knowing through the senses is only barely distinguishable from these recognitions of particular objects that are known. The logical difference between these two concepts resides in that recognition designates an affirmation of the individual identity of the newly observed object with another observed previously, whereas knowing indicates a subsuming of the object under a concept already well known.[20]

Aloys Müller gives expression to his thought in similar terms. He maintains that we perceive much more than we see or touch. The perceived apple is much more than that actually seen in the thing we call an apple. No doubt there are sensations in perception, for without them there would be no distinction from representation. But these sensations are completed with a certain number of representations that are forged with them and with judgments or with the sediment of judgments.

> Never in our awareness of an object do we have a pure complex of sensations and representations; rather in such cases there is always immediately added at least *one* judgment. This does not need to be a formulated judgment, but rather a knowledge of something. When we know, for example, that what we see there is the color red, by that very token we place it in the class of objects of sensation, and we have in this knowledge an unformulated judgment. Calling the thing an apple also contains a judgment. Let us think now about the sediment of judgments, about the wealth of knowledge previously acquired, which is enclosed in spatial intuition.[21]

The number of interpretations that are more or less in agreement is enormous. We could add many names to those already cited, including those of J. P. de Crousaz, I. H. Fichte, P. Jessen, A. Höfler, J. K. Kreibig, J. Bergmann, A. Riehl, K. Stumpf,

[20] Wilhelm Wundt, *Compendio de psicología* (Madrid: La España Moderna, n. d.) , p. 320.

[21] Müller, *op. cit.,* 53.

W. Enoch, W. Jerusalem, H. Maier, K. Jaspers, A. Meinong, F. Brentano, and W. Dilthey.[22] All these men, as well as those previously cited, accept the interposition of judgment in perception, in one way or another, but not always with the same import that we attribute to it. To establish this point unequivocally, even though running the risk that the insistence may seem useless, let us point out that our primary interest is to affirm that every objective presentation is constituted by an act of judgment. The objective presentation may be an external or internal perception, or the apprehension of an ideality, a concept, a conclusion, or something imaginary. The apprehension of the states of the subject is also an objective presentation, if the states are brought to consciousness so that they do not lose their condition as states.

This problem alone is our immediate concern. It is well to make this clear, because some mentioned investigators have not sufficiently isolated this problem and others have stepped over the problem, going beyond the face-to-face relation of the subject and the object, which is our immediate interest. Notions such as the reasoning of causality, to which one has recourse in the attempt to establish the existence of a reality which, as its effect, produces perception in us, or the notion of resistance, on which one leans to justify the existence of reality so far as it is independent of consciousness, exercising its pressure on it—these have little or

[22] For many reasons it may be well to provide a clarifying statement concerning these last three. Meinong has extensively studied certain psychical acts to which he assigns an intermediate position between representation and judgment (*Ueber Annahmen* [2d ed., Leipzig: J. A. Barth, 1910]), which would give the impression that he decisively separates judgment from all else. However, he maintains that perceptions are judgments, properly speaking. (*Die Philosophie der Gegenwart in Selbstdarstellungen* [2d ed., Leipzig: 1923], I, 128.) Brentano also would seem to separate judgment from everything else, on the basis of his three-fold division of psychical phenomena. But he states explicitly that "the fact that perception should figure among judgments also shows very clearly that predication does not belong to the essence of every judgment. In effect, perception is knowledge or assent, even when it is erroneous." (*Psicología* [Madrid: Revista de Occidente, 1926], pp. 118–119.) As for Dilthey, who in referring to this problem discussed it with others in which he was more interested, we rely on his adherence to and support of the thesis that Helmholtz had already stated. (Dilthey, *Gesammelte Schriften* [Leipzig: B. G. Teubner, 1924], V, 94. Spanish trans. by Eugenio Imaz, *Psicología y teoría del conocimiento* [México: Fondo de Cultura Económica, 1945], p. 159.)

nothing to do with the problem before us: that of objectivity as pure perceptibility.

Neither emotion nor will can provide the foundation for objectification. They may push toward it, stimulate it, but objectification is accomplished through judgment alone. Yet here, without undue inconvenience, we may confess to a certain primacy of the will, which, though in no way affecting the thesis we defend, tends to join with another thesis that permeates in a general sense our understanding of man and of reality as a whole. The appearance of intentionality in the realm of psychical states testifies to a thrust, to a tension, in which intentionality finds its source. Indeed, one could speak of a *will to consciousness* that makes itself present and is conceivable as one of the forms of that thrust which produce in reality, from the physical level up, real strata that are increasingly rich and complex, more differentiated and inwardly developed, and even—there is no reason to recoil from the expression—more valuable. We refer to this impulse or thrust and the acts in which it is manifest as transcendence.

INTELLIGENCE AND OBJECTIVE SIGN

The fundamental aspect of objectification, which has been the principal emphasis of our discussion thus far, is limited to acknowledging presences, to raising the lived to the level of the known. If we wished to give verbal expression to this fact, we would choose the formulae "that is" and "that is present." The state or complex of states is recognized as being, as existing, and nothing more. Normally, however, the objectifying act is not merely the bare recognition of an undifferentiated presence; it also particularizes the presence. As has been indicated, the process of particularization or determination takes place in part on the transcendental (unconscious) level and in part on the level which, for convenience, we have called logical (conscious).

On the transcendental level, objects are constituted as pure presences and receive their broadest determination through the categories. Objects are recognized first of all as temporal-spatial, temporal, ideal, and so on. While objectification presents the object in its totality and fullness, the recognition of its more particular modes of being occurs on the level we have referred to as logical. This is the conscious level whose processes, once they are clarified and objectively systematized, are studied in logic. We distinguish, therefore, between the single constitution of the object and its two types of determinations: those given together with the object itself, of categorical origin, stemming from the transcendental level; and those attributed to it on the logical level through processes that have their parallel or their reflexive duplicate in determinative judgments.

Although we will not be able to cover all the problems pertaining to intelligence, we wish to point out that its entire function rests on the ability to objectify. The functions of the intelligence tend to be examined as though they consisted in a certain kind of handling of previously given elements. This is an erroneous assumption. The intelligence is the same whether creating objects or speculating on the ultimate and most abstruse problems. What has been said with reference to the function of judgment in perception puts us on the proper road. It has shown us that judgment, the principal logical element, is not at work in the logical sphere alone, but that, before this, it has also had a dominating role in objectification, in the creation of the object as such for the subject—in the object as perceived.

The fundamental objectifications are those of whole or complete objects: this tree, that house. Such objects, which are strictly individual, are functional and entitative units profiled by experience itself. And in man's capacity to distinguish these objects, to individualize them, and to attribute existence to them, he is already widely separated from the animals. Animals do not apprehend cognitively; rather they functionally "take into consideration" certain complexes that assume a vital importance for them—for their food, reproduction, and physical well-being. These complexes are taken into consideration as wholes, with no isolation of the components, not even those that would seem to be of primary interest. Frequently, for example, the animal does not recognize its customary prey if the prey is not confronted in the complex in which it is usually hunted. For man, however, the objectifying task is continuous and, in principle, unlimited. In the objects we have referred to as whole or complete, man perceives the parts, properties, processes, modes, and relations, objectifying them separately, and attributing to them that being or consistency which is inseparable from any objectification. One does not find it strange or surprising that he can speak of the color or form of an object, of its weight or its size and space in relation to another object in the same way as he can speak of things existent in themselves, although the former are qualities or modes with no real consistency and are given only as moments of the fundamental objects. Thus, the objectifying faculty of man, having recognized objectively the complexes naturally profiled in experience, fulfills the task of striving for the objectification of all that comes within its range, that is, of objectifying in an unrelenting manner. There is a tendency to use the term "abstraction" for this operation. This is convenient as long as one keeps in mind that the operation is not restricted to an activity of separation, but is rather the objectifying perception of what is being separated, a recognition that attributes being. This is precisely what enables one to handle what is abstracted as subsistent in itself, to handle it as object.

The perception of these objects obtained through abstraction, through isolating perception, leads man to discover a basic condition of the warp and woof of reality, which could be referred to as the logical structure of reality. Namely, reality is constituted of elements entering into the composition of individual and contingent complexes (this tree, that rock, this man), but, on the other hand, these same elements constitute "natural" families, groups which can be ordered hierarchically. The primary objects have color, form, numerable parts, determined physical properties, which, grouped in a given manner for each object, define it, in its singularity and specificity, as an individual and as a species. Yet, these elements can be linked together of themselves, completely independent of the concrete complexes that they form in reality. Not only can they be isolated from the real complexes, and not only does objectification confer being on them as it discerns them, but it recognizes immediately that for each there is a specific place in the ontological panorama. There are natural families of numbers, forms, and relations, of each order of qualities or properties. Objectification functions here in two successive steps: It isolates each one of these instances in each individual object of common experience (a given color in a particular rose), and from this single, isolating objectification another object is lifted out, though it is the same one. This is done by attributing to the object a new condition—universality—through the recognition that it is not only an element in a real, determinate complex, but an element common to many, one of the common components of the whole. (The color perceived in the rose is repeated, or can be repeated, identically in innumerable objects.)

Results of two different orders are obtained through this kind of isolating perception or objectification of what in itself is not an empirically delineated natural entity. On the one hand, as has been said, there is an ontological order that is recognized and established as natural and not created by the human mind, but which is totally distinct from that revealed in real complexes, with its conformation and distribution in space and time. Thus, one can observe the families of numbers, forms, colors, sounds, densities, and temperatures, each with its special order. On the other hand, through the objectified synthesis of the common features in related entities found in basic experience, they are grouped in species and these, in turn, in genera, and so on successively, that is, they are classified in species for ontological or structural reasons and in still larger groupings in a step-by-step, pyramid fashion according to the rigid canons of logical classification. By this classification one also proceeds to reconstruct a fundamental ontological scheme that corrects and surpasses anew the arbitrariness of the actual distribution of things in space and time.

In keeping with what has been said, we are able to distinguish three types of objectivities: first, complete or whole objects, such as the sheet of paper I am using now; second, objects isolated within the complete objects, yet perceived in them, such as the white color or the form of the sheet of paper. I am able to consider such an object either individually as a single fact or in its universality, as something identical with itself, regardless of the complete object in which it may appear; and, third, objects created through the synthesis of the features common to many primary objects. Many objects of this type are referred to as specific objects. All this is the consequence of the same objectifying capacity, though exercised on different levels, which is constituted simultaneously with man. That is, what we call man is the being capable of these objectifications.

If the intelligence had had to get along with nothing but single objects, with complete objectifications, it could not have advanced far. What has further promoted the formidable advance of human intelligence has been the transition to objectifications of universal or general scope, under each of which many empirical examples are subsumed. The dictionary is the great collection in which these ultraindividual objectifications are registered in the form of common names. Such words as "house," "rock," and "horse" include all houses, all rocks, and all horses—past, present, and future. Also found are such words as "number," "condition," "quality," and "withdrawal," which are also general in scope. And from the point of view in which we are interested, all verbal expressions also come to be common names—"you run," "he was talking," "I would finish"—because they describe determined kinds of actions in the different ways in which they occur, but with a generality that includes all the actions of a corresponding kind. A general dictionary includes the great mass of objectifications achieved by man, not only in his ordinary activity, but also in scientific and philosophic activity where these have been incorporated into common usage. This means that the objectifying and nominating functions emerge side by side and work in harmony. In effect, objectification requires or gives rise to nomination and would seem to be imperfect without it. The original function of significant language appears to be that of reinforcing objectification, of underlining it, of completing and solidifying it, binding it to the material concreteness of the sensible sign. It does not matter that significant language may stem in some way from the nonsignificant, from the language without objective content which we find in animals and which is still retained in some modes of human expression. What cannot be doubted, so far as we are concerned, is that man emerges at the same time as does significant or objective language, since this language not only expounds its objectifications immediately, but it is indispensable if objectification is to be perfected and consolidated and thereby is to function in a continuous and normal fashion. The primary function of language, then, would be expression; but it also includes communication, which is understood as the communication of the subject with himself, his saying to himself that he perceives, that he is aware of a presence, that he has something in sight. Man possesses nonsignificant language, in common with the animals, yet the superiority and the fullness that it attains in him is due to that in the emotions and volitions which is specifically human. It stems from the fact that emotions and volitions are phenomena which occur in a subject who is ever conscious of a vast world of objectivities. Communication in the proper sense, which is the transmission of objectifications to other subjects through signs, may undoubtedly stimulate nomination, and, perhaps by reflection, it may stimulate the objectification contained in the foundation of nomination; but this is only an incentive to continue the task that the subject already carries on by inclination and even by intrinsic necessity. To perceive in terms of objectivity already implies something akin to telling oneself that something on the horizon of consciousness stands out. To speak is to tell it to oneself and then to tell it to others.

The correlation and reaction between intelligence and language are evident at every stage and show the indissoluble alliance between them. Significant or objective language seems to emerge with the perception of whole objects. Thus, the child tends to invent words to designate those objects which impress him and whose names he does not know, and if he knows the name he tends to pronounce it when the object is placed before him. However, if the human mind did not perceive objects of an ultraindividual scope, language would have become stagnant and would not be anything like it is because it would have become only an interminable collection of proper names, one for each thing. The capacity to perform general objectifications, which makes possible versatile intellectual activity, is also the founding condition of human laguage. For, just as a single thing is thought of with the help of general notions (in thinking of a determined man, we are tacitly attributing to him that which pertains to man as a species), so also language designates the particular with the help of the general by means that vary and through which words, each of a general meaning, are compelled to name situations or objects that are rigorously individualized.

The perceptive function stimulates language, and language in its turn supports the continuation of the objectifying task. What is intuited seems to demand a verbal sign naturally and immediately. If the sign does not exist, if it is vague, equivocal, or changing, the retention of what is objectified suffers as much as does its transmission. Perception is always objectification. Verbal expression reinforces objectification, making it more objective for the subject himself in that he is thus able to say something to himself as if he were someone else. The tendency toward linguistic expression is an aspect of the universal fact of expression, which in this special case is subordinated to the modes of intentionality. It is the same impulse found in the immemorial foundations of the representative arts, of the picture writing of the primitives, of the spontaneous drawings of infants, and of all the developments of objectified culture. The sign is indispensable for retaining objectifications in a stable and ordered multiplicity, because the purely psychical tends to evaporate, and the sign fixes it through the superior stability and concreteness of what is sensible and externalized in comparison with what is only intuited or presented. In principle, one is able to intuit and to think without words, and objectification, of course, precedes nomination; but what is intuited or thought will neither be neatly outlined nor retained, nor, by the same token, will it be possible to advance in a progression of thought that requires the foundation and support of some thoughts upon others. If man is the only being who speaks, it is because he perceives objectively and no one else perceives in this fashion. If he is able to progress indefinitely in his objectifications, which are not only of separate instances but also of their connections and, in the long run, of the whole web of reality, it is because he speaks. We shall see, in addition, that speech gives rise to what is peculiar to the human community, making it possible for the species to take advantage of the achievements of individuals for the benefit of every member of society. From all these points of view it is obvious, as has been said somewhere, that the question how man created language is lacking in meaning, because language is necessarily simultaneous with humanity. Stated in other words, speech is one of the functions whose appearance gives form to the being we call man. Man completely mute can only be imagined as a sketch, as an unformed design of man. We refer, of course, to a muteness that precedes the appearance of language, not to the accidental muteness of an individual within a speaking community, since in this case the mute is able to take advantage of the speaking activity of his forefathers and his contemporaries. The extraordinary reach and significance of speech consists in that, as it brings out what is intuited or thought, it confers upon it an existence of its own. This permits communication and makes it possible for objectification to grow and become securely anchored in each subject, while integrating the objectifications of all subjects in the community.

The whole function of the intelligence can be reduced, in the main, to processes of analysis and synthesis and to attribution of existence to what is analyzed and synthesized. The perception of a whole or primary object is the result of an analysis which outlines and separates it from the continuous web of experience. We have already seen that animals do not profile objects but keep them interwoven in functional complexes within which the objects do not possess autonomy. The isolating perception of parts, modes, properties, relations, or aspects of any kind is also the consequence of analytical processes, made possible through the ability to objectify. Analyses alone, however, would not permit the work that is peculiar to human intelligence. They would separate and atomize reality, transforming it into a huge conglomeration of objectifications before which we would be at a loss. The practical and theoretical handling of these materials becomes possible only through a correlative synthesizing operation. This operation creates objectivities of a general kind and orders them according to their own nature by subsuming them under ever more inclusive generalities, thus arranging what is objectified in rigorous classifications. But the synthesizing capacity goes beyond this in creating new complexes, according to man's intentions. To treat this point, however, we must distinguish the different uses of the intelligence.

In its practical function the intelligence works out the problems that each moment of life sets before man. Let us take an example. If the problem is to hang a particular picture on some given wall, the wall is seen as "an extension" within which the proper place is to be chosen and as "a given resistance" capable of holding up the picture. This "resistance" will also influence the selection of support and the manner of suspending the picture. The picture will be seen as "something heavy" or as "a weight of a certain magnitude," which, for its part, will contribute to determining the quality and sturdiness of the support needed. With the problem limited to these specific terms—"to hang a particular picture on a given wall"—everything pertaining to the wall or the picture that is not a factor in the problem is ignored. The analysis has separated and retained in each case only those elements that take part in the proper composition of the dynamic situation of hanging the picture. Within this situation the wall is only a surface and a resistance and the picture something extended and heavy. The numerous remaining aspects of the wall are ignored; everything about the picture which does not pertain to the specified purpose is set aside. Temporarily, we create an *ad hoc* situation, an original synthesis composed of certain elements discovered in the wall and in the picture. These elements we recognized as similar to others previously recognized in reality, though abstracted from it, and whose nature and function are familiar to us. In general, we know what extension, resistance, and weight are; and we must understand clearly how each of these should be taken into account. The process of hanging the picture presupposes a special dynamic synthesis of the necessary elements leading to another synthesis, which is preconceived as a project yet has a static nature, that is, the new condition of the wall adorned with the picture. In all practical activity, therefore, there are two syntheses, two situations created by man through the proper arrangement of the component parts, each of which is first imagined and then carried out. There is the final situation—the picture hanging on the wall; a given industrial or handmade product; being at a particular place at a specified time—and the dynamic situation by which it is possible to obtain the desired and anticipated result—the procedure of hanging the picture; the industrial or manual process; the acts and the means necessary for our travel. The elements used are extracted from the present reality, but only so far as they are recognized as previously isolated and are our conceptual possessions. We could not handle the resistance of a given wall or the weight of a particular picture if we did not already have a general idea of how resistance and weight behave. The *intelligent* use of the intelligence in its practical application consists in the invention of final syntheses, in creating new objects, and in finding more adequate dynamic or operational syntheses for creating them. To limit oneself to objects that are produced by habit through inherited resources is a traditionalism bound by routine. In this, there is neither the attempt to exercise the capacity to project new objects nor that to revise current procedures in order to correct them or replace them by better ones. In this procedure, the analytic and synthetic functions are at rest, and there is a blind repetition of what was done before. The use of "models," the solution of problems according to established patterns, is inevitable and permits the intelligence to keep itself ready for new demands. Yet the models or patterns still need the approval o the intelligence, which created them and must preserve them, authorizing their continued function. The practical intelligence is itself a constant inventor, unceasingly analyzing and synthesizing. Properly speaking, an inventor, whether so by profession or by avocation, is one who is engaged in innovating and worthwhile syntheses by having within his reach many objectifications pertaining to a given sector of reality; by being able to perceive objectively the existing and possible connections between these objectifications; and by his imaginative aptitude for formulating objective syntheses that had not occurred to others.

Once the principal steps have been established and fixed, the functioning dynamic syntheses and the procedures for reaching final situations give place to operative models or "methods." A method, therefore, is the scheme of a procedure established by the intelligence in order to achieve some goal, a procedure that has been fixed and is valid for all similar cases. In turn, those aspects of the methods which can be so embodied find concrete expression as tools, which, when simple, are interwoven as parts of the method and, when very complex, become mechanized methods. Operations such as hitting, cutting, and perforating, which were originally done with what happened to be at hand, suggest the construction of instruments conceived as something for hitting, cutting, or perforating, in such a way that the material of which they are made is only the support and agent of the operations for which they are made. It has been said that man is a tool-making animal. As we have seen, this is a matter of a derived ability that stems from the capacity for intelligent action—the capacity for fixing goals and for imagining means of attaining them. In turn, the prerogative of intelligent action has its ultimate foundation in the objectifying capacity. Without it, the analysis of reality which provides the elements for *ad hoc* syntheses would not be possible. Instruments form but one of the classes of such syntheses. Let us remember that something similar may be said with regard to language. It has also been stated that man is a talking animal. Significant language is exclusive to man, but it presupposes the analyses and syntheses that are based on the objectifying activity—even though significant language may operate in these analyses and syntheses in an auxiliary fashion.

Let us turn to the examination of several aspects of the purely cognitive or theoretical activity of the intelligence.

Theoretical knowledge is developed in a series of stages. The first stage is based on common or spontaneous knowledge, and each stage makes reference to the following one, until the statement of ultimate problems is reached. In common experience, mankind has carried out an analysis of reality followed up by countless syntheses. Rarely does one turn one's attention to the extraordinary magnitude of this task. Notions of increasing generality, such as horse, quadruped, animal, are achievements of spontaneous objectification, and the same is true of all common terms in the dictionary except those developed in the sciences. Not only are these objectifications general in scope, but their generality is set up in succeeding levels that finally reach the limit of total generality commonly referred to by the words "something" or "thing." [23] In the study of nature, the basic sciences are the descriptive-classificatory sciences whose primary purpose is to define general objects and groups of actual entities and then to order them according to their nature or structure, that is to say, ontologically. Systematic mineralogy, botany, and zoölogy are good examples. One cannot doubt that they stem from common experience, though, to be sure, they correct it and add to its depth. Many of the mineralogical, botanical, and zoölogical species have been established through common observation. Common observation, however, tends to be governed by practical interests and, also, to fall into error, frequently making mistakes. Practical interest gives rise to groups such as "eatable animals," "wild animals," or "harmful bugs," which are of little interest for theoretical purposes. Common observation ignores the world of microbes, and, when a marked dimorphism occurs, animals that belong to the same species are placed in different species. In addition, common knowledge is accompanied by errors and misconceptions because of its

[23] We do not refer to the word "thing" in the sense of a material thing, but in that vague and very general sense that becomes evident in expressions such as the following: "Now just get busy with something"; "What you may think is something in which I am not interested."

lack of method and critique.[24] Yet, in all, the amount of knowledge that it accumulates is enormous. The intelligence must clarify this knowledge and add to it, eliminating the errors stemming from the interference of other faculties (emotion, will, imagination); it must serve as its own critic and question reality unceasingly. Such a task is carried out in the first place by the descriptive-classificatory sciences, which in turn refer to tasks of greater difficulty that penetrate more deeply the constitution of reality, to a group of sciences that is above them in the hierarchical scale: biology, chemistry, physics.

These sciences do not attempt to define species of real entities, to give form to superior natural groups, and to place them in systematic pyramids. The problem at this point, stemming from the break down of reality into its elements, consists in doing with these elements what was previously done with the whole entities of immediate experience—in recognizing, defining, and investigating their basic being, ordering them into successive natural groupings. These entities are not isolated in nature, but appear as compounds, functions, properties, or relations of whole entities. Simple bodies and the reactions that chemistry studies, physiological conditions, color, sound, gravity are all entities [25] stemming from a more difficult objectification than that which provides whole objects. And, by the same token, the sciences investigating them belong to a higher order than those sciences dedicated to the study of whole objects. Yet even here, common observation provides the point of departure in presenting rough notions that must be examined, deepened, reorganized, and explained. Color, for example, is differentiated into its kinds and varying shades; science determines these distinctions with precision and sets up the spectrum. The facts of weight, accepted on the basis of common observation, are corrected in the law concerning falling bodies and in the understanding of weight in terms of gravity. The examination of whole objects stimulates the examination in common

[24] See "Saber ingenuo y saber crítico" in Romero, *Filosofía de la persona* (2d ed., Buenos Aires: Editorial Losada, 1951).

[25] Here the word "entities" refers not only to entities in the classical sense but to process. This is inevitable, particularly if one maintains that perhaps everything in reality is inherently process.

experience of the elements of these objects, and on the theoretical and critical level these two stages of spontaneous knowledge correspond to the two types of sciences we have distinguished, although generally they remain on the level of so-called sensible perception. The awareness that this experience is conditioned by the structure of our sense organs provides a forward step, which is most evident in physics with the transition to interpretation in depth and to universal theory, which attempts to go beyond perceptible reality. The phenomena given in experience are now explained by other facts, which are essentially quite different, but which are capable of producing in us, as their effects, the perceived phenomena. Such phenomena as color, sound, and heat are explained in this manner. This transition is achieved in the main through reasoning and calculation, with the help of new hypotheses that lead to new kinds of experimental exploration. Until recently, the ultimate level of interpretation consisted of a mechanical conception. When this was set aside, compromise interpretations that found little acceptance, such as the energeticism of Ostwald, were proposed. Finally it was proposed that a pragmatic and skeptical view be taken of all interpretation (Duhem, Poincaré), Today, new conceptions are elaborated which are, in part, contrary to deeply ingrained mental attitudes, and which demand an effort of adaptation on the part of the intelligence—for example, the collapse, long anticipated in philosophy, of matter into process; the wave-corpuscle association; and the new concepts of space and time.

The continuity of the intellectual task manifests itself in a very evident manner. The gradual withdrawal from common experience is, in itself, a critique that makes sensible knowledge relative. The preponderance of rational methods seems to lead to a deep and exhaustive examination of the whole rational world of man— the critical justification of reason, logic, and mathematics. Physics, as an analysis of the perceived, leads to its rational interpretation; and this interpretation, in turn, demands that its own foundations be investigated. If the inquiry into human knowledge has not been previously assumed by philosophy as one of its central problems, scientific progress would have demanded it as a necessity for the theoretical perfection of knowledge. That is to say, the development of the critical approach to reality gives rise to questions that inevitably lead to the statement of ultimate problems, including that of reality "in itself," since the consciousness of the relativity of sensible knowledge brings with it the demand for a nonsensible knowledge, which ordinarily adopts the form of a rational metaphysics. When reason itself is called into question, either the absolute is sought through an irrationalist metaphysics or the possibility of metaphysics is denied, though the latter solution does not exclude the metaphysical as much as it denies its accessibility, its potential for being known.

In the actual or historical course of knowledge, the stages have not necessarily been completed successively. As is quite evident in the history of metaphysical speculation, thought, spurred on by intrinsic demands, has not waited on a completed description of immediate experience before risking a hypothesis concerning the ultraempirical or rational nature of things. Nor has it waited to exhaust the rational interpretations of reality before stating the problem of the relation of knowledge to reason. Even as an ontological order can be perceived in the scattered and disordered reality of nature, so in the diversity of the problems to which it leads, a logical order is discovered, an order determined by the nature of the problems themselves and different from the sketch that is drawn by the occasional, that is, historical, appearance of these problems in the mind of man. In summary, just as the intelligence finds in reality a system toward which it is projected, by the same token it finds a coherent system in its attempts to apprehend reality. In both cases, the systems demand a reorganization of facts that come forth spontaneously in a confusion which is not only characteristic of the natural and the human universe but which constitutes the actual structure of this universe in the double perspective of space and time. The intelligence, therefore, confronts two different tasks that are nonetheless intimately connected: the exploration of reality in its spontaneous arrangement, in its immediate and existing order, as a group of phenomena in space and time; and the ontological inquiry into that reality, discovering in it a consistency and order distinct from those revealed in the multiplicity of entities within the boundaries of space and time. The second vision is derived from the first by a kind of decantation. Yet the first vision of reality is neither intelligently interpreted nor even practically dealt with except with the aid of the second.

It is hardly necessary to point out that all intelligent activity presupposes judgment and language.[26] Our thesis is that intelligence does not begin with the handling of previously given objects, but that the mere giving of objectivity is an intelligent act akin to others so far as these acts are founded on the same principle—objectification. We have already referred to the original, active presence of judgment and the consecutive appearance of nomination in the first objectifying acts. So much the more must one recognize the constant presence of judging and nominating activities in the latter developments of the intellect.

Although intelligence has its own function which obeys certain relations stated in the so-called laws of association, it is a great error to consider these laws to be the essence of the intelligence. All intellectual activity—including perception—objectifies, and it is therefore inherent in the intelligence to open itself to objectifications, investigating and registering them for cognitive purposes, as well as projecting and creating new syntheses for practical purposes. Thus the suggestions of the spontaneous associations of images or thoughts are continually controlled by objective verification. Objective projection of the intelligence, as has been stated, has two sources: that which tends toward the empirical aspect of experience (toward that given as existent and present), and that which tends toward the ontological order, which uncovers what we might call the essential or logical structure of reality. This opening to the objective is precisely what confers on the intellect its greatest significance and in a certain way places it above what is usually referred to as "reason." The intelligence is an actual function, a fact; reason is an ideal, the group of requirements or norms in which the supreme demands of the intelligence are believed to find their fulfillment. Whereas intelligence is defined primarily by its acceptance of the objective, by its ability to mold itself to what is, a

---

[26] Language is born as a direct expression of objectifications that are actually achieved, though they may be imaginative or even fantastic. Language, in itself, provides certain directions for imagination precisely because of its original tie with objectifications. The connections of language with myth and the supposed actual relationship between expression and what is expressed, which in turn feeds the important events in verbal magic—habitual in primitive thought and abounding in curious survivals—are pertinent to the theory of culture and not to an anthropological investigation limited to the foundations of what is human.

single definition of reason cannot be given because the great number of ideal demands that go into its makeup are very diversely conceived. There is a Permenidean reason, a Cartesian reason, a Kantian reason, a Husserlian reason, a vital reason. . . . Without considering the difficult problem of the relationship between the intelligence and reason, let us say this: It is the intelligence which, down through the course of philosophical thought, has constructed these various images of reason—images of itself in its desired perfection and purity—and it is also the intelligence that has confronted the contradictory enigmas of irrationality.

It is well to insist that the functions which provide us the knowledge and interpretation of the objective world compose a series whose continuity is not interrupted. The purely intentional aspect and the spiritual aspect of these functions will be distinguished later when we discuss the spirit, but one must keep in mind that this difference does not stem from the internal nature of the functions themselves. It stems rather from their ultimate intention that depends upon whether the corresponding acts contain a positive reference to the agent, to the subject of the act. When this reference is completely lacking, the act is spiritual. Since the intelligence is inconceivable without the aprehension of the universal aspects of reality, the grasping of essences is not a special attribute of the spirit, as Scheler thought, but rather a condition of any intelligent activity, even that linked to very common practical chores. This must be strictly understood as pertaining to the intelligence as we have restricted its meaning and not to functions of another nature, even when these, by the complexity and certainty of their results, give the impression of intelligent behavior. If a considerable part of the intellectual activity here described undoubtedly belongs to the realm of the spirit, it is only because the spiritual attitude thrusts the intellect along certain lines and not because there is a spiritual intellect with a structure and principles of its own.

INTENTIONALITY AS ACTIVITY

Everything that composes the sphere of reality, that exists in time, is active. The real does not know rest, and when it gives us the impression of peace and quiet, we are being deceived by an appearance that we are not able to unmask, a covering that is only the hint things reveal to a knowledge that is practical, unconcerned, and trivial. As soon as reality is looked upon with close attention, with considered reflection, one begins to suspect a dynamism. As the reflection increases in depth and as it is pressed on to disentangle the true aspect of things, this dynamism becomes patently manifest.

Greek philosophy, though its general propensity was for perceiving and valuing the static rather than the dynamic, recognized early in its development the internal anxiety and movement of things. Yet, with the exception of Heraclitus, it attributed the mutations to the phenomenal aspect of the real and looked beyond this aspect for the true and stable foundation of things. The verification of change was precisely one of the reasons that gave rise to the affirmation of the superficial nature of what is grasped through sensible perception; it also initiated the tenacious search for immutable substance, a search that makes up nearly all the history of ancient metaphysics. All in all, however, activity was not conceived in every case as a property of the phenomenal order. In philosophers such as Democritus and Aristotle, change occurs on more profound levels; and in Heraclitus it becomes fundamental, constituting the basic condition of the metaphysical core of things. The clearest example of the preference of Greek philosophy for immutable substance is found among the Eleatics, and it documents a propensity of the intelligence: the demand for identity, concommitant with the human mind, which is contained in the first logical principle. In one of its earliest moments the experience of activity, change, and process comes into conflict with the rational demand for identity and collapses before it. What changes is denounced as appearance or phenomenon, and the attempt is made to apprehend rationally—underneath the crust of change—that which never changes. Later, a compromise is made and a minimum of change is admitted, movement, a mere change in the arrangement of parts that in themselves remain unchanged. Thereby, even if the rational demand for complete stability is set aside, the immobility of the parts when taken separately is maintained, and one is able to explain satisfactorily the multiplicity of all phenomenal changes by deriving them from movement. Finally, there is the confession of a full measure of change, found in the deepest levels of being. The most daring interpretations are not limited to affirming the reality of change in substance; rather they conceive of the real as pure process, as activity that needs no other support than itself. By way of summary, the experience of change—or rather of activity, since change is an expression of activity—gradually succeeds in overcoming the rational demand for stability and immutability.

Beyond the realm of the immediately real, of the perceivable, where change is the rule, there is a vast field of the immobile. Ideal entities, numbers, mathematical figures, essences, pure relations are stable and foreign to any change. Many contemporary thinkers ascribe this same or a similar immutability to values. As to the metaphysical foundation of reality, it has already been stated that certain philosophies increasingly stress an influence that could well be called Heraclitean, and one might add that these philosophies seem to be those with the most promising future.

The idea of stability has been metaphysically bankrupt since Hegel's nontemporal evolutionism, especially since the daring Bergsonian innovation that has plunged time into the very center of everything that exists. In parallel accomplishment, physical science now seems to have reduced all substance to pure activity, though in mechanism it adhered, in the past, to the identity of mass, interpreting all change as a perceptible image of movement, which is taken to be minimum change or, at most, quasi-change. Incidentally—and to make an observation that corrects an erroneous position—one must be aware that the apparently definitive establishment of process philosophy, as opposed to the substance philosophy of ancient vintage, does not necessarily mean that existences should exile and completely demolish essences. To be sure, essences were too closely associated with, and many times were even identified and confused with, the substantial elements, which in classic fashion were regarded as perennial and stable. But one merely needs to think of Husserl to realize that such an identification has only a shadow of justification. Essences set forth only those aspects of reality that are consistent—they do not predetermine the level on which that consistency occurs; and they are compatible with the most extreme philosophy of process. To admit that there are essences is no more than to recognize that reality has different modes of being, that it has an order, a cosmos, which is the same as saying that *there is reality* in the commonly accepted sense. Only if there were no reality, only if reality, with its multiple and wondrous procession of entities, with its generic aspects and its individual attributes, its sequences and orderly links, did not exist, if there were only chaos, would there be no essences—in the plural. But there would be, for all that, a single essence, the chaotic essence. The passionate friends of chaos must admit at least this one essence.

The process or activist interpretation of reality is becoming more widespread. In the progression from the inanimate to plant life, from plant to animal life, from animal to human life the cosmos acknowledges an increase and a complication of activity. At least process is given to us in this way in the part of the cosmos that we are permitted to observe on our planet. There is no reason for believing that our terrestrial world is a special or privileged realm, distinct from the rest of the immense cosmos, and distinct in the major directions of its development, in the primary impulses that give it form, or in the possibilities that its evolution converts into realities. And though it may be sensible and prudent to maintain that the circumstances which have made possible the gradual ascent of reality from the physically inanimate to the spirit are found only on our world, this would not invalidate the thesis of total cosmic identity, just as the existence on the earth of vast deserts where life is not present does not prevent life from being a fundamental fact on our planet. As a reality on this earth, as something that can be assumed where the conditions permit, it seems justifiable to postulate a progressive increase of the cosmic processes. We relate this increase to transcendence, which is the positive element of reality.

Setting aside those increases which, with passing time, may have occurred or may continue to occur in the rhythm, differentiation, and complication of processes in the physical order, it is obvious that the appearance of life is indicative of an increase in the total process, an evident acceleration in the throbbing of the cosmos. Vital events, so far as they give evidence of irreducible peculiarities and unique principles, can be theoretically separated from physical events; but it is not feasible to separate them actually from the physical events, because the vital events include the physical events. Just as living beings are an addition to the physical environment in which they appear, so life in general, in the totality of its manifestations, is a *plus* superimposed on the inorganic. It is not a form or kind of reality placed materially beside inorganic reality, but rather something implanted in it or constituted upon it. The ultimate constituent elements of a living being are all bodies that may be found in inorganic nature, though, to be sure, we refer not to those which a biologist would isolate in his search for ultimate portions of life, but to those which can be separated and defined through the analyses of physics and chemistry. The properties of these elements—their specific inorganic being—are not suppressed upon becoming parts of an animate being. Life takes possession of them, keeping them at its disposal. It organizes, distributes, and places them according to its modes and demands, or, in other words, encloses them in the environment of life. It does not, however, annul or transform their structure as physical beings. Within molecules—which sometimes are extraordinarily complex —the atoms continue to be what they were before they were converted into living substance. Intact in their own existence, they move in and out of the vital orbit without being modified, without interrupting or altering their activity. When the pumping heart forces the blood upward, physical gravity is not violated but a new task is imposed upon it. Life has created a motor that did not exist in the realm of the inorganic. With life, then, there emerges a duplication of the natural function and, one might even say, a duplication in two senses. A new form of reality—the vital form— appears; this new form takes the raw materials of the inorganic level, which, following their own inclination, in one sense continue their physical operation as before, and, in addition, yield themselves to the function proper to life.

Let us clarify these assertions. The inherent processes of the universe are increased, in the first place, by the clear and obvious appearance of the vital—a new form of reality essentially different from the inorganic. From one point of view, the elements of the biological realm emerge and grow alongside those of the physical realm. The enriching of the cosmos is evident—on a stage that up to now has been empty, life makes its appearance at a given moment and begins to produce species of plants and animals. There have been repeated attempts to bring the inorganic and organic orders together so that eventually the difference between them would be abolished. It is not infrequent that some phenomenon or other which characterizes life has affinity with or is similar to events that take place in one sector or another of the physical world, and this is sometimes taken as support for the contention of the continuity of the inorganic order with the vital order, of the absence of an essential difference between the two. This idea found ready support among scientists and philosophers in the second half of the past century, and it is not lacking in defenders on the contemporary scene. It found support in well-known theoretical positions of scientism, finding concrete expression in biological mechanism which allowed no components or principles in the events of life other than those that make up and control physical events.

A contrary opinion, which maintains profound diversity between inanimate and living beings, seems to be more in accord with the results of an unbiased experimentation. Some biological facts, when taken separately, may certainly be compared to specific physical phenomena, but the complex of the phenomena that characterize life constitutes a functional unity whose originality seems undeniable. The physiologist Wilhelm Roux, who takes this viewpoint, maintains that an appropriate idea of life is given in the following terms:

> Living beings are certain bodies in nature which (1) take in matter that is foreign to them (incorporation); (2) change this into substances that are similar to them, as living beings (assimilation); (3) modify that matter through means which they possess (disassimilation); but (4) through elimination of the modified substances which they have modified, (5) by the substitution of these substances through nutrition and assimilation, they are able to maintain themselves either completely or partly unaltered; and (6) through an excess of what is assimilated over what is disassimilated they can grow. In addition, (7) through means that are to be found principally within themselves, they are able to move (spontaneous movement and reflex action), as well as (8) to divide (reproduction), and therefore (9) are able to transmit completely their properties to the product of their division (hereditary transmission). Add to this (10) self-regulation in the execution of all

the special functions, among which adaptability, in particular, should be included.

Karl Sapper, from whom we take this passage,[27] does not find this synopsis, as set forth by Roux, to be completely satisfactory even though he recognizes the correctness of the characteristics included in it. He feels that this synopsis slights the most obvious and peculiar characteristic of every living being—the defined, profiled form with respect to the surrounding world. Actually a living being is above all a psychical form, a form which, as we shall see later on, is an individual. The formative power, a part of life which is constantly at work, is a unique activity. Through it, there is ushered into the cosmos a rigorous *novum* and with its appearance the cosmos gains an additional dimension.

Having affirmed that the appearance of vital activity, with the characteristics we have just indicated, and the individualizing power, which will be treated later, give rise to a new kind of natural function, let us again turn our attention to a separately discernible aspect of this fact: the control that vital activity exercises over inorganic reality. Through this control, motion in the cosmos is increased because inorganic reality is compelled to perform new tasks and functions, to work in determined directions that formerly were unknown to it—all of which may be added to its primary physical function. Undoubtedly, all chemical elements a living being appropriates and uses are mobilized by life, and so far as they have to do with life, they are subjected to a more accelerated activity than in the physical realm.

At this point we stumble on a situation of major interest. Beginning with the vital order, it seems to be a recurring fact that the orders of reality are *colonizers,* in different ways and degrees; that is, they take advantage of a given order, settling down in it and using it for their own purposes, and forcing it into a kind of subservience. Interconnection is an essential principle for the whole of reality. It is that intricate complexity which associates and welds together the real, ideal, and valuable elements. Of the various ways in which the whole is interrelated, let us turn our

[27] Karl Sapper, *Naturphilosophie, Philosophie des Organischen* (Breslau: F. Hirt, 1928), chap. i.

attention now toward this colonizing dependence. In it life subdues inorganic nature just as intentional psychism subordinates life to itself, molding it in accord with its purposes. The spirit, in its turn, takes root in intentional psychism and imposes its own regulations, thereby subduing the whole realm of nature.[28] In situations where colonization occurs, the colonizing entity does not encroach from the outside, imposing its norms and purposes on a state of things that may be foreign and external to it; rather it stems from and takes root in the very midst of the reality that is being colonized—it feeds on it, governing and directing it from the center of the subdued reality itself. It emerges as a parasite of superior heritage which doubtless eventually enslaves the very complex that bore and nourishes it, yet at the same time rises the complex to a greater dignity, forcing it to coöperate in the task of forging a meaning for totality.

Inorganic reality, life, intentional psychism, and spirit are the divisions in reality as temporal being. Each one of these orders, beginning with life, takes root in the order immediately below it and colonizes it, taking it as the matter on which it imposes new form and new principle. This general fact provides one explanation for the progressive increase in cosmic activity: The colonized level adds to its original function what is imposed upon it by the colonizing entity. This does not necessarily mean that what is colonized will increase the performance of its own specific function; at times, the intensification may be limited merely to channeling the activity in new directions and for new purposes without modifying its natural "tempo." Plant and animal life impose special functions on physical reality as they mobilize it for their own benefit and take advantage of it for purposes heretofore unknown, the purposes of life. The animal realm, in turn, colonizes plant life by feeding on it and in this way submits certain vegetable products to more intensified and diverse processes than they would have undergone if the animal realm had not benefited from them. In addition to the general colonization of the lower stratum by the one above it, more special cases of colonization exist within the realms of plant and animal life. These are carried on by

---

[28] Concerning the distinction between nature (including mere intentionality) and spirit, see the discussion on the spirit on pp. 144–161.

particular species or individuals and also result in the growth and acceleration of the cosmic rhythm. The whole is thus comprised of very active and complex cycles of colonizing labor, which often occur in consecutive stages superimposed on each other with the physical world as the lowest level. All of this means that life, a vast reservoir of forms that are autonomous and centered in themselves, in addition to and as a result of possessing a unique configurative capacity, activates large parts of the inorganic realm, putting them to work and thrusting them into unknown directions. The atmosphere of the earth, for example, assumes new functions and undergoes more rapid and complex changes when it is colonized by life, when there are living beings to breath it. Its elements enter into new series of transformations: they are used directly by plants and animals and indirectly when the animals consume plants or other animals.

A new, active, colonizing principle emerges with the appearance of intentionality. Marvelous though the psychical operations of the animals may seem, particularly those of many insects and the superior vertebrates, they are not a new form of reality, but only an important, essential attribute of life. All the surprising aspects of preintentional psychism must be considered as a part of life, with which it is born and progresses, and to whose realm they belong completely. The vital sphere encloses this psychism within its limits and keeps it strictly subordinate to the demands and modes of the vital sphere in a servitude primarily apparent in instinctive behavior. Intentionality does not follow as a mere refinement or improvement of preintentional psychism. There is no continuity between these two psychical modes, but an abrupt and revolutionary change, which, in creating new instances—a field of objects and a subjective center—and a completely distinct kind of functioning, gives rise to a psychism partly free from the tryanny of the vital order. This psychism has horizon of its own which extends far beyond the system of stimuli within which animal psychism functions. We find ourselves, then, in the presence of a new form of reality, an activity completely distinct from all of those that existed before its appearance. The characteristics of the *natural man*, the entity governed by intentional psychism but who excludes any principle superior to this psychism, will be examined later. For the present, we are interested in making only a brief reference to the intensification that intentionality introduces into the cosmic order.

In the first place, the cosmic process is increased by the simple fact of the addition of a new kind of process. But not this alone. The intentional processes constitute an activity more intense than any physical or vital process. The subjective center shaped by these processes is the stage for a drama without parallel in the rest of reality. Perception and thought applied to a task infinite in both extension and depth; the interplay of feelings and passions, sometimes peaceful and sometimes stormy; and the inclinations of the will, which has before it an extensive range of requests—all of these serve to convert the subject of intentional acts into such a compact of reality that the tensions reach a tremendous potential. This subject is in no way like the psychic organ of the animals, which is ignorant of itself and is unconditionally devoted to conserving and extending life. The subject knows itself and creates its own purposes, so that, even though it continues to be a part of the great natural complex, it is no longer a submissive instrument of strictly vital interests. It is like a mirror in which reality is reflected, but a living mirror capable of rearranging its images according to its own criteria and of reacting to them in very diverse ways. The colonizing inclination occurs here in an exceedingly broad manner, with practically unlimited claims. Perception and cognitive elaboration are colonizations of a particular kind. The reality that is known is left intact, but a kind of duplicate is extracted from it through which the subject, and thus the whole of reality, is enriched. Heretofore, everything was merely what it was, but, with intentional activity, reality not only continues to be what it is but, in addition, it is its reflection in intentional consciousness. Everything, therefore, has been duplicated, though not in the sense that hereafter each thing should be accompanied by its own graceless, neutral shadow. For even if it does not possess the actual consistency of the corresponding reality to which it refers, intentional duplication is infused with the light of consciousness, throbbing in the shifting confines of the subject as if it were the thing itself animated by a new life. It would even seem that perception bestows upon the perceived an unexpected dignity, an unspoken meaning. Strictly speaking, intentionality is only consciousness in each subject, but in some way it also comes to be a cosmic consciousness, a reëncounter of reality with itself. It is not satisfied with a passive recognition of what exists, with merely holding before the world the mirror that reproduces it, because the world recognized by consciousness comes to be the field and the storehouse for an untold number of activities totally impossible without an objectifying perception and analysis—operations in which man's being is actualized and developed. Thus man is occupied with progressively producing an order that he superimposes on the spontaneous order of things. This order is culture, whose activities and products are not entirely included in the spiritual realm, as has often been believed, because, although the spirit may be what gives rise to the most pure and elevated cultural expressions, many of them are explained by mere intentionality. By means of culture, man engages in grand style in the conquest or colonization of reality, including that unique segment of reality which he himself constitutes. Culture includes an unlimited series of acts and products through which man gives expression to and makes concrete his own inner reality, giving form to it, feeding it with things collected from everywhere, and elaborating a world that is his own. These cultural objectifications, which are external expressions of the soul—some of them movable and fluid, others more or less solid and stable—in their turn serve man as support and backing, and, through them, as through a natural river bed, man's existence flows. Cultural colonization occurs within very wide margins. Cultural self-colonization is every human function that attributes consistency, profile, and depth to the formless, psychical substance as with the babbling of an infant, crude drawings, and the development of myth; and it is also true of all learning and in the long run, of all education. All knowledge, all technical development is colonization of reality. The superior expressions of culture, such as religion and art, which generally include the agency of the spirit, are also colonizing activities. They are the result of impressing human molds on aspects of the real or, in some cases, the transformation of impressions received by the subject as he relates himself to the vast objectified world. Everywhere, due to the basic act of intentionality, a powerful, ever-stirring energy is introduced and flows in the world, modifying it, reorganizing it, and making it human.

In this section, our purpose has been to emphasize the gradual increase of the cosmic process and the role that intentionality plays in this increase. Such an increase, although it may occur within each level of reality, is most visibly manifest in the stratified, hierarchical structure of totality, where on each level another is superimposed that takes root in it, feeds on it, and compels it to be of service. This is the event which we have referred to as colonization, in which the colonizing principle or agent imposes a new and appropriate form upon what is colonized. Colonization is accumulative: the living engages in a general colonization of the inorganic as well as in a particular colonization of portions of the living itself; intentionality colonizes the inorganic and the organic directly and, in addition, colonizes indirectly the inorganic already colonized by the organic—and it colonizes itself. Up to this point, the colonizing principles have not gone beyond the natural order; one might say that nature is colonizing itself. This successive interweaving, this embracing on an ascending scale, gives rise to a complexity, an increase in the cosmic process, in which the element of intentionality takes on an exceptional importance so that colonization is universalized, creating for itself the most efficient resources and instruments, even making itself conscious. Yet the realm of nature is not surpassed. As we shall see later, the spirit is also a colonizing principle, the ultimate and supreme colonizing principle, but of a completely different quality. With it one leaves nature and enters a new realm.

INTENTIONALITY AND INDIVIDUALITY

The real is always individual—individual in the broad sense, which is juxtaposed to the general or the universal. General or universal instances do not properly belong to the domain of the real. Concepts taken from experience by empirical comparison or generalization are general; essences, whose absolutely identical presence is recognized in the particular, are universal. The relation between the universal and the particular is an old and permanent problem for philosophy. One needs only to remember the basic difference between Platonic and Aristotelian philosophy: for the former, what truly exists are the universal ideas, and single entities are copies or imitations of them which have being only through

participation or reflection. In the latter, however, particular entities are fully real, and the essence is found in them as a component
part. The dispute over the nature of universals—a corollary to the
disagreement between Plato and Aristotle—and the discussion concerning their place and significance in the texture of reality formed
a considerable part of the work of medieval minds. It was by no
means an idle labor, as was believed more than once, but rather an
effort to clarify a fundamental ontological problem. Philosophers
of our own day, such as Husserl, return repeatedly to this difficult
problem which existentialism, also, has stated anew in moving
terms and with immediate reference to man's being and destiny.

For the present, let us leave the problem of the relation of
individuality to universality, which in a sense is the relation of
realities to essences, and examine some aspects of individuality on
its own ground, that is, reality, limiting ourselves to those aspects
which relate to our topic.

First of all, it is well to define or limit the concept of individuality—to leave aside its vague customary uses and enclose it within
strict boundaries. From one point of view, every particular or
single entity, every example that is included in an ultimate species,
is an individual. This is the logical-formal use of the term, which
places the individual in juxtaposition to the species. In this respect,
therefore, everything that is a single thing is individual and has
above it a species that includes it. A rock, a plant, an animal, a
human being, a picture, a number,[29] a value, an institution, a social
group, and a historical period are individual things, contained as
such by the corresponding general concepts that refer to the
respective species. As can be seen, this formal notion of individual
includes without exception everything conceived as a particular
thing, regardless of the objective level on which it occurs. From
this point of view, by the same token and with equal right, a thing
as well as a process, a stone as well as a number, a man and a norm,
a microbe and the universe are all individual things.

In this respect it is well to note that important distinctions are to
be made within this broad concept of individuality. Without
delaying to enumerate them, let us keep in mind that in some

[29] Any number is a single thing. Although it may include a plurality of
units, this plurality fuses into a single thing with its own characteristics.

individuals, individuality and universality coincide. The number five and the equilateral triangle are unquestionably individuals of the class "single number" and "triangle" respectively, but because of their nonspatial and nontemporal quality, they take on a ubiquity and a supra-temporality that permit them to hover above concrete reality in a universal manner. On the other hand, real units, that is to say, entities linked to time, are individual things in a more precise sense. They are in a way prisoners of their particularity, because even the moment of universality that occurs in them—the essence—is made particular and single by the very moment of existence. In our opinion, the series of real beings reveals a movement toward universality which culminates in the spirit. But this does not restrict the singular fullness of each one, and we go so far as to believe that the strengthening of singularization and of individualization is the procedure through which beings obtain gradual access to the universal. When limited to a comparison with ideal particulars, real particulars are undoubtedly individuals in a more strict and rigorous sense. But with these distinctions we leave aside the logical-formal criterion, which sees in the individual merely a particularized instance included in a species.

It will be well to introduce at this point, however, a distinction of considerable importance. The general notion of "real individual" does no more than juxtapose existing particulars to abstract generality, referring to those separate and distinguishable portions of reality—regardless of the sphere of reality to which they belong —as individuals, so far as they are distinguished from the genera and species, being classified indirectly under the former and directly under the latter, though these "genera" and "species" are not necessarily scientific terminology. The predominant criteria are those of real particularity or singleness. Under these circumstances, individual is equivalent to real unit—an example that has been made particular, an instance that has been isolated but endowed with actuality and is thereby interwoven in the complexity of impulses and reactions of space-time or merely of time. Taken in this further, rather extensive sense, individuality is characterized by temporal or spatial unity and continuity, by the separation or the outlining of each object that distinguishes it and isolates it, relatively speaking, from its environment and converts it into an example of a particular species.

An inspection of reality convinces us of the necessity for distinguishing, at this point, between two very different kinds of individuals: those whose individuality stems from something external to them; and those whose individuality is dependent upon the action or control of an internal principle. The first are merely real units, single or particular objects. It is preferable to reserve the word "individual" in its fuller meaning for the other kind of entity, in keeping with the etymology of the word: *Individuum* is equivalent to undivided or indivisible, and only the object whose organization and structure obey an inner principle residing within itself can be considered indivisible. By this criterion, a rock is a particular or a single object and, also, an individual in the logical-formal sense, but not in the true or ontological sense. If it falls over a cliff and breaks, the pieces become so many separate rocks by the same right as the whole rock—and we are well justified in believing that the rock that fell could easily have been part of a larger rock. Nothing essential has been lost in such alterations, whereas something important is always lost when a true individuality is broken. We could cite as an example of an individuality that is complete or founded on an immanent principle an atom, a plant, or an animal. Individualities of this kind are the only ones that should be considered as such.

However, there are difficulties in this view that make it advisable to seek a more satisfactory approach to a concept of individuality. A plant is an individual, but a graft taken from it will likewise come to be a complete individual when it is planted and takes root. The grafted part would seem, therefore, to have had a certain individuality when it was still part of the plant. The earthworm, which becomes two worms when cut in two, seems to have had a certain potential duplicity that becomes evident when it is cut in two and when both parts are reconstituted into perfect individuality. In such cases there functions that power of regeneration which appears to be concomitant with life. The event that caused the separation was accidental, since the individualizing tendency of life is natural and normal. In the given instances, this tendency has found a way to complete two individuals, whereas in the common instance of a wound it is limited to restoring the wounded part. The problems presented to the biologist by individuality do not concern us at this point, for manifest throughout them is the thesis that life is found only in individualized forms, and it seems to aspire, or as Julian S. Huxley conclusively states, "It aspires to a perfect individuality." The difficulties that stem from some ambiguities in individuality will be obviated if we keep in mind the criteria of the 'present situation' and of 'the point of view,' depending on the circumstances. The use of these criteria is made clear below.

Individual, as we have said, is the undivided and indivisible real complex—that is, what ceases to be what it fundamentally has been when it is divided, not only in form and size, but in all that pertains to its proper and complete existence. The plant from which the graft is taken is a wounded individual, and the worm cut in two is, for the present, a lacerated animal, an individuality destroyed. This is the 'present situation' that must be accounted for, according to the first criterion we referred to, and if eventually the graft and the worm segments are restored and even reproduce themselves, this happens precisely because of the individualizing principle—the power inherent in life to organize individuals and to restore wounded individuality. This latter property is one of the salient characteristics of the vital individualizing force. The capacity for regenerating broken individualities is not perceived anywhere in inorganic reality. In the physical order, atoms are individuals and so, perhaps, are their defined elements, as well as molecules and crystals. The other inorganic aggregates are not individuals. Physical individuality, less definite and more multiple than organic individuality, seems to have been halted in the first steps of the developments leading to the creation of a regular order—steps which were indispensable for overcoming the original confusion—leaving to life the task of continuing with individualization.

Unity of function (and of purpose, if we accept what Eduard von Hartmann proposes) at times demands that distinctions be made between one phase and another.[30] From one point of view, for example, the individual or the unity of function and purpose, in

---

[30] This is the second criterion to which we have referred—that of the point of view.

some animal colonies, is the total colony, whereas from another point of view each component part may be considered an individual. It seems equitable to accept as valid a similar distinction that considers certain functional collectives as individuals, such as an ant hill or a bee hive, a crowd, or any form of human grouping with its own order and purpose. The criterion of an actual functional unity, dependent on an internal principle, weeds out any fictitious individuality and shows the true individual as a compact centered in itself and organized by an inner necessity. Referring to some surprising groupings of cells, Huxley states:

> But in the second case one could say there was a strange super-organizing force, an idea of the whole existing in the parts. Yet again there comes to mind the image of a general commanding his army or that of an architect arranging his materials. But again we ask ourselves, Where is the general? Where is the architect? We cannot accept that there exists something similar in a normal sponge and less still in the little groups of cells scattered in disordered groups.[31]

Usually an individual is made up of lesser individualities that sacrifice, to a greater or lesser degree, their own autonomy and individuality in forming the superior or encompassing individuality. Connections and subjections of very different kinds bring together and order the atoms in a molecule, the molecules in the cell, cells in a multicellular being, and men in society. Atoms, molecules, cells, multicellular beings, and men are individuals because they have, in addition to a functional unity, an autonomy that separates them from everything else, an autonomy which, as Huxley well noted, is not absolute enclosure or isolation such as that of the hermit or the ascetic, but an active autonomy that assumes an interchange of materials and influences from the surrounding reality. However, those complexes lacking autonomy are not individuals—as is the case with the everyday objects or those organic complexes whose structure and function reveal their con-

---

[31] Julian S. Huxley, *The Individual in the Animal Kingdom* (New York: G. P. Putnam's Sons, 1912). Spanish trans., *El individuo en el reino animal* (Buenos Aires: Pleamar, 1945), p. 98. The other quotations from Huxley are from the same book.

dition as parts given over to the exclusive service of a whole or a real individual. This is true of the tissues and organs of a living being, which have no more meaning or significance than what they contribute to the individuality of which they are instrumental parts.

A traditional definition of individuality is, *Id quod est indistinctum (indivisum) in se et distinctum (divisum) a quolibet alio.* Two basic characteristics of individuality—indivisibility and separation—are set forth here; but autonomy, on which we have been insisting, has been omitted. The individual, in effect, is one in itself and is separated from the other individualities as well as from nonindividualized reality, in spite of the many relations that it maintains with them. The first characteristic is fundamental and primary. An individuality is cut out and affirms itself as separate from all else to the extent that it is a unit of action and of meaning and not an arbitrary portion of homogeneous or heterogeneous substance. It cannot be denied that this functional unit is such only when it is truly autonomous, though it is granted as presupposed that, within the natural order, this autonomy is necessarily relative. Total autonomy is reserved for the spirit.

Each individual is a circumscribed, closed unit, although there are entrances to it and exists from it. It is an object inherently distinct from all others. We refer to objects as "distinct" when there are many of them and only because there is a plurality. The distinct and the different, which in common usage amount to the same thing, should be distinguished in instances where it is convenient to have a fairly strict terminology. "Distinct" objects are distinguished from each other by the fact that each is a unit, whereas "different" objects are such because of structural or functional diversity. One can think, therefore, of objects that are distinct but not different. It is obvious that each object is distinct from all the rest, because whatever is not distinct is one and the same. It is quite another question whether each individual—for this is the type of object with which we are concerned—is different from another individual or from all others. The difference, for real objects taken in a general sense, rests on two aspects: the aspect of position of each object in space and time; and the aspect of composition or structure. There cannot be objects—in this case individuals—which differ in absolutely nothing, for if they had identical positional aspects of space and time, they would be superimposed and thus confused. It remains to be seen if it is possible to have individuals that are relatively identical—that is, having different positional references but having structural and functional aspects that are absolutely identical. We have examined this problem elsewhere and it is not necessary to restate our conclusions at this point.[32]

Leibniz maintains that there are no identities in what is real, that every individual or every monad differs internally from the rest. Taken all together, these constitute, for him, a series in which the differences between units, although exceedingly small, give rise to a continuous gradation. Undoubtedly, this thesis rests on metaphysical and even theological foundations and implies that value judgments are involved, for the repetition of anything identical would have no justification whatever in a universe governed by meaning, in "the best of all possible worlds." The truth is that no valid argument justifies the rejection of the possibility of relatively identical individuals—that is to say, individuals that are structurally and functionally identical yet different in their positional reference—although their existence may prove highly improbable.

The existence of the world as a cosmos, as a consistent and persistent, varied yet ordered and regular reality, seems to be related intimately and from the beginning to individuality. Before any physical individuation occurred, one must presuppose a temporally or at least logically earlier chaos. In all cosmogonies, religious as well as philosophical and scientific, the "world" is born and progresses through a process of individuation, and one cannot see how it could be otherwise. The first cosmic elements, the atoms, are individuals. Perhaps the original physical material should be imagined as the undifferentiated and chaotic *apeiron* of Anaximander, which later was individualized into stable yet diverse structures—the atoms—producing, when associated in molecules, the extremely rich variety of substances of which the world is made. And yet the world moves in regular and harmonious processes. The capacity for individuation is limited in inorganic reality. The appearance of life means, above all, such a powerful

[32] Romero, "Contribución al estudio de las relaciones de comparación" in *Papeles para una filosofía.*

increase in individualizing energy, that physical individuals appear as little more than rudimentary sketches of the organic individuals. They appear as blind attempts of an ability to give shape to things, an ability that finds in life the opportunity for developing with incomparable splendor.

In the preceding section we spoke of the capacity for form, which seems to be unceasingly manifest in life. Let us keep in mind now that the forms thus engendered are individuals—realities singularized and centered in themselves, each of which asserts its own existence as separate from all other beings and things. Individuation gains in life a meaning that it did not achieve on the inorganic level. Living realities are in a sense self-realities, complexes with a self-regulated structure, which, although without consciousness, might be said to have an inner center. They are neither systems constituted by physical bonds or principles, nor are they mere configurations, in which the flood of vital activity is partly or temporarily circumscribed and collected. Rather, in effect, they *are,* existing by themselves and for themselves, as if each one were in charge of life, administering it for the period of time conceded to it and leaving some or much of itself to its descendants, its heirs. Above all, organic individualization makes possible the two vital levels, as opposed to the single level possible in physical reality. This double phase of life is the sum of unique processes, and it is also the reflection of those processes in a focus or center, which little by little becomes more resonant, more compact, more organized, more self-possessed. Stated in the solemn words of Max Scheler, "It would seem that there is a gradation in the architecture of the universe whereby a primitive being turns ever more toward itself, growing in its inner relation to itself by degrees that are ever higher and dimensions that are always new, until it understands itself and totally possesses itself in man." Life seems to be, *par excellence,* the great producer of individualities, an incommensurable laboratory destined to elaborate, diversify, and perfect them in a task in which creativeness and tenacity compete. "La vie," Bergson has written, "manifeste une recherche de l'individualité et tend à constituer des systèmes naturellement isolés, naturellement clos." This opinion of the great French philosopher has been taken up and endorsed by Huxley, who has placed it at the head of one of the chapters of the book previously mentioned.

It would seem at first glance that there are no degrees in individuality. An object is individual or it is not, depending on its fulfillment of the requirements of individuality. But an individual, because it is a unity of structure and function, increases in individuality in proportion to the intensification of that unity. According to this consideration, the living individual is more of an individual than the inorganic individual. Coördinating functions are greater in the living individual, and, most important, it has extended its outreach, elastically defending its individuality, making use of its environment, restoring the individuality if it is broken, and creating new individualities. To all of this is added the element of psychism, whose extraordinary significance becomes obvious when one is aware of its growth in the scale of living things. The animal is more of an individual than the plant, the vertebrate more than the insect, the mammal more than the fish. With these considerations in mind, one can correct the observation that all individuals are similar with respect to their individuality. Individualization in the realm of the organic corresponds to the coördination of parts, the harmony and unification of the functions, and all of this is parallel to the constitution and the consolidation of an inner center. The gradual leaning of primitive being toward itself, of which Scheler speaks, occurs only in the process of individualization, which gives rise to and strengthens inner centers of increasing complexity.

Individualization is particularization, the formation of private nuclei closed and separate from all others, not in the manner of the monads of Leibniz, to be sure, without doors or windows, but with provisions for strictly regulating and investigating everything going out and coming in according to its own norms and interests. The progress of individuality is, therefore, the progress of particularity, but at the same time—and this is what is paradoxical and surprising—it is an advance toward universality, toward liberation from enclosure in the particular. This contradiction can be resolved without difficulty. The increasing individualization is an increase in the potentiality of the single center, a concentration, a gradual self-domination, an illumination of the psychic sphere, the culmination of the cognitive mechanism. As a result, there is an increase in the radius of action of the entity, which while it becomes more itself, intensifies its jurisdiction, its capacity to project itself into areas increasingly varied and extensive so that it gradually amplifies its relationships with things and beings. The meaning of the direction of this development is seen when one thinks of the ordered series of individualities, from those of plant life and animal life in the most primeval ages to the anthropoids. With their more active processes, with their mobility, animals are far ahead of plants in their relations with things. Psychically, the animal species in general gradually open up to the world as they climb in the zoölogical hierarchy, and we are able to imagine something like a fog between them and reality, which little by little is dispersed. Intentionality releases the gust of wind that blows the fog away completely and with it pure animal life has come to an end.

With the appearance of intentionality, individualization takes a gigantic step—indeed, a jump. Preintentional psychism in the animal is already an energetic element of individualization as an element of creating inwardness, as an instrument of correlation and meaningful conduct. In general this psychism is inseparable from the forces and tendencies that promote and maintain living individualities. Intentional psychism constitutes in man an individualized center which cannot be compared to that of the animal. This center engages in activity of a new kind. It creates a nucleus— the subject—which is the pivot or axis supporting the whole conscious life of the individual and referring it to himself. Of all the changes brought on by the birth of this new psychism, the first that should be mentioned here is the extraordinary condensation that gives rise to a focus, a point which comes to be the determining factor in this kind of individuality. In addition, this individuality, condensed and thickened, is pregnant with a content without parallel in the earlier stages of psychic life. All objectifications, with reference to the external world as well as to the inner organic and psychic activity of the individual, come to be his own possession, through perception and through memory, retained in a dark background from which they are extracted either voluntarily or involuntarily. The whole of these objectifications, which include all the dimensions, apprehensions, emotional reactions, and movements of the will, make up a subjective world elaborated, selected, and shaped according to the standards of each individual, including his world view and outlook on life. The knowing of oneself—self-consciousness—which for us is an attribute of intentionality and not an exclusive property of the spirit, introduces an individualizing component of immeasurable consequences. Although the subject might lack a world and possess only the reflexive datum of his own self, he would thereby have reached a very high level of individualization in living and knowing himself in his oneness. In self-consciousness there is no less than a new dimension of reality, which is developed into a supreme individualizing resource; and thus the individualizing impetus that seems to run throughout reality, creating a meaning in it, would seem to have reached its apex and fulfillment.

The spirit carries individualization beyond mere intentionality to its limit, enlarging and ennobling that duality of self and the world which, as we have seen, are almost inseparable aspects of human individuality. In addition, with the coming of the spirit the particularity of the individual is reconciled, precisely at its most extreme expression, with universality. Matters pertaining to the spirit, however, must wait for later discussion.

II

THE HUMAN COMMUNITY AS AN OBJECTIFYING COMMUNITY

The human community will be our concern only with respect to those aspects and characteristics which are indispensable for complementing or corroborating the determination of what is essentially human. In addition to excluding what is not directly related to our problem, we will try to omit those aspects which border on this problem but which truly belong to the order of the spirit. We will discuss all that pertains to the spirit later. The sociologist strives toward the exhaustive study of human society; we are interested solely in the aspect of society that pertains to the qualities in man which are the foundation of humanity.

The comparison of the human community to animal societies, which for a while was quite attractive to philosophers and sociologists of a naturalistic bent, no longer seems to have many supporters. In our opinion, just as there is a basic difference between man and the animals, even when man is considered as deprived of his spiritual dimension, so there is a profound and irreducible difference between animal and human communities, even when the latter are considered apart from the influence of the spirit. Man is defined as an intentional entity, as the being who is a subject and who has an objectified world. This basic situation, as has been stated, determines and conditions the specifically human element in the feelings and behavior of man. Man's emotional as well as his volitional activity, separated though they are from the corresponding aspects in the animals, do not contain in themselves their differentiating principle. They receive it from the subject-object structure which is original in man, in fact the only thing original in man, unless we go back to the *vis judicativa*, which would seem to have engendered and promoted the correlative poles of subjectivity and objectivity. The subject-object structure is not only essential and determinative in man—in what might be called his individual constitution; it is also essential in the community or collection of men and in man's objective product, that is, his culture. The capacity of this basic structure to provide a satisfactory explanation of everything human is precisely what assures us of its truth.

What is proper to the human community derives, without exception, from the fact that man is a subject and that he perceives or conceives a world of objectivities. Social life, as such, is not exclusively human. Not only do many species of animals live in societies of diverse kinds, they also reveal some of the conditions investigated in human society by sociologists—positive and negative tensions, leadership, stratification, division of labor, and so forth. The parallel can be drawn with particular reference to family complexes. No animal grouping, however, regardless of the aspects which it may have in common with human society, can reasonably be equated with it; only human society is a grouping of subjects, each with its own world of objects, and each one, therefore, capable of objectifying the group and of objectively conceiving each of his companions.

To state that human society is a grouping of subjects is not equivalent to asserting that these subjects are constantly and fully conscious of themselves as subjects. Man is not, either at birth or in principle, a being who understands and possesses himself, though certainly he should and does reach this goal through his objectifying capacity. Indeed, if he does not attain self-consciousness he shows a deficiency or a halt in the objectifying progression. In the subject-object structure—the foundation of what is human—objectification is essential to the object, since the object is constituted by it. But objectification is not essential to the subject, although self-consciousness is self-objectification. It is only essential to the subject to be a subject, to have objects in a relationship of perception and, as regards other behavior, to be the center of activities which are directed objectively (intentional activities) within the emotional and volitional realm. The subject may perceive objects; he may even give form to his objective experience in the realm of external reality and even of internal reality and develop it to a considerable degree without confronting the unique experience of the self, the conscious and explicit affirmation of his very self. For what constitutes the subject is knowledge in general and not knowing oneself in particular. Ordinarily, inner experience should not be confused with actual self-consciousness, which is also inner experience, but inner experience of a particular kind, probably mixed with a strong dose of interpretation. There is no subject without some inner experience since many of the basic objectifications belong to the realm of inner reality. But these experiences do not necessarily imply the perception of the self, either when they occur as isolated and occasional experiences or when they are organized in broad complexes. Indeed, the perception of the self presupposes the objectification of inner identity and permanence, a persistent glance directed toward itself, which discovers and in a sense brings about the concreteness, the articulation, and even the hierarchical organization of its contents in their relation to the center which supports them and around which they are arranged. In order to avoid misunderstanding, it needs to be made clear that, although self-consciousness is not a basic element of the human, eventually, and in all probability, it becomes a necessary element without which the humanity of man would be incomplete. What constitutes man is objectification as an uninterrupted activity and not as a fragmentary or chance function. Therefore, any interruption or limitation in the objectifying activity is also an interruption or limitation of what is human. All of the necessary extensions and consequences of objectification belong to human nature, even though they may be delayed or may not even appear, because man is the being who makes explicit, historically or temporally, everything that is implicit in his essence.

It is in keeping with the natural order of things that self-consciousness in its full and proper sense is not a primitive posture but a somewhat late one. The spontaneous orientation of the perceptive glance is direct, going from the subject toward what comes before him. The turning of the subject toward himself is a sign of maturity. The experience of one's self presupposes many previous experiences of the other, and a sufficient strength to attempt the reflexive movement that in a certain sense violates and contradicts the proper course of perception, which is normally a perception of something opposite to the subject or something offered to him. In order to perceive himself, the subject must skillfully change himself into an object, open himself up, modify his nature. A different movement takes place in the common perception of subjective content when this content is not the self, since there is no inversion of the perceptive glance in this case. If the subject turns his attention to a kinesthetic state, if he relives some past event, if he dwells on some image and is conscious of its fiction, he is doing no more than what he habitually does in any perception—giving his attention to what comes before him. But it is something quite different to conceive oneself as an inner individuality, as one who persists throughout the changes of life and consciousness. A certain parallel in the succession of basic philosophical attitudes may serve as an illustration. Metaphysics is inquiry in the direct sense and is concerned with the being of things. Normally, it is prior to the theory of knowledge. The latter is an investigation of an indirect or reflexive kind. Here, the philosopher must turn back toward himself, freeing himself from things and concerning himself with his knowledge of them, giving attention to the modes by which he apprehends and interprets reality. Something similar also occurs in the development of man in the first stages of his existence: the child is more lucidly aware of the external reality than he is of himself, and the so-called crisis of adolescence, in large part, is the discovery of one's own inner reality. The delay in the appearance of self-consciousness confirms the role of objectification, which, understandably, falls first on what is external, on what is foreign, on what comes before the subject (a category that includes the subjective things which are not the self), and only later turns to the hidden reality of the ultimate subjective being.

"Social intercourse is not what distinguishes man from the animals," writes Morris Ginsberg, "because there are animals which have a complex social life. What makes man's position unique is the notable combination of individuality and social intercourse, his capacity to rebel against the will of the community and to gain an internal independence which in turn permits him to react on the community." [1] Though perhaps in its early manifestations the community held sway over the individual, the objective perception of the group which man attains—and which the animal never achieves—already signifies a beginning or a possibility of escape or release. By the same token, the objective perception of his peers helps to smooth the way toward his own self-perception. It seems undeniable that both the consciousness of the 'we' and of the 'you' are prior to that of one's own self. The conceivable group of one's peers and the individuality of each one of them are perceivable in acts of direct apprehension. Each one's external perception of himself, of his own body as well as of the complexes of his inner experience, leads him to feel incorporated into the group and in this manner to constitute the being of the 'we' which, on the other hand, each one may conceive and understand with reference to his own experienced life, though this does not necessitate a reference to a clear consciousness of the self. A kind of transitory reappearance of that original situation occurs in mob phenomena, which present, in addition, other obvious traces of primitivism. Practical self-affirmation and egoistic sentiments do not require the objectification of the self. The most impudent egoism possible may be found just as well without self-consciousness as with an exasperating self-consciousness. Thus, at least in principle, practical self-affirmation of the subject occurs independently of the conscious or objectified self-affirmation. Yet it can be presumed that the two are related, as for example in the feelings of responsibility and in some kinds of striving toward meaning. We have some reports of the appearance of the perception of the self. Concerning the memories of his childhood, John Paul Richter writes: "One morning, when still a young child, I was standing at the front door, looking toward the left, toward the wood shed, when suddenly the inner vision, 'I am a self,' burst over me like lightning from the sky. It has remained radiant ever since. It was then that my self saw itself for the first time and for eternity." That child who was to be *Jean Paul* had not needed to conceive of himself as a self in order to exercise all of the acts characteristic of a human individual who is different from the others, including the act of distinguishing his individuality from that of all the others.

[1] Morris Ginsberg, *Manual de sociología* (Buenos Aires: Editorial Losada, 1942), p. 109.

Once the priority of the consciousness of the 'we' and of the 'you' is admitted, we are aware that objectification is involved in it, the same objectification that, in a very particular form, carries with it the consciousness of the self. In the lower levels of social life, society prevails over the individual and absorbs him. Many well-known facts testify to this absorption: for example, traces of the notion that the group should be held responsible when one of its members commits a crime are still found, even in very civilized societies; then, too, more generally speaking, there are legal ordinances which still ignore individual rights.[2] This form of subordination of the individual to the whole is quite different from the bonds of loyalty which an individual may later establish with a social group in recognition of his debt to the group and as an expression of his alliance with the men to whom he feels bound through an identity of heritage, interests, and destiny. In the first instance the community has been objectified, and the individuals lack a self-awareness and a self-evaluation to counterbalance the objectified community. In the second instance, the individual perceives himself at the same time that he perceives the society. It is probable that the perception of others stimulates the perception of oneself and leads each one to recognize oneself as a self, and from here one is led to recognize a self in others. In social and cultural exchanges these movements, which shift back and forth with increasing intensity and range, are frequent because man constructs a reality external to himself which is his own projection, and in his association with it he reinforces and improves the inner source from which that external reality comes. Let us remember that, because it is a community of subjects, the human community is, in fact, one in which the subjects perceive each other and that it may and probably ought to become a community in which each member perceives himself and conceives of each one of the others as a self.

Although we recognize the partial truth of Ginsberg's assertion referred to earlier, the essential characteristic of human association stems from something other than man's capacity to rebel against the regulations of the community. The human community is an

---

[2] Felix Krueger, *Zur Entwicklungspsychologie des Rechts* (München: C. H. Beck, 1926). Abbreviated version, Romero ed., Krueger, *Estudios psicológicos* (Rosario: Universidad Nacional del Litoral, 1939).

intentional community. This is what defines it and separates it from any kind of zoölogical community. Man perceives objectively, and he constructs an objectified universe—through his total experience, through his memory, through his suppositions and foresight —which is broadened and completed with the world created through culture. All of this, so far as it is the possession of each individual, can be transmitted or communicated because it is of an objective nature when it comes to him and because it also seeks objective or significant expression. A considerable part of the inner life of each individual is thus transmitted to others and in a certain measure to the whole community, which recapitulates the objectified experience of its members. From this point of view, if man is a subject, a being who apprehends objectivities, the human community is an association of subjects and a common storehouse of their objectifications, which are at the disposal of each member so far as he is capable of receiving them as significant things. This is the basis for the extraordinary scope of objective language in characterizing the human community, which is a community of those who speak, of beings who share their objectified content of consciousness.

What is merely lived is not only on a lower level than objectification, it lacks the actual possibility of transmission. States are externalized in involuntary expressions. When recognized, they are understood by those who apprehend then as signs that many times are equivocal with reference to the phenomena from which they arise. Yet these signs do not actually signify the phenomena, and, unlike the signification of objective language, the phenomena when translated into a representation are not the precise content of the sign. Thus, between a psychical phenomenon and its nonsignificant expression (for example, between a strong feeling of danger and the shout which externalizes it) the relation is immediate and from cause to effect. For significative expression, however, a situation must have been objectively perceived or conceived, and the signs which relate to it must be freely used. Normally these signs will be a sentence or the articulation of sentences, although it may also be a single word with the value and scope of a complete sentence. Objective language not only makes it possible for the subject to give precision to his inner experience and be capable of extended development of his thought as well as communicating it to other subjects, it also makes possible the preservation, the indefinite conservation of these matters in an oral or written tradition. To a considerable extent, a community is a tradition, an accumulation. This tradition has a cumulative character not only because the experiences are added to each other and superimposed on one another, but because these actual experiences permit and suggest others which would not be possible without some precedents. The series is not linear, but that is not to say it cannot be cumulative. One experience may invalidate many earlier ones, even though these were its natural antecedents, or this experience may corroborate those earlier ones and confer upon them the seal of a more profoundly established certainty. Sometimes the awareness that a particular quarry is nearly exhausted will arouse the desire to search for others. Different though some experiences may be from those that precede them, they are not therefore less dependent upon them. There occurs at this point an interesting relation between tradition, which is a cumulative and unending process, and what is currently called traditionalism. Tradition is augmented and enriched with the passing of time. Traditionalism seeks to crystallize given stages of tradition, and, in crystallizing them and presenting them as definitively valuable, it goes against the very grain of true tradition, which is a continuous process, perfecting itself with each passing day. No one will deny that the tradition of mankind in the higher civilizations is infinitely richer and more complex than that of primitive man or the animals. But in primitive man, and to an even larger degree in the animals, there is much more of the "traditionalist" than in the highly civilized man, who is an untiring contributor to his traditional heritage. Tradition increases to the extent that the species or group gathers and conserves the experiences of its members. It is founded, therefore, upon objectifying activity whereas what is commonly referred to as traditionalism is founded on laziness, apathy, the incapacity for new objectifications, and the explicit intention of adhering once and for all to what has already been done and achieved. In opposition to this static traditionalism there is a legitimate traditionalism which respects the past without attempting to convert it into an eternal present. This legitimate traditionalism, in loving and respecting tradition, thinks at the same time in the inherited tradition, in the tradition which is being forged with each passing moment and in which man's unceasing activity will continue to build.

In a certain sense, and yet with all the mental reservation needed to prevent the elements of collectiveness from being converted into mythical hypostasis, one can say that the human species or its groups, as the case may be, possesses an objective representation of reality as given. This representation is made up of individual conquests, though the representation does not attain the same scope in any individual that it attains in the group. This representation is maintained in the group through distribution in the memory of its members; it is elaborated in myths, recorded in its documentary archives, as well as concentrated in some individuals who either by vocation or professional occupation store up large segments of the experience of the group. The group, whether it is the species or partial groups, does not have a psychic organ. It is in individual psychism—the only one that can be proved—that the purely individual as well as the collective moments are given. The difference between these two is not important at this point, since in speaking of a collective accumulation we refer without differentiation to the so-called collective representations and to the sum of those which continue to be strictly individual. These collective representations, so far as they are individual, are fragmentary but they integrate and complete the representations of each individual with those of the others when they come to form part of the common heritage. Many distinctions can be made in this accumulation, if the quality of the representations and the sections or levels of groups are kept in mind. Let us limit ourselves to distinguishing between the content of consciousness of which we are conscious and which is clearly perceived, and that pertaining to a "world view," which occurs on the level of belief, with its interpretations and implicit evaluations. Another important aspect is collective self-perception—what a man thinks of himself as a man or of men in general, what he thinks of his racial group, national group, and so on. The individual experiences of each member of the group are extremely limited and weak when compared to those he receives from the group through various means. The possibility of communicating one's own experience to others—to the group—and receiving their general accumulated experience occurs in man to a degree and extent so different from that given in animals that any attempt at comparison is ludicrous. In addition, by objectifying everything, man also objectifies the very transmission from the group to the individual, making himself conscious of it, conceiving of it as a convenient and necessary process which he perfects and accelerates. The resources of a systematized pedagogy are only the most evident part of the human educative processes, which begin with learning the language and listening to the stories told by the mother or a nurse. The whole human community is a vast school, which teaches and instructs man from the time his intellect is first kindled until the time it finally goes out.

We are not in a position to discuss to what extent there exists in animals, or at least in some species, a traditional heritage, transmitted through imitation and learning, alongside the merely biological heritage conveyed through organic media. For man, who is an intentional being, the heritage that is peculiar and exclusive to him is not the biological one—that he shares with all the living beings—rather it is the intentional heritage, which is a heritage of what is acquired. Thus intentional heritage contributes in its way to man's surmounting the unyielding law of enclosure within one's own psycho-physical organization. In the other beings, this law does not seem to allow handing down to one's descendants what has not been converted into a biological element. What man inherits in his capacity as man is not only certain dispositions or predispositions enclosed in the germinal cells, though indeed much that is specifically human comes to man through this channel, including his fundamental psychical structure. By means of external objectification and expression man makes public what he objectifies through communication and cultural creation. In community life what is objectified and expressed is retained and comes to be the common possession of the contemporaries and an inheritance for the descendants. Thus, what man inherits is the world as the species or the group has perceived and conceived it, in addition to all the accumulated cultural objectifications. These become his to the extent that he is able to understand and use them, to the extent that he appropriates them for his own enjoyment or benefit. His heritage does not come from his parents alone, but from the whole group and, in the long run, from the whole human race.

In the human individual, there is already an evident historicity because he accumulates the objectifications and also because he is modified in making them, as Husserl states in a passage referred to earlier.[3] This historicity, which is, one might say, private, is notably augmented, for the community and for the individual to the extent that he is a part of it, by the increase in the communized mass of objectifications upon which each one lives as on a platform which unceasingly is raised through the combined efforts of all. Human experience is not only the experience of the objectifications thus treasured, and of the total, varied contributions to the common treasure and of its increase; it is also the experience of living in each age on that rich legacy in which the experience of all and of each day are deposited. Western man, above all, is the one who has become aware of this continuing dynamic growth. It has made possible the belief in progress and even the whole concept of history, and has led some to maintain the radical historicity of man. This last belief is a dissolving of human nature into its historical becoming, which disregards that this undeniable historicity cannot sustain itself; rather it is constituted on the objectifying structure and depends on it.

The distinctiveness of man gives rise to other consequences for the life of the group and for each individual because he is a member of the group. Not only is the group as such objectified, deriving from this objectification abundant related phenomena, which we cannot stop here to discuss; there is a more decisive objectification which occasions or makes possible the passing from those aspects of community in the strict sense, or from a grouping which is preferably lived, to those of a society, a grouping with norms and purposes more clearly established. In general, from this point of view a human grouping is properly a community which, through the objectification of ends and means, engenders a great variety of partial, well-defined groups, but in addition tends to change from the communal to the social because of the objectification of the communal relations. In some cases, the level of socialization achieved at the expense of communization is felt as a loss, and a return is effected—or at least there is a demand for a planned attempt at a return—to the communal situation which was abolished or weakened. The odd thing about this fact and the important point for our thesis, is that these same forces with their

[3] See pp. 32–33.

objective direction resolve to retrace the steps that were taken in advancing from the communal to the social. What they propose to accomplish is the restoration, through highly conscious means, of a situation which itself is characterized by the predominance of unconscious and merely lived dimensions. The innumerable repercussions and the fluctuating phenomena are normal in man, and they derive directly from his specific mode of being. In all these processes an increase is evident—in group consciousness, as well as in the objectification of groups, of their goals, and of the relations between their components. At this point, a fact of exceptional historical and human importance—the self-consciousness of each group—should be mentioned, though only briefly. This is not merely the consciousness that the group exists, but rather that it is this or that kind of group, that it has certain qualities. This consciousness is normally produced or intensified through proximity and contrast to other groups, the contrast of Greeks and barbarians, of Christians and pagans, and the class consciousness of our own day. As yet these diverse collective consciousnesses have not been subjected to a systematic investigation which would trace them down through the ages, which would describe them as they were and yet bring out, so far as it is possible, their accord or lack of accord with the social reality they reflected. When we have such a study, and when we know how each group has conceived itself and others by way of comparison, we will no doubt have an instrument that will provide us with new and unexpected assistance for the understanding of the historical process.

Thus far we have been concerned with the community as a receiver, integrator, and transmitter of the experience of the given world, of that world which is naturally present for man's apprehension. Yet it is evident that this topic cannot be separated from that of the community as the environment within which culture is produced. Here culture is defined as the series of creations that are specifically human, a sphere which, strictly speaking, can neither be isolated from the perception of the objectified world nor from the very existence of the community, which, though it may be very elementary and primitive, nevertheless presupposes an order which is itself a cultural creation. For the moment, we have preferred to dispense with the discussion of culture; we will refer to it in a subsequent section because this will enable us to treat its own characteristics more thoroughly, and also because we are aware that the tendency to associate reveals a propensity already present in the animals, although man's uniqueness provides his group with characteristics which make the groups unique and convert them into something completely different from that of animal associations.

The preceding discussion was restricted to dealing with some of the facts which, with regard to the phenomenon of community, have a close connection with the fundamental structure of man. They are of interest because they are the consequence of that structure and because reflexively they rework this structure and strengthen it. In addition, we believe that these facts are determinative for human groups, important as other facts may be. Other social phenomena, fundamental as they may seem, either stem from some form of these facts or go back to prehuman tendencies or factors which receive their specific aspect either directly from man's fundamental structure, which molds them, or indirectly from it, since they adapt themselves to situations which that structure establishes.

Sociologists give a fundamental place in social life to certain dispositions, tendencies, or attitudes which they consider basic and irreducible. Primary as these may be, man's unique nature undergirds them as a common condition or presupposition. The human is the first and general condition of everything socio-human. This can be stated in the following formula: man is a subject, man is the being who perceives an objective world. If human society is not a mere perfecting of the animal societies, it is because man is not a perfected animal, but rather a being with a unique structure. Within society, regardless of the level of the communal integrations which may occur, man behaves as a subject who exercises his native objectifying function on his human environment also. Many of the social processes derive, directly or indirectly, from the manner in which and the extent to which each one objectifies the others, whether as individuals or as a group, as well as from the relationships he maintains with them. It is not difficult to retrace social relationships to the source of all that is human. Vierkandt,[4] for example, distinguishes between social attitudes directed toward

---

[4] Alfred Vierkandt, "Sozialpsychologie," *Handwörterbuch der Soziologie* (Stuttgart: F. Enke, 1931).

a concrete goal and other attitudes which involve a given mode of behavior, particularly with respect to the social environment, identifying the former and the latter with the tendencies or impulses which Oppenheimer refers to as final and modal. It is evident that what distinguishes and conditions these two types of attitudes is the perception of two diverse kinds of situations and the objectification toward which the individual is inclined in each one. In the former, this objectification is directed toward a determined end, a special purpose, and in the latter, toward the community or, more aptly, toward a segment or aspect of it. Tönnies is well-known for distinguishing energetically between community and society, a separation on which we have commented elsewhere. For him, community relationships are those of domination and companionship, and those in which domination and companionship occur together, as in marriage. The societal relationships may stem from the formalization or the loss of warmth in the community relationships or they may be societal when governed by contracts or agreements similar to the contact.[5] Undoubtedly, in all of these relationships, the objectification of the situation comes first. This objectification is the perception of the individuals with whom relationships are to be established, who, in their respective positions, are juxtaposed to the one who establishes and lives the relationship. The relationships of domination, companionship, and marriage are not constituted primarily by an undetermined impulse which is totally blind. Rather, these relationships are constituted on the basis of some conditions and qualities recognized in the dominating individual; or there may be an affinity or coincidence that links those who see themselves as companions; or perhaps the attraction to a person of the opposite sex with whom one desires sexual relations leads to cementing the bond between them.

[5] Ferdinand Tönnies, *Comunidad y sociedad* (Buenos Aires: Editorial Losada, 1942). Also published under the title *Principios de sociología* (México: Fondo de Cultura Económica, 1942).

III

CULTURE

Preliminary considerations

In the examination of culture, we will proceed as we have in the examination of the community, limiting ourselves to aspects closely connected to man's being and intimately linked with the foundation of what is human.[1] Our primary intention is to show how culture stems—one might say by necessity—from the objectifying capacity and, therefore, is a part of the fact that man is a subject who grasps and conceives an objective world. The unity of man and culture is manifest in many ways, and we are especially interested in pointing out, in the correlation between them, culture's influence on man.

Let us first define the distinction between objective culture and cultural life. Objective culture includes all of man's creations that achieve substantiality and autonomy with reference to their creator and thus have a relatively separate existence, such as institutions, works of art, theories, and customs. By cultural life is

---

[1] For methodological reasons, we are limited to considering only those aspects of the theory of culture that are of interest to our task, so we will have to skim over many important aspects and omit others entirely. It is our purpose to publish a book in the near future which will deal with the whole topic, a work on which we have been working for some time. [Romero was not able to complete this work.—Tr.] For historical and bibliographical suggestions and a general, though brief, statement, consult F. Romero and E. Pucciarelli, *Lógica* (13th ed., Buenos Aires: Espasa-Calpe Argentina, 1951), chap. xii.

understood the life that man lives in the midst of the objects he has created. If the merely organic—in which man coincides with other living beings—is left aside, then the whole of man's life is cultural life. What continues to be purely organic in man is not clear, for, since man is immersed in culture, much in him that originally was organic has taken on cultural implications. For example, the digestive functions are modified by diet and regularity, which are the products of culture; sexual activity stems in part from peculiarly human motives occurring within a framework in which the agents are subjects, and their activity takes place in specifically defined situations usually under strict social regulation.

The reference to culture at this point provisionally sets aside its spiritual aspect. From our point of view, culture is not necessarily spiritual, even though throughout it seems to be dominated from above by spiritual motives, and even if in effect it is spiritual in many of its expressions. The spiritual implications in culture will be discussed later.

All specifically human activity is cultural. It presupposes cultural objectifications and it manipulates them in the processes of creation, modification, comprehension, and development. Human life is inconceivable apart from culture. The notion of culture includes, then, every human product and all human conduct. The strictly organic is not human, just as the physical is not organic. Yet weight, a physical trait, is something no living body can escape. The notion of culture is at times placed alongside that of civilization, as marking off, for example, a special area, including man's more practical and concrete activities and projects. In keeping with this terminological distinction—which is a value judgment— art, philosophy, religion, and so on, would be included in culture, and all technical activities would be included in civilization. Aside from other difficulties, however, this division does not provide a criterion clearly indicating the distinction. We will therefore adhere to the single but broad concept of culture.

Culture and community
The breadth of this concept includes the community and all facts pertaining to it, for if we classify all of man's activities as cultural, there is no reason to make an exception of those relating to human associations. Thus, all facts that sociology studies are

facts of culture. In addition, the community is the field in which culture occurs. There is no contradiction in maintaining that the community is a part of culture and at the same time, that it is the area in which all culture occurs. This kind of double and mutual implication may be surprising at first glance, but one must recognize that it appears at each step along the way of philosophical and scientific thought. Complicated relationships exist between the various cultural districts, and one of the most noticeable we refer to as "of involvement," whereby particular cultural activities involve others—sometimes all others—in a manner and to an extent varying widely.

In our opinion, the community, as much as any group, is a cultural objectification although of a particular order and only so far as its content or elements are men. Sociology is one of the special sciences of culture that studies human association and the complexes which arise from it. All cultural activities unfold within the community and smaller groups, yet this does not mean that the element of community or of association should completely absorb and condition all these activities. In addition, because the tasks of culture within each cultural region entail special forms of human association, material is provided for subordinate branches of sociology, such as the sociology of religion, knowledge, art, language, and technology. Sociological pretensions which attempt to dissolve all of culture into the social dimension, to explain it only in terms of the social, are continuously renewed. Some sociologists of knowledge attempt to interpret the whole structure of knowing in terms of the influence of social factors. There is such a school among language scientists and similar ones in other areas of culture. Despite strong social pressure, each inclusive group of cultural events stems from a special human demand determinative for it. And there are other factors. First, the fact that in some instances the subject of culture is collective does not imply an absolute domination by the social. This is true since, in the identification which produces collective subjects, a specific incentive has been previously at work, one that corresponds to a given cultural position or specialization, although the consolidation itself is completed socially. What are referred to as "the folks," "the people," "the public," for example, are groups which, once constituted, can be described sociologically; but if they are constituted differently, it is not for social but for cultural reasons, stemming from the particular content that each has in view or the purposes that are pursued. The same human group that is identified as "the public" in an art exposition or a theatrical presentation becomes "the people" in a church or a political gathering. This is not merely a matter of words but a real difference in the character of the groups. Second, the community itself does not necessarily impose a strong community relationship—it does not naturally tend to increasingly enclose and subdue the individual. On the contrary. In its evolution through the ages it apparently tends to replace aspects that are properly communal with those that are social, in which the relation of the individual to the group is less fixed. In general, it is the social life which in various ways, some direct and others indirect, promotes the development of individuality and thereby progressively promotes a perfection and a humanizing of the social through increasing affirmation of man as a subject and reinforcement of his autonomy, initiative, and responsibility. All of this overflows into the diversification of cultural activity and its liberation from a tight and unilateral community.

Culture and intact nature

Culture is a result of man's objectifying activity. Everything that man produces or changes in some way, everything on which he places his own seal more or less permanently, is objective culture. At times the culturalizing process is not visible in the object itself but rather in the new relationships to which it is submitted. The rock we place unchanged on the desk and use as a paperweight is a cultural object because we have introduced it into our human circle and have given it a place there—we have given a meaning to it. A paradox that incessantly pursues man appears, in this regard, in a curious fashion: when man, through love of "nature," of what is alive and spontaneous, attempts to defend this untouched nature from himself, he only achieves his goal by contradiction—that is, by making it a cultural object. Not only do we find culture in the garden that we lay out skillfully around our house, but also in the forest whose natural state we protect with regulations and forest rangers. This is also true with regions we set aside as national parks in order to maintain the native state or the plant and animal species found there.

Knowing is the only human activity that does not culturalize the object to which it refers. It is inherent to pure knowing not to alter its object but rather inquire into it faithfully; and it is the result of this inquiry—data and systematic organization of data—and not the object itself which becomes one of the most extensive and exalted spheres of culture: that of knowledge. Emotional reactions to an object do not culturalize it in a strict sense, although they establish an attitude toward it which usually occasions culturalization. Thus the object may be purposely frequented and changed to a regular source of enjoyment, entering into the human circle, or its appropriation and development may be achieved in a still more deliberate manner. Normally, cultural creation presupposes an activity that in some instances is decided voluntarily and in others is obscurely obedient to a need felt by the subject.

Speaking of objective culture brings to mind primarily what is produced or notably modified by man. But the radius of cultural objectification is much greater if we include in culture not only what man produces or purposely alters but also everything to which he actually ascribes a meaning by his own self and his needs, everything that in one way or another he brings into his own environment and places in reference to himself. According to this criterion, the whole earth is culturalized because there is not a square mile on it that remains outside of judicial and boundary disputes. One would have to fly up to the stars to find nature unaffected by culture. As for our own examination of culture, since we do not wish to become engaged in an excessively strict theoretical investigation that would lead to subtle distinctions, we must forego those somewhat vague types of culturalization and must focus on a more concrete and immediate interpretation. This interpretation will consider only human artifacts and actual modifications of things. The oceans are vaguely culturalized, so far as navigation is dependent on them and their use is regulated by maritime law. This broad sense of culturalization may be provisionally omitted, however, in order to retain only such definite examples as a cove or a bay converted into a natural harbor, an artificial harbor enclosing a part of the sea with breakwaters, an area of the sea conditioned and used for cultivating oysters, or a beach used for recreational purposes.

Culture and nature

Usually, culture is juxtaposed to nature. Culture, it is said, is what man elaborates and produces, whereas nature is the whole of natural reality that subsists independently of man. This separation is comfortable, for undeniably it brings together two groups of facts, each from its own point of view, which differ profoundly, and which should be described not only with regard to the aspects characterizing them but to the ways of knowing that should be applied to them. It could be said, for example, that natural objects are subject to causal interaction and cultural objects to relations of meaning. Natural objects, which in principle are not individually of interest since value is not assigned to them, are collectively referred to, in any knowledge of them, by a generalizing concept. Scientific knowledge cannot deal with each one in particular, but must deal with homogeneous groups, such as types of entities or laws of succession (Rickert). Furthermore, natural objects are *explained,* investigated through causal recurrence or through analytical breakdown. Cultural objects are *understood,* they are interpreted by taking the external reality of the object as the expression of its internal reality or meaning (Dilthey).

Although much of this represents a solid and definitive conquest, we are neither in agreement with the stated order nor with the terms on which the distinction between nature and culture appears in it.

It is not sufficient to differentiate culture and nature by maintaining that the cultural object is a creation of man and is distinguished in this manner from the spontaneous natural object. A bird's nest, in the same way as an object of human culture, is a product of the activity of a being who builds it in keeping with a purpose. If, as some adherents to an extreme naturalism maintain, man is an animal—much more intelligent and developed than the others, but nevertheless an animal—his creations are natural in the same sense as are those of some animals. The construction of dwellings, nests, and even dams is not exceptional in the animal kingdom. Some ants raise ants of other species and domesticate them, a procedure we consider to be cultural when carried out by man.

If man is not an animal, and if, as Scheler and others maintain, he is separated from the zoölogical order through possession of spirit, what would be characteristic of cultural objectification would be a shaping or polarizing by the spirit, which is man's differentiating characteristic, according to that theory. But it should be noted that there seems to be a lack of accord. For example, in Sombart only the spirit is capable of objectifications in the proper sense; whereas for Scheler, practical intelligence is common to man and to animals, and therefore everything in culture which depends on that intelligence—vast areas, needless to say—should be included in the animal order and not the specifically human order.

For us, temporal reality is divided into two large sections: nature and spirit. The characteristics of each will be defined later. Man is by heritage a natural being, but with this most important exception: in him, nature either remains natural, thwarting the law of its development and in a sense denying itself, or it develops until it reaches spiritual attitudes. Man is an objectifying being, and spirit is the complete fulfillment—the perfection of objectifying activity. This fulfillment or perfection does not presuppose a continuity with what precedes it, but rather a jump, a break; the foundation continues to be the same, but the direction changes at a given moment and is even inverted. The spiritual attitude comes to bear in a variable way without ever annulling the nonspiritual motivations in its environment. Man is always, in part, nature, and he may be man and be restricted to nature. Normally man is both nature and spirit, and this duality explains many peculiarities of the human condition, of society, and of the historical process. Man is never pure spirit.

The nonspiritual component of man is nature, but not animality. What we have said has been in an effort to characterize the human substance or structure which is not yet spirit but which differs profoundly from all subhuman nature. This component is the objectifying structure, and it justifies reference to this area, which is set apart within the totality of nature, as "intentional nature." For us, then, nature is divided into inorganic, organic, and intentional nature. And, except when its objectifying activity is interrupted and its proper course is broken, intentionality flows into the spirit.

Objective culture includes all externally objectified creations of man. Thus it presupposes intentionality, though not primarily in its spiritual expression, even if one presumes, with good reason, that culture as a whole tends to recognize the primacy of spirit. An object that is produced is culture if it stems from intentional activity. Therefore, one cannot speak of culture with reference to the products of nonintentional beings, even though they exhibit a markedly purposive character. Purpose in all its expressions poses a serious metaphysical problem. The purpose of the nest or the ant hill would lead us to that of the liver or of the tonsils and perhaps to the purpose of the inferior species in permitting the appearance of the superior species and of man, and this in turn to the purpose of the whole cosmos. Purposiveness in itself, therefore, is not a suitable criterion. Cultural purpose will always be a representable or objectifiable purpose.

With this observation, we believe we have clarified the systematic position of culture. The unqualified juxtaposition of nature and culture is not valid unless we qualify the nature that we are considering as "untouched nature." If creation or cultural activity is alien to spirit, it is nature; if spirit takes part in it, it will be a combination of nature and spirit in varying proportions, which is common to man and to everything human. One should not forget that when we speak of nature in relation to man and culture, we do not mean animality, but rather nonspiritualized intentionality.

The object of culture

Man's activity produces and uses the so-called objects of culture: institutions, norms, language, works of art, formulated knowledge, artifacts, and so on. All of these classes should be understood in the widest possible sense, so that together they include everything objectively created by man. Thus, we would include in language— in its current meaning as an oral language—every system of signs with an objective content. The concept of an artifact will include everything that is used either to make or to achieve something made through the use of instruments such as tools and machinery, but it also will include a boat, a street, or a cultivated field.[2]

The object of culture is not an object of culture unless it is

---

[2] Cf. Hans Freyer, *Theorie des objektiven Geistes* (Leipzig und Berlin: B. G. Teubner, 1934), especially, part i: "Objektiver Geist als Sein."

objectified and made fully external. A poem may be complete in the poet's imagination, but it does not become a cultural entity until the poet provides it with an oral or a written form and projects it out of himself. Until that happens the poem is only a private possession, an instance of the poet's own inner consciousness. A norm, which is an imperative of conduct demanded by a given social situation, may be conceived simultaneously by different persons. It does not become a reality of objective culture, however, until it is formulated and sanctioned by general observance. Usually, the object of culture comes to be such when it breaks the mooring that binds it to its creator and takes on an autonomous life. One of the parallels between culture and community is derived from this. Objective culture is a possession of the community; it exists so far as it is a communal reality. The creation of the object of culture includes not only the actual formulation in the mind but also, and in particular, what we might refer to as "the cultural birth"—the act that thrusts what is created into the external world in such a way that it is given a life of its own, separate from its creator.

This separate and independent life would not be possible if the object of culture did not have a material base or component. A word, for example, needs sound or a graphic sign in order to be a word for all and to have a uniform meaning. The dumb and blind word, which is pure meaning and is related to nothing accessible to the senses, will be a representation or a concept that an individual thinks of or remembers in solitude. It will never be a collective possession, an entity within the reach of everyone, or at least of many, an entity that is communicable and generally understood. For certain cultural entities—language and the mental constructs that acquire body in it, such as knowledge and literature—the material base serves primarily to crystallize and provide communicability.[3] But the rule is that the material base must be an essential and constitutive part of the object, even if it is not the principal part. In a poem, for example, whose substance is not exclusively conceptual, language not only crystallizes and makes

[3] It must be kept in mind that we are continually faced with the necessity to simplify. See pp. 46–51.

possible transmission but is the bearer of certain auditory or rhythmical characteristics that contribute greatly to the meaning. In a work of musical or plastic art, the material base—sounds, forms, and colors—that is arranged in each case is decisive, and "translation" [4]—the substitution of one material base for another —implies a detraction that is extreme if the transfer is to an entirely different medium (the oral description of a painting) and relative if the change is to a similar medium (a photographic copy of a painting). In an instrument—such as a tool—the material base is usually irreplaceable, but the tool can be perfected—that is, its material component can be better adapted to its operating purpose. But in spite of all this, the principal thing in the object of culture is not the material base, but the meaning that is materialized in it, the whole of the intentions that animate it. On this basis, it is legitimate to say that a cultural object is predominantly a psychical or psychospiritual reality and not a material one. What really makes a chair, for example, is not the materials of which it is built, but the purposes and intentions that are harbored in it, that define it and form the organizing principle of the material parts. These shape it as a piece of furniture on which one sits, ascribing to it certain characteristics that are first of all intentional and then functional. These characteristics distinguish it from any other piece of furniture with a similar use, such as a bench or an arm chair. If someone who had never seen chairs or known that they existed should see one for the first time without understanding its purpose, he would not, strictly speaking, have seen the chair,

[4] Some concepts, habitually used in a restricted sense and for a limited group of facts, are opened up and generalized when they include all cultural phenomena. This is the case with the concept of "translation," which includes all of the acts of replacing the material base, of transferring meaning or content from one bodily form to another. This problem requires investigating the bond and relationship existing in each case between the meaning and the material base. The much-discussed question of the extent to which an effective verbal translation is possible is, therefore, only a part of a much more extensive problem. The notion of "revolution" in the theory of culture is also extended and generalized, and is applied to all cultural orders. These problems will be taken up in the book on culture now in preparation. Here I have merely touched upon them, in order to show the nature of many topics that I cannot treat in detail because they have their proper place in a thorough study of culture.

even if he were gifted with perfect vision and should have seen the material makeup of the chair in all its details. On the other hand, if someone accustomed to seeing chairs and using them should perceive this same chair, he would have seen it, even though his vision was quite poor and only offered him a very vague outline of it. To summarize: the cultural object is always something with a soul. To grasp it is to decipher that soul, to interpret the material aspects of the perceivable container through which content is apprehended. The technical name for this kind of apprehension is "comprehension." To comprehend, then, is to pass from something significant to something signified. The material aspect of the base should not be understood, literally, as matter, but rather as something that in some way belongs to the material world. For a painting, the material base consists of elements that are directly material: the canvas and the coloring substances. For language and music, it is certain acoustical phenomena. For a ritual or a custom, it is movements or attitudes that stem from the behavior of material parts.

Some cultural structures have an ultraindividual objectivity, but it is not materialized or made external. For instance the "spirit" of an age or a group, so-called world views, and public opinion are not materialized or made concrete as is a linguistic phrase, an institution, a dogma, or a creation of art or technology. Provisionally—since this is not the time to discuss the matter thoroughly—we will say that there is no concern here with cultural objects, but with matters of a collective conscience, with something pertinent to the subject of culture rather than the cultural object.

The material base is as real an aspect of the cultural object as the meaning or content. In addition, every cultural object has an ideal element, a reference to a value, which is not an actual part of the object but rather a direction or a polarization.

This orientation toward value gives rise to one of the criteria currently used to classify cultural objects. A classification is imposed, such as: religious value—religion, myth; theoretical value—science, philosophy; aesthetic value—all of the arts; ethical value—law, custom; utilitarian value—all of the technical sciences. These rudimentary classifications have been further elaborated and more or less profoundly modified by the current philosophy of values.

Recall, for instance, the well-known classification of Scheler and the less well-known one of Rickert.[5]

However, the difficulty of placing each cultural expression under the protection of a single value appears at this point. In law, for example, some maintain that a special legal value is at issue. In many cases the intrusion of ethical values seems undeniable; in others the necessity for implanting order, which can be interpreted as social convenience, as purely utilitarian, is primary. Cultural entities—the products of the activity of man, a single being with many different facets—tend to give evidence of this unity and diversity; and although in each case they may polarize toward a given value, at the same time, other values are exercising an influence over them. This, of course, is apart from the instances in which they are sensitive to a constellation of diverse values. To avoid these ambiguities, Freyer has proposed a classification that considers only the primary direction of the objectification, ignoring any subordinate value or motive which may be present, despite the chance that the latter may be of greater importance than those initially defining the object. According to this division, cultural objects are classified as follows: (1) creations or formations, that is, objects sufficient in themselves and making up relatively closed and complete entities, such as a religious or scientific doctrine or a work of art; (2) every kind of sign with objective content; (3) social forms or complexes; (4) artifacts, that is, everything that serves to make or achieve something; (5) education, so far as it includes objective structures instilled in the subjects through pedagogical processes. Freyer believes that this provides access to a firm criterion, since anything that might cause fluctuation in the order is rigorously set aside, and each object enters undisputed into one of the sections. If one keeps the dominant value in mind, a sign majestically painted by a great artist would have to be counted among the works of art, even though this is contrary to its practical purpose. There are, then, two values, each of which pulls in its own direction and makes

[5] Max Scheler, *Der Formalismus in der Ethik* . . . (3d ed., Halle a. d. S.: M. Niemeyer, 1927), pp. 103–109. Heinrich Rickert, *System der Philosophie* (Tübingen: Mohr, 1921), I. Cf. the systematized table added to the end of the volume.

difficult the classification of the object. If we are guided by the principle proposed by Freyer, the objectifying intention was utilitarian and should predominate, regardless of other important values that may have been superimposed on it. The object, therefore, is undoubtedly an artifact. In such a procedure one yields to the nature of the object. If it were a painting, a pure work of art, it would attempt to attract and hold one's interest. As an artifact, its purpose would lie outside of itself; and if it also tried to attract attention, its purpose would be to direct attention immediately toward something else, toward the object whose purpose it is to advertise. With Freyer's classification, one avoids some of the difficulties that accompany other classificatory systems. However, difficulties with which we cannot be detained at present, do appear.

Relations between cultural objects

From one point of view, objective culture—the whole of cultural objectifications—is the result of man's humanization of the non-human, a transformation of reality which colonizes it, on a grand scale, to the advantage of human demands and necessities. This colonization, in a broad sense, affects not only the world external to man, but the prehuman in man, in order to make it human, and even extends to what is already human in order to make it more human. In changing a part of the earth's surface to a cultivated field, in constructing a bridge from pieces of wood, in organizing sounds into a melody, man manufactures culture from an untouched nature. He does the same thing in educating his phonation for articulate language and singing, and his muscles for work and recreation.

From another point of view, objective culture is the external projection of man's inner reality. The animal cuts out his environment in the surrounding world; man builds an environment in his own image and likeness. Yet it is questionable whether the animal passively accepts an environment. The animal's environment is never simply the common surrounding environment, the complex of what surrounds it. It is an environment peculiar to the animal and dependent upon his specific nature, which selects what is of vital interest and establishes relations and interaction with it while ignoring the rest. At times, when the interaction becomes intense, this environment is influenced or even modified by the animal. But the animal never actually creates an environment. Man builds an environment—indeed a world—because he carries a world within himself, a complex of objectifications that he is able to project outside himself. Since the animal does not have an inner reality populated by objective instances, it establishes a relationship only with what is external to it, from which it receives impressions, and to which it reacts through the states that it lives.

The world of culture, because it is a creation of man, bears his seal in each of its parts, and all these parts testify to a unity that is a reflection of the unity of man—a dual unity, as will be seen later.

We should not be surprised, then, if we find unifying motives in each aspect of culture. Man is an objectifying being, and the existence of culture as an extremely varied gallery of objectifications testifies to this basic human condition. The directions of the objectification, since they derive from the common human nature, are not arbitrary, for there are traces of similarity with groups that are quite remote in time and space. The ordered community, language, custom, religion, art, and technology belong to man regardless of era or country. Some cultural creations, such as science, appear only in certain cultures, but the fact that others have not attained them must be attributed to their incomplete development. This is proved by the scientific ability demonstrated individually by many men who come from cultures without science of their own into those with it. On the other hand, there is no culture without some body of knowledge which, rudimentary and fantastic though it be, is a sketch of and an advance toward mature, scientific knowledge.

Each of the historical cultures—that is, the cultural complexes developed in the great human communities—presents a character or blend which particularizes it and distinguishes it from the others. The classical Egyptian and Greek cultures, for example, give us an impression of coherence and affinity among their respective components. They reveal a style that reflects the way of life charactristic of the people of each culture—their particular way of conceiving the world and human existence. Thus, within the fundamental unity of culture, there are cultural orbits and even periods of time or stages which define more or less harmonious cultural complexes, governed by specific interpretations of reality, and of man as a part of reality.

The different sections of cultural objects within each cultural orbit or period do not have merely a parallel relationship to each other—they do not merely live side by side. There tend to be dominant motives in each conception of reality, which impose their seal on some or all of the cultural expressions and in this manner are converted into unifying motives. The factor of magic, religion, war, or economics, for example, may predominate. In the medieval community of the West, the primacy of the religious motif strengthened the institutions concerned, directly or indirectly, with religion, and, in addition, it subjected to itself those sections that were alien to religion in the proper sense of the word: art was essentially religious; science and philosophy adhered strictly to the tutelage of dogma, placing themselves at its disposal. In sum, in each cultural season, the purposes of the various sections of culture do not shape each section independently; usually, there is an intermixture of these purposes with the predominant motifs, whose greater energy exercises a primacy that can become enslaving and absorbing. The various dimensions of man are not actualized in a neutral or balanced way in culture; rather, the collective subject works by means of a special world view, and every world view is affected by a partiality or a polarization inherent in it, and testifies to the presence of a predominating principle or group of principles.

Alongside these elements of cohesion and uniformity, other elements are at work in the midst of each culture, binding the parts together and establishing other kinds of correlation and dependence between them. From among these correlations we select the phenomena to which we will refer as the phenomena of involvement. Through the unity of the agent—man—each cultural instance—in a manner proper to it and within its special domain—exercises sometimes a relative primacy over other instances, involving them and subjecting them. The community, and to a lesser degree the state, include all culture to the extent that all culture occurs within them. Language expresses all of culture verbally and is an indispensable link and vehicle for the whole of culture. No culture could avoid instant paralysis if objective communication among its agents were suppressed. Aesthetic feeling is not manifest exclusively in the arts. Consciously or unconsciously it colors almost all cultural life, although frequently in a shade that is barely perceptible. The vast quantity of learning is also a universal component, and there is no cultural activity that can dispense with it. The economic concern is present in most cultural tasks. Those which seem to be free from it have already developed a solution that makes it possible to ignore the problem. No section of culture is absolutely autonomous and indifferent to the others; all depend on each other and each one affects the others. On the other hand, many are motivated by an imperialistic intention which the others try to counterbalance, and which is evident in many situations. If the circumstances are favorable, the imperialistic intention establishes itself in a privileged situation. We do not believe, as has been proposed, that the desire for power is man's principle characteristic. Yet self-affirmation, the centering in oneself, is innate to the individual, and this affirmation of one's own entity, which is the consequence of being a subject, is manifested in many ways, in keeping with the circumstances. Among these ways is the desire to be worth something, as well as the desire for power, and one should not disregard the peripheral longing for appropriation of material goods and the accompanying joys and advantages. All this is at work in the professional or specialized groups responsible for the different tasks in culture and to a notable degree when they are institutionally organized. From this stems the tendency to place their cultural activity above the others and to establish for it a position of preference with respect to the whole, relegating the others to subordinate positions, at times even to servitude.

The cultural texture, as can be seen, depends on factors quite varied in influence, dignity, and even legitimacy. Cultural progress consists partly in the increasing imposition of a just estimate and of a social discipline that are capable of assuring a balance in which each part of the culture may satisfactorily fulfill its purposes.

Cultural objectification

Culture, as we have stated, does not consist solely of objectifications or realities, such as institutions, works of art, or instruments, which, separated from their creator, take on an autonomous life and are thereby converted into a common treasure. Culture, in the proper sense, is human life, both spiritual and nonspiritual, which develops according to its peculiar modes of being and necessarily includes the production and use of cultural objectifications. As the dynamic and the flow of life—of human life, not the life that biology studies—culture requires objectifications. It circulates among them and leans on them, taking advantage of their human content. It moves through their interiors—completely in cases such as language, which is in a continuous process of modification and growth, and at other times in ways that are more partial and circumspect. Because of the immediate prestige and the greater visibility of what is concrete and stable, culture as a complex of objectifications is frequently understood to be "culture." Evidently this objectified cultural reality enjoys complete existence only in cultural interchanges, in its involvement with the life of the group. If a cultural entity maintains its full significance after its cultural complex and its corresponding group have disappeared, it is because its content has universality, and by this means it rises above the incompleteness of the original complex and comes to be accepted as belonging to another. This happens to some eminent creations in philosophy, literature, and the arts. At this point there need be no concern for investigating whether the meaning remains the same in passing from one complex to another. This is part of a larger and most difficult problem: that of the valuable characteristics which a creation may develop with time through the discovery and emphasis of values that previously had hardly been perceived, or the problem of the change of historical perspective.

It is not too difficult to demonstrate the necessity in culture of the objectified moment. An appeal to elementary common sense will be sufficient. It would be impossible to imagine communal life without an ordered community, without legal and institutional organization, without the tacit customs and norms established through common consent. Equally unimaginable would be normal religious and artistic activities in which the corresponding objectified aspects did not exist: namely, dogma, ritual, and religious institutions; literary, plastic, and musical creations that are understandable and within the reach of many. Scientific activity and, in general, everything pertaining to knowledge are inconceivable without objectification and the accumulation of successive conquests, without formulated methods, without means. Technique is principally the production and use of materialized resources. Culture is much more than the series of cultural objectifications, but it cannot even be imagined without them.

In asserting from the beginning that man is an objectifying being, we have not intended to say solely that he perceives an objectified world, even though this is the aspect that should interest us at first. Undoubtedly, the beginning of what is human in man is both the capacity to perceive objectively and the correlative constitution of the percipient as a subject. But the perception and conception of a given world, in the terms of objectivity, carry with them a type of cultural activity—the formation of externalized objectivities in an immediate fashion and with a necessary continuity. What permits man to apprehend objectively what is foreign to him bestows on him in like manner the gift of objectified creation, and both functions are joined and inseparable. The most obvious nexus between both operations is the tendency to express objectively what was perceived objectively, in naming, and in all the basic representative functions such as the picture writing of the primitive, the spontaneous drawings of the child, and perhaps some imitative attitudes. To perceive objectively is to harbor something within. However, full objectification, which is merely persistence in the attitude that produces it, requires an emphasis and a setting apart that are not satisfied by merely remaining within the inner forum, for they demand a form and an embossment which overflow from the maternal enclosure. Here, as in physiological generation, to conceive and to give birth are aspects of the same process. At the beginning, the intimate impulse of the objectification is sufficient to bring it forth; but the build-up of the objectifications that surround the individual, the culture perceived in one's surrounding as a habitual environment, also stimulates and favors externalization with the example and power of custom. There is also a special need that the content be made public, since it is necessary for communal life and for obtaining from the community a sanction strongly desired by the individual. Thus there is both an impulse from within and a pull from outside.

Let us compare for a moment the apprehensive or perceptive objectification, of which we have been speaking in the foregoing sections, with the creative or cultural objectification.

Perceptive objectification is a recognition, an active admission of something, the assent to an existence. Its formula, as we have stated, might be: This is; or this is here. If involves an affirming aspect, and without it there would be no recognition. The subject recognizes the existence of a tree before him, he recognizes the form and size of the trunk and the branches, the green color of the leaves, the distance between the tree and the objects that surround it. All of this, so far as it is perceived, comes to be the property of the percipient who keeps it in his memory.

Let us see what creative objectification is. The subject imagines or forges in his inner reality a song, a tool, a new scientific explanation. He sees them objectively, as realities existent in outline, animated by a secret life that wants to make itself evident; and sometimes he feels as though he were possessed by his creation. The song sings in his soul; the tool seems to move in his fingers and accomplish the function for which he had conceived it; the scientific formulation seems to inspire him to publish it with its claim to elucidate the facts to which it refers. A thousand imaginations pass through a man's head in a continuous and obstinate review. Of these imaginations, a few—sought for and forged with intent and with tenacious exertion or seemingly appearing spontaneously and of their own accord—take on a position of privilege. They are not content to be more or less fleeting aspects of the conscious life of the subject, but they are strengthened in themselves—they aspire to persist. They come to the subject with a special validity— justified or not—for accurate expression, for beauty, for the splendor of unexpressed truth, for the good or the utility they are capable of bringing about. It is not absolutely necessary for the subject to be clearly conscious of all this. Many times, what he has objectified, whether perceptively or through his imagination, blindly impels him, by the splendor and energy with which it is given, to make it external. The internal or imaginative objectification is followed by the externalizing objectification—which for a song is embodied in the words; for a tool, in the wood or steel; for a scientific theory, in conclusive propositions or formulae. Much the same thing occurs in this psychical procreation as in biological procreation: many of the seeds are not properly fertilized; and they never become more than private instances, moments that belong exclusively to the inner life of the organism. Others, however, are granted complete germination; and their development leads them to mature as complete entities, to gain a separate and independent existence, and at last to emerge from the womb and take their place in the world. The birth may well be an abortion that places in the world an embryo which is not acceptable; and once the product is cast upon the world—upon the community—the world decrees whether it is deserving of life. Once the cultural creation has been externalized, its existence or influence depends no longer on its creator but on the collective consensus. The song that says nothing to anyone, the tool with no possibility of gainful use, the formulation that is obviously in error or incomprehensible find no place in the realm of objective culture, though they may endure in its lower levels as oddities or curiosities or, on occasion, linked to the biography of their authors or in some other larval state without true cultural objectivity. The real process of inner creation is much more complex than what appears here, for not only have we barely sketched this, but we have limited ourselves to the simplest and clearest examples, dodging processes that are collective and unconscious (myth, language). In addition, there is a constant interchange between the internal source and the external actualization, for the latter ordinarily demands or suggests elements for the former.

In objective perception, one recognizes without exception that something is or is given through a judgment of existence or presence, generally tacit and unconscious. Likewise, in cultural creation it is as if one recognized that something ought to be, that something belonging to private jurisdiction has the right to an autonomous existence, exposed to the light of day. At times this ought to be is implicit in and at one with the obscure, externalizing impulse, while on other occasions it is a conscious, well-defined conviction. The one who conceives of a step for the common good believes that he *ought* to assure its observance, and, if he is able, he will make it known through speeches or attempt to have it formulated as a law or regulation. The one who invents a machine judges that it *ought* to be built. The theorist understands that his theories ought to be made known. In other cultural areas, such as art, the consciousness that what is conceived ought to be made external is often lacking. However, the conception itself carries with it as a component or directive the tendency to be expressed, so that in its genesis the will is present not to remain a prisoner of a creative subjectivity. Since the fullness of the conception is achieved through its actualization, the inner creation and its externalization come to be aspects of the same process of elaboration. In all of this—and it bears repetition—the objectifying function is what is decisive, and, as we have indicated, some kinds of cultural creation show, in a special way, the identity of the root source in this type of objectification and in perceptive objectification when they make evident the immediacy of the transition. Thus, he who perceives an object names it or tends to name it, and the same may be said of him who, more or less unexpectedly, becomes aware of a relationship. An infinite number of words in a language refer metaphorically to an object, and those archaic metaphors, forgotten when the word refers directly to the object, were, when first used, only the immediate expression of relationships of similarity. These relationships were grasped perceptively even though the objects were dissimilar, and later the relationships took on the autonomous existence of cultural objects.

Man is man so far as he is a subject. To be a subject presupposes having objects, having everything that can come before one's glance appear before one—before the court itself, because the subject is always a judge. This includes parts and properties of things, relations and modes of being, one's own subjectivity and that of others. Cultural creation, so far as it gives an external character to creations, is also the process of making what is created appear before one in a new type of relationship and at a new distance, in providing it with a form and a concreteness that attribute to it an existence outside ourselves. Thereby, the apprehendable world is considerably enlarged with a kind of objectivity that is exclusive to man, and which is, strangely, his own reality that has been cut off from him. It is projected outward, at first, and then from the outside it is presented to him, estranged yet intimately knowable, situated beyond him but allowing him to see it and understand it from within—something that is not conceded to any other reality—so that through it he probes more deeply within and becomes more cordial with himself. The details of cultural creation will not be examined here since they are not directly related to our present concern. That study is the concern of the theory of culture and is one of its most important chapters. It is sufficient to point out that the genesis and the final embodiment of objects of culture—that is, the process which leads from the first beginning or germination of the object to its acceptance into the cultural sphere with its own independent life—is quite varied, depending on the particular case and the kind of connection between the meaning and the material base of the object. There are, no doubt, obvious differences between the series of operations that must be completed in order to produce a work of art, a bridge or a road, a religious doctrine or a scientific theory, a popular song, a refrain, or a regulation. The creation may be conscious, or totally or partly unconscious. Sometimes it is individual, sometimes collective. Collective creation does not mean a single kind of process, but rather a variety of influences on the part of different kinds of human groups in the creation, modification, and destruction of cultural objects. These problems are linked to some that belong to the same circle and to others tangential to it. Such is the theme of the internal coherence and consistency of any cultural creation, which seems to be evident already in the progression of the creative process, imposing on it a direction, as if the nascent object were collaborating with the one who is creating it. This is also the theme of evolution and of revolution as means of cultural change, and likewise with progress—that is, evolution with an increase in values. In cultural creation we are concerned primarily in emphasizing its most general character: that it is an objectification and frequently even a double objectification, interior and exterior. We might mention even a third objectifying moment indispensable for the functional fulfillment of the object: its perception by the community, which recognizes and understands it, and which takes account of it as existing and given as an entity in the cultural environment.

The reaction of culture on man
If man creates culture because and to the extent that he is an objectifier, culture, in its turn, is creating man. Man's relation to

objective culture is not limited to his producing, understanding, and using it in common and easily identifiable terms. There is also the more profound effect that culture has on the individual man.

The most perceptible effect that culture has on man is exercised in the everyday processes of life, in permanent cultural intercourse, in the mere fact that each objectivity fulfills its purposes. Language is useful for communication, and it also enables each subject to clarify and organize his thought and then develop it. Religion satisfies man's needs in facing the unknown and the absolute, and provides channels for his feelings with regard to them. Judicial regulations and the institutional apparatus give order to our society. The works of literature and of the arts are appreciated and give joy to those capable of understanding and feeling them. Accumulated knowledge not only satisfies man's inherent demand for knowledge, but it permits a multitude of practical applications, without which civilized life is not conceivable. From this point of view, objective culture allows man to live culturally—which is equivalent to living as a man—on a certain level and with a special attitude toward the world and toward life, in keeping with the cultural realm to which he belongs.

If, as has been indicated, we are restricted to the interplay between man and culture, we will have considered only the most visible aspect of the help provided for the individual by the cultural objectivities that surround him. To be sure, these objectivities make it possible for man to live culturally, but in addition they make it possible for him to be and to achieve within himself his own nature. Let us not forget that objective culture comes from man. If there are linguistic, judicial, artistic, technical, and cultural realities, it is because man is a being with abilities and corresponding needs, and because he develops through engaging in these activities. Within the corresponding sector, each objectified realm is the achievement and the experience of the species or the group. Each individual, with his varied cultural capacities, confronts the whole mass of culture. What he takes in depends on the breadth of his comprehension and his particular situation, but it is obvious that the perceived whole is infinitely beyond his capacity. His linguistic capacity confronts the existing language; his artistic aptitude, so far as it has found expression, confronts art, and so on successively. This means that each ability of the individual has access to what has been achieved in that area by a colossal individual far surpassing him—that is, the group in its multisecular existence. The consequence is an influence of a strength and a stimulation whose impact could hardly be exaggerated. If the linguistic vocation and desire of man have been creating language with individual contributions of infinitesimal import, the common treasure—one of extraordinary complexity and size—is now organized and functioning in the presence of each one's linguistic capacity. It educates through its presence and use, and it stimulates and awakens the linguistic ability to some extent, raising this ability to its own level. This procedure is repeated for all aspects of culture, and it is decisive for the connection between man and culture and essential for man, the primary heir. As we have noted, animals inherit only what is organically embodied, what is consubstantial with the matter of the organism. Although it may develop and grow over an extended period of time, the legacy that it receives is only what comes to it enclosed and sealed in its matter, within the space defined by its living segments. The fortune which is thus transmitted from fathers to sons hardly allows for any increase; it is as if ossified. On the other hand, it is solidly entrenched, and there is hardly any risk that it will be dissipated. The inheritance that is man's exclusive possession is of a quite different kind. It does not come to him through a somatic but through a psychical process, and to a large extent he finds it distributed around him in vast repositories covering everything his glance encounters. The legacy is enormous, but so also is the risk. The animal benefits leisurely from his heritage, which is rather meagre in comparison to man's, yet the animal has no concern for it, for he carries it within. Man finds himself frequently in danger of losing a large part of his heritage, either because it may be hidden or taken from him, or because he may be careless in appropriating it. His individual power amounts to little when deprived of the protection of the treasured belongings. If for some reason he is cut off from a section of acquired culture, he frequently succumbs to a dark primitivism in that area. It is well known that the "colonist," the man from a high civilization who transfers to a geographical area where he is not surrounded by the cultural complex which is his proper environment, tends to fall apart even morally, unless he is bolstered by a strict discipline. All weakening of the influence exercised by the cultural environment loosens man's resources. This weakening may be caused by the scarcity or absence of some cultural mechanisms—as in the colonist—or to the loss of vigor and prestige of one or various parts of the culture, which, although they may continue to be nominally accepted, in reality are undermined, as in times of crisis. The major danger of crises does not consist in the death of some aspects of culture and the necessity for replacing them. It consists, rather, in that for many persons, during the interval between the extinction and the restoration, the area in crisis seems simply abolished, nonexistent, and that phase of the human soul which looked toward it and was nourished by it remains empty and at times retreats to much earlier stages and, in some instances, to a lamentable primitivism.

There are, therefore, two kinds of influence or reaction of objective culture on the individual. On the one hand, it creates him culturally, raising him up to the average cultural level, obliging him to link each one of his faculties or abilities to the corresponding objective sector, educating it, forcing it to develop to the level reached by the group. This influence is of a pedagogical type, we might say. Culture that is due to the effort of all is now turned toward each one, and the common legacy becomes the heritage of each individual, not only as a possession but as a disposition, an attitude, an inner quality. It is as if the soul were becoming richer and more intense through association with realities that speak its language, with creations that no doubt respond to its own needs; for that reason the soul understands and accepts them. But these realities also represent an accumulation of content that the individual could never have achieved on his own, and to which he adapts himself through a psychical activity that strengthens him. Planned education leads toward this end, methodically hastening and facilitating the inclusion of the individual in the cultural situation of his group by smoothing out the path and guiding his first steps. We distinguish this kind of influence, which we call pedagogical and which is of a humanizing and formative character, from another that we might call coercive, and which consists in the actual domination of each individual by culture through the tacit obedience which it imposes on and demands from him, and which each individual generally accepts.

In silence we trust the culture that surrounds us. All culture, or considerable sections of it, must enter into crisis before we come to question it, or before we limit or condition our assent.

Man, therefore, is submitted to a continuous process of culturalization. Culture is made by him. It is made by the average man in his infinitesimal contributions and by the exceptional man with his outstanding conquests. In this way a whole is composed and organized which, in turn, reverts toward each individual, enriching his development and sustaining him at a certain level by a silent compulsion and a complicated interplay of sanctions, external and internal. These sanctions are identified with the individual in normal situations, but they always tend to disappear if the external pressure decreases very much. Sombart has said, "The nature of man is art." One might concede that this is so if by the nature of man one means his culturalized reality, forged by communal and cultural interchanges. Strictly speaking, man's basic nature is not art, but one—as a being that both objectifies and is a subject—which pulls to itself yet carries with it that inclination toward art to which Sombart refers: that of being an agent of culture, a creator and user of it, and at the same time recreated by it through a reflex action which is the natural consequence of man's own primitive nature and which, because of the inherent strength of the bond, is identified with that primitive nature.

IV

THE SELF AND THE WORLD
THE NATURAL MAN

In the previous chapters we have tried to describe the fundamental structure of man. We have shown that this structure presupposes a judging attitude, that it introduces into the most profound levels of man what later becomes the explicit judgment. We have attempted to show that intelligence and significative language, just as much as the human community and culture, are based on that fundamental structure; and we have referred to the role of intentionality in the acceleration of activity and in the process of individualization which seem to provide the essential directions to the cosmic process. The problem of the spirit has remained a separate one thus far, since it is to be the theme of Part Two. But it has been indicated that intentionality leads to the spirit and is perfected in it, and that intelligence, society, and culture, if indeed they can be maintained on the level of pure intentionality, take on the forms in which they are familiar to us as well as their characteristic human dimension when they are integrated with the spiritual dimension.

To be constructed on the intentional structure yet to be deprived of the spirit, is neither to be an animal nor, strictly speaking, to be a man in the full sense of the word. It is not legitimate, on the other hand, to deny absolutely a human condition to such a being. Perhaps we might say that we should attribute that condition to him in the light of the promise of the spirit which is latent in his intentionality. Such a being has undoubtedly existed in the inferior stages of humanity, perhaps existing normally in minimal cultures and, perchance, in isolated instances, enduring in the superior cultures. We refer to it as *natural man* and, as we have stated, characterize it by the total lack of the spiritual factor. We do not preclude that the spiritual attitude may arise suddenly and unexpectedly in intentionality, influenced by inner motives, by an example, or by some external appeal. The natural attitude is maintained only until the first spark of spirit appears. Habitual persistence in overtly natural attitudes, if in some way one has assented or assents to the spiritual attitude, does not constitute a true natural attitude, but rather a special situation related to the duality peculiar to man. This duality is discussed in Part Three.

Let us consider the principal traits of the natural man—that is, man so far as he is deprived of spirit.

This man, built on the subject-object structure, is a self surrounded by a world of objectivities. The self-world pair represents a step up from the subject-object pair. The subject is converted into a self through the reiteration of intentional acts which organize the subjectivity, granting it consistency, continuity, and identity with itself. The world is the result of habitual objective experience.

The self can be dissolved into the 'we' or affirmed individually. The consciousness of the self is just as natural when the individual incorporates himself into a natural complex with which he identifies himself as when he sharply distinguishes his own natural individuality from that of his fellows. The universal projection, the turn toward the "other," exclusively constitutes the nonnatural or the spiritual attitude. The self can be dissolved in the group, can feel that it is *his* group or that he is *of* the group, and can appropriate it in this indirect fashion without breaking the subjective particularity. Both cases are only extensions of the concrete self, particularities broader than the strictly individual particularity. If the self conceives of itself as individualized, the self-consciousness that it achieves is not of a spiritual dimension unless it aligns its own self with the selves of others (breakdown of particularism; universalism). The spiritual dimension does not arise because other selves enter into certain effective relations with one's own self, but because of their pure condition as selves. The merely intentional subject is not only capable of self-consciousness, but he tends to fall into extreme and exaggerated forms of self-consciousness or self-interpretation, sometimes with a morbid intensity. What is characteristic of the nonspiritualized self is that he lives candidly as the focus of the world, as the central point to which everything leads and to which all is referred. He professes an egocentrism that should not be understood as an all-embracing egoism, because there is a natural behavior—found even in animals—which is altruistic. Perhaps a background exists in him, lived absolutely, that leads him to consider himself a reality not comparable to any other, that is, a substratum of states which, from its depths, directs all his intentional behavior and imposes on it the particularity akin to nature. The practical absolutism, the control and subjection which he imposes on the beings and things in his environment, probably stems from the fact that the substratum of states functions in him as the ultimate frame of reference. Given spiritual self-consciousness, each self undoubtedly feels that he is a real, unique, and incomparable instance, because the self he himself is is the only one he asserts and lives from within. But as a self, he places his selfhood on the level of the others, and in order for the self-perception to be spiritual, the indispensable prerequisite is the consciousness of the community of selves as identical entities, with regard to their being and meaning. The spiritual attitude, as will be explained later, is one of absolute transcendence. In the reflexion toward itself, the self is transcended in that it turns toward itself as toward another, which makes it possible for it to place itself on a level with the other selves. In the nonspiritual affirmation of the self, this movement of full transcending is lacking. The self remains referred to itself, with no true exit to the other selves, and remains at an infinite distance from them. If it associates with other selves, the association is natural, and the selves included in the group feel associated only with their own selves which are clearly separated from all the others. All reflection presupposes, in some measure, a special transcendence. The nonspiritual reflection of the self on itself is an imperfect transcending that leaves a whole mass of states intact. This mass of states or lived immanence is the determining element, from which the self is affirmed as an absolute reality, a reality before which—and to whose benefit—everything else is made relative.

Subject is the correlative term of object. It is not difficult to concede that in some superior animals, in the apex of the zoölogical scale, a subjective attitude appears from time to time with the correlative emphasis on objectivities. Yet, though such acts may occur, their scarcity and above all their discontinuity prevent them from bridging the gap separating the animal from the human individual. They are the thrusts toward humanity which the animal exercises, blind attempts of the very few species that are somewhat similar to man in body and behavior. The occasional subject that appears in these beings is a far cry from the constant subject which defines the human in man. The permanent subject—that is, the continuous and normal subjective function— constitutes the self; its objects, so far as they are an interwoven complex of subjectively tinted objectifications, compose his world for him.

This world is the result of his experiences, and it does not stand before him only when it appeals to him as a totality that engulfs each particular experience. Rather, in a certain way, it accompanies each single experience. Thus, just as each act of man is the act of a subject constituted before the act, so each objective situation is, for him, a parcel of his world, a unity within the plurality of situations rebounding in it and partly integrating it. Individual situations are not apprehended in the isolation of their immediate presence, but they are apprehended as prolonged and complicated with others. The prolongation and complication are the natural consequences of objectifying activity, of the constant storing of objectifications, and of the objectification of the conditions and general boundaries under which the experiences have been presented. The objectification of relations, of time, and of space brings with it the supposition of causal function beyond what is proved and the extension of objective reality into the space-time realm. The admission of a vast world on which one depends in many ways is supported by the objectification of the formal conditions of actual experience. Once the general requirements of experience have been changed to objectifications, one can accept on a varied foundation, and with differing degrees of intensity of belief, other realitites that are not perceived but are presumable— either by analogy or on the basis of an interpretation reaching back to that in the actual and the present which is judged to be the effect of the remote, the vestiges of the past, a seed or a cause of the future, as well as to what is constant in memory. The world of man is thus organized as the extension, in different directions, of an experience which, frequently, serves primarily as a base or an argument for the conjectural constitution of what is not experienced. Man's life develops to a large extent in this reconstituted world, in contrast to the life of the animal which takes place in limited, present situations and in those of a greater temporal scope, which are given to it organically and not cognitively, a scope in which the instincts are rooted.

For man, the world of cultural objectifications is added to the given and reconstituted world. We have already spoken of the former with the stipulation that, for us, objective culture, at least in part, is foreign to the spiritual element. What was previously said about the relations between man and culture should now be kept in mind. In thinking of the relation between the self and the world, one must take the word "world" in its broadest sense, as everything that man finds or presupposes in his environment. The world, therefore, includes everything that is understood to be natural reality, as well as cultural reality, which men have been creating, but which each man—each self—confronts as a realm endowed with its own existence. A principal part of the world for each self is the other human units, which abstractly come to him as his fellow creatures—though the likeness is really and effectively apprehended only in the spiritual attitude. In actual practice, however, these human units are ordered as groups either to which man feels a stranger, or in which he participates. Each human unit is included in a great number of groups (family, social class, profession, nationality), and generally he is active in each situation. More particularly, his behavior as a member of the group is oriented to his companions in the group, though to a varying degree, for in some extreme situations the suppression of the individual element may result. One should keep in mind that not only the actual connection—that is, the vital or emotional aspect of the relation—but also the cognitive objectification of the group by each self, its perception as an objective reality, is influential in this group relationship. Intentionality is present in man in every aspect, and without it man is incomprehensible.

All human activities that do not have their equivalent in animals derive from the fact that man is a self, endowed with consistency, continuity, and self-perception, who faces an objectified reality. The egoism of the animal is fragmentary. Always it obeys its needs and organic impulses within the possibilities of the situation defined for it as its immediate surrounding. The egoism of man is that of a self with all its complex psychical density. His organic requirements come to him filtered through intentional psychism, and they receive from it their specific quality. One needs only to recall what happens with such primary and overbearing physiological demands as hunger and sex, which are bound up, in even the most primitive civilizations, in a tangle of institutions and customs, whether ceremonial, judicial, or otherwise. To the egoism of a biological root, which in man is shaped in accordance with the intentional structure, is added another that stems from man as a self. Many feelings, such as vanity and all those awakened when the self feels neglected or wounded, can be placed in this category, as can the desire for wealth and power, the attempts to become important and famous. The self aspires to affirm and strengthen itself, to dominate, to be something more, and it would be vain to try to reduce all this to the organic foundation, since many times these impulses contradict it and in some instances may even require a sacrifice of the individual's biological appetites and pleasures. Even in dismissing entirely the spiritual moment, man is still defined by the intentional structure. He is fundamentally a self, and he has before him a world that beckons him with its expanded spatial-temporal perspectives, and all his behavior must be referred to this general situation, which is peculiar to him.

The same can be said of attitudes that are not directly egoistical. The so-called altruism of the animal (toward its young for example) is blind and instinctive. It is not difficult to attribute to it powerful, emotional reactions which, from a distance, might respond metaphysically to the consubstantial unity of the cosmos. Properly speaking, however, these movements are not transcendent in an absolute sense, but rather immanent in the reality in which they occur. They are immanent in life, for example, in that they stem from centers that are scarcely individualized, and life through them is, therefore, unified and vitally in harmony with itself. Particularism, as will be seen later, is the rule of what is natural and inevitable in natural instances, regardless of the length of its radius. In a strict sense every natural attitude is egoistical, referred to itself and not to the other as other. The natural altruism (nonspiritual) of man follows these norms. One might restate, with reference to him, what was said about strictly egoistical conduct. This natural altruism functions in accord with the general situation in which man is a self surrounded by objectivities, among which are beings similar to him that he takes as such, but without decisively turning toward them. Many feelings of affection and solidarity, which sometimes lead to the sacrifice of the individual in a deeply moving way, belong to the equipment of the natural man; and they do not need any reference to the spirit. They presuppose the constitution of a concrete 'we,' which, undoubtedly, is often a noble broadening of the individual self, yet without the absolute projection toward the other which defines ethical purity. It is thus affirmed that the distinction between the natural and the spiritual in man is in no way to be identified with the distinction between what is good and bad morally, even if absolute morality belongs exclusively to the realm of the spirit. The difference between natural behavior in the animal and in man (whether considered egoistical or altruistic) thus remains clearly established. Psychically, the wild beast that rends its victim apart is an appetite demanding satisfaction. The animal that takes loving care of its offspring is the blind agent of a vital impulse. The man who acts with impudent egoism or tender sympathy is a self who acts in keeping with his own individual being—a being that exists prior to the act—and who acts in the presence of a vast objective world imposed on him in its solid contexture, a world to which he responds. What is natural in man is not the organic demands and impulses, but what stems from the intentional structure that gathers and draws these demands and impulses to itself and adds to them other motivations, equally natural but alien to the biological order.

The world of man is a world whose elements are some experiences unquestionably his own, but a world inevitably completed through extension and interpretation. As a matter of fact, each experience includes an element of interpretation which forms a part of it as it is constituted, but which, when constituted, undergoes additional interpretative processes. The conceptions of reality are individual, but they are in keeping with specific standards and are guided by specific types or models. From one point of view, the conceptions of reality could be imagined as arranged in a linear series. At one extreme would be the conceptions of the primitives, abounding in phantasy, and at the other the critical and refined conceptions of those who, in our own day, take into consideration all the conquests of the mind in order to construct consciously an image of the whole. Yet the multiplicity of the conceptions of life and of world views cannot be entirely contained by this one-dimensional approach. There are specific sketches of a world view which correspond to different human types and which are re-iterated in every time and place. There are sketches corresponding to the great cultural areas and others more specialized, dominant in smaller areas. There are world views ascribed to the great periods of history which decline and fall with each period. The major difficulties in the almost untouched problem of world views stem principally from the interconnection and the superimposi-tion of these different sketches. Man never confronts a neutral reality. At the first contact, reality begins to be transformed into a determined world view, which assimilates successive apprehen sions of it. Neither does man create culture by pursuing separately the development of each cultural motif or value. Rather, in each instance, the world view works as a whole for him, in such a way that in any of his cultural creations the principal features of his world view are manifest—at least in its own attitude and atmos-phere.

The world view does not necessarily include the spiritual ele-ment, although, to the actual man, it may normally presuppose it. Mere intentionality is sufficient to give account of it, if indeed in this case it seems incomplete, characterized by that imperfection which the absence of the spiritual principle entails for everything human.

We do not believe that one can doubt the existence of natural man. Spirituality, whose essence and characteristics we turn now to describe, presupposes mere intentionality, completes and perfects it. It is legitimate, therefore, to admit that there is in humanity a level or a state in which intentionality might exist without the spiritual element. Perhaps this is occurring at present in the contemporary remnants of primitive humanity. It is probable that a rudiment of spirituality will appear in every culture which has evolved at all, though it may be barely distinguishable from the higher forms of the natural state, and even coöperate with them. The spirit is inevitably present in the great historical cultures, and it is that which bestows on them their evident preëminence. The question of whether the existence of a purely natural man is possible within the higher levels of human association is difficult to answer. It is undeniable that many attitudes of man, of every man, in any time or place are strictly natural, but the natural state of the self exists only when the privation of the spirit is complete—that is, when spiritual behavior never existed and when any inclination to assume a spiritual posture is lacking. It is undeniable that the social-cultural complex, on first surmounting the most elementary levels of primitivism, finds itself satiated with spiritual essences, and that human conduct, enclosed within these complexes, receives from them either directly or indirectly the breath of the spirit.

PART II: THE SPIRIT

V

THE SPIRIT IN GENERAL

INTENTIONALITY AND SPIRIT

In preintentional psychism, the individual lives his states obscurely, without referring them to a subjective center. In intentional psychism, consciousness is organized as a differentiated structure in which a subjective pole exists that grasps objects and projects itself actively toward them. The subjective pole, in keeping with its normal function, is constituted as a self surrounded by a world, that is, an environment of objectifications linked together objectively. The acts of the self—cognitive, emotional, volitional— flow into this world, which determines them in part, both by the situations that it presents to the self and by what the latter owes to the accumulated experiences of that world with respect to its own constitution. In merely intentional psychism, the world is only the objective field in which the self affirms and develops its existence, governed entirely by practical interests, by incentives of an individual sort which are referred to the concrete and unique being of the self. The situation does not change fundamentally, as has been said, when these interests are referred to complexes or groups with which the individual is concretely identified rather than directly to a single individual. This is true only to the extent to which the identification with the group stems from concrete and practical motives and not from ideal intentions, for in the latter case one crosses over from the natural to the spiritual attitude.

Merely intentional activity creates objectivities for the subject but subordinates them at once to the immediate goals of the percipient, who catalogues them under the earmark of interesting or indifferent, useful or useless, agreeable or disagreeable, attractive or repugnant, and so on. The emphasis on some of these objectivities and the blurring of others, the direction and energy of the objectifying glance, depend on practical factors. These concrete incentives are at work, primarily, in subsequent cognitive activity, in intellectual elaborations. The emotional and volitional acts are oriented in the same manner, depending on and yet to the advantage of the psychophysical reality of the agent. Thus, intentional acts are launched toward given objectivities, but a return to the subject is within them.

The principal characteristic of the spiritual act is the lack of this return. The spiritual act is projected toward the object, and it remains there. In cognitive, emotional, and volitional activity, the self is concerned with the objectivities for what they are in themselves. In merely intentional activity the subject places the objects and then takes them to himself, whereas in the spiritual act he places the objects and then yields himself to them. In order to give profile to the spiritual act at this point, let this provisional and incomplete definition be offered: the spiritual act is that intentional act in which the subject yields himself to the object. A more precise specification of this kind of act requires that one determine its what, why, and how—that is, its internal nature, the presumed motive of its appearance, and its manner of functioning.

Because the spiritual act is an act of a special nature, of a superior kind, hereafter, when we refer to nonspiritual intentionality, we will say "mere intentionality" or "pure intentionality," or we will use some other expression distinguishing it from intentionality made spiritual.

At first glance, according to the preceding summary description, the spiritual act seems more simple, more direct, and less complex than the act of mere intentionality. Actually, one element in the nonspiritual intentional act is lacking in the spiritual act—the subjective return, the practical reference of what is objectified to the individuality of the agent. When the naked acts are taken in themselves, they undoubtedly present this difference. But this is not so if, as is only just, attention is focused on the self and its corresponding behavior in mere intentionality and in intentionality made spiritual. In the first, the self lives its natural state spontaneously, leaning over the object and bringing to bear its own reality as a concrete individual who takes himself as the universal and ultimate point of reference. As can now be well seen, what we have referred to as subjective return is not something that can be superimposed on its act by the self; rather, it is an intention operative within the act itself—it is the final polarization of the act toward the agent which is inherent in the "natural" attitude of the agent. In the spiritual act, on the one hand, this intention is suppressed, but what occurs is not, properly speaking, a simplification, but a purification of the act. On the other hand, the spiritual act enlarges its radius with respect to the nonspiritual act, because, in freely turning to its object, it finds a more extended area than that circumscribed by the relatively limited register of the practical interests of the agent. Mere intentionality redirects reality to the midst of man's natural state, whereas, in the spiritual attitude, man turns to whatever is and participates abundantly in totality. The self, particularistic in the first attitude, rises above itself and is universalized in the second.

The difference between the psychism of states and intentional psychism is self-evident if one accepts the proofs or assumptions we have previously set forth. The first is a flux of psychic matter with no clear distinction between cognition, emotion, and the will, and without a subject before whom objectified instances might appear. Intentional psychism is an intimate aspect of the activity of a subject to whom objectivities are presented, who recognizes them intellectually and projects on them, as objectivities, his acts of emotion and will. The difference between these two psychical realities is enormous in itself, even if one considers only their internal structures. Such a difference is increased when one considers its mode of functioning. Preintentional psychism finds itself inevitably at the command of organic life. It is an instrument of regulation and adaptation for the individual, in that it adapts the individual to the surroundings and also in that it partly adapts the surroundings to the individual—so far as it limits the environment and makes it functional in view of the implicit demands in the constitution of each species. High as one may ascend the scale of this psychism, though occasionally and exceptionally the rudiments of intentionality may be found in the individual, such an individual never passes beyond the level of the purely vital, it does not come to be a self surrounded by a world that it can recognize and within which it conducts itself with a free choice, taking into consideration the wide perspective of objects extended in space and time. Intentional psychism, however, draws the individual out of the strictly organic level, converting the individual into a self gifted with a world in which he develops an action overcoming the biological levels to the extent that the incentives of this order are partly transformed into motives of another kind. It is essential not to ignore that intentionality entails cultural objectification whereby a realm of a new kind is constituted around the individual, the realm of culture, thus creating a complex, untested situation; for the subject lives simultaneously in the world of the spontaneous natural state and in that of culture, and he works in virtue of them both. Even in the lowest levels of civilization, however, a notable preëminence of the cultural influx exists, an influx that defines his evaluation of basic, natural reality and his behavior in its presence. The distance between the nonintentional and the intentional entity, from the point of view of structure and activity, is sufficiently large to justify a strict ontological separation.

The preintentional psychic field and the intentional psychic field differ profoundly. No structural difference between the merely intentional and the spiritual exists, however, because the foundation, the self-world pair is the same in the second as in the first. Intentional consciousness is the common field of the purely intentional and the spiritual acts, so that one cannot speak accurately of a spiritual consciousness that could be opposed to the other. The spiritual act is an intentional act of a special kind, an act that not only turns toward objects but is governed by them and is exhausted in them, though this should be said with the reservations that will emerge later. What is essential in it is the full objective direction. In functioning as the agent of such an act, the subject does not change in what we might call his subjective makeup but rather in his implantation within reality, in his meaning, in his posture or attitude. One cannot say, however, that for the subject the spiritual state is only a mode of working and not a mode of being, because the subject is constituted by his acts, and what he is depends on the character of his acts, with reference both to actuality and to acquired habit. The differences to which we have been referring find support in the awareness that nonintentional acts are easily distinguished from intentional acts on the basis of external factors, whereas an intentional act may appear spiritual without being so and vice versa. At times one may be in error about the nature of one's own act.

From one point of view, then, the difference is minimal, from another, and undoubtedly more justified standpoint, however, it is immense. The difference between the merely intentional act and the spiritual act seems minimal because many times the two are confused, and the only difference between them may rest in the final subjectivist intention of the former and the objectivist intention of the latter—nothing more. But with the step toward radical objectivism which defines the purely spiritual act, the natural level is abandoned, and even a particle of the divine—nothing less—is restored in humanity.

It follows that between the purely intentional and the spiritual there is an identity of real contexture, but a difference of intention or purpose. In other words, we might say that there is an identity of matter or content, but a difference of relation or form. The same occurs in the two previous strata of reality—the inorganic or physical and the organic or living. The constitutive matter of the inorganic and the organic is the same. Not one single component can be discovered in the organic level that cannot be reduced to elements existing in the physical order. But the relation or form differs, and, with its functional consequences, it serves in each case to define the entity, to locate it in the level of organic reality or that of life.

The philosophical problem that appears at this point could not be more important and exciting, yet we must not be detained by it. The problem of matter and form, of their relation and respective scope, emerges in great philosophical systems, but it has not yet been adequately examined either separately or as a whole. The thought of the Pythagoreans is a great effort to explain reality in terms of form. One can find some incisive comments in Collingwood [1] on the significance of Pythagorean thought as a forerunner

---

[1] R. G. Collingwood, *The Idea of Nature* (Oxford: Clarendon Press, 1945).

to recent concepts. The relation between matter and form is one of the principal and most interesting characteristics of Aristotle's system, in which the supremacy of form gives rise to a hierarchy of beings according to the degree of predominance of the formal element. The basis of the Aristotelian theory of knowledge is constituted on the element of form. In noting the essential difference between the physical and organic orders, Schopenhauer pointed out that matter is decisive for the former and form for the latter. Not only does structuralism, so alive and promising in most recent thought, have to do with this general problem, but so does all actualism, all resolution of being in act; for what is thus proposed is the release of being to a pure acting, which should be conceived as a dynamic form. The culmination of the structuralist and activist interpretations in contemporary science and philosophy may well be perhaps the definitive triumph of formalism.[2]

Essentially, our whole conception of reality leans toward structuralism and actualism. The distinction we make between matter and form, between content and relation, refers to the way in which the real is given, to the duality of the entitative and the functional, and it does not hinder the final resolution of the entitative into actual moments. With this reservation, the four grades or levels of reality compose two genera, the genus of spatial-temporal entities and that of temporal entities, each with two species. What we refer to as matter is identical in each of these two genera, but the relation and the form differ from species to species.

Setting aside the ultimate reduction of being to act, which we assume is universal, one must admit that the visible entitative moment becomes weaker as one ascends the scale of reality, to the advantage of the relational and formal aspect. That is, that the latter is more important and decisive in the living than in the physical, in the intentional than in the living, and in the spiritual than in the merely intentional.

The metaphysical problem of freedom need not be confronted here, but there is one aspect that should be mentioned. It is not difficult to see that the temporal genus (mere intentionality and spirituality), by the simple fact of not being spatial, escapes strict

[2] See the important work of R. Frondizi, *Substancia y función en el problem del yo* (Buenos Aires: Editorial Losada, 1952). The English trans. is *The Nature of the Self* (New Haven: Yale University Press, 1953).

determinations and strict mathematical regulations of space. Thus it enjoys more freedom than the other genus (the inorganic and the organic), or, at least, it avoids certain compulsions of a rigid determinism. As no more than a suspicion, and adhering to the impression that emerges from the inspection of the scale of reality, one can maintain that the qualitative moment increases and the quantitative moment decreases as one moves from the first species —the inorganic—to the others. And since mathematics is the form *par excellence* of determinism, this movement would correspond to a progressive liberation of being. In our opinion, as will be seen later, this scale implies an increase in transcendence, but let it be stated now, without dwelling on the point, that it may be interpreted as a moving from the more to the less determined, from fatalism to freedom, by the gradual decrease of the mathematical implications, as seen in the following diagram:

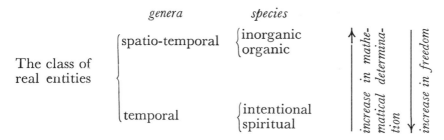

This diagram should not be taken as an exhaustive classification of real entities because it does not include objects of culture. Its only purpose is to present schematically some of the preceding thoughts.

In asserting the reality of the spirit, we affirm its temporality. On occasion, the nontemporality of the spiritual act has been upheld. In opposition to that interpretation, we maintain that the spiritual acts of knowledge, of ethical behavior, of aesthetic creation or enjoyment not only endure in their most simple modes, but ordinarily have a development, frequently long and complex, that cannot be conceived except in time. The subject who executes the act is a living spirituality to the extent that he maintains that attitude, which cannot be broken up into timeless instants.

Passing from pure intentionality to spirituality not only carries with it a distinction capable of giving shape to a new ontological species, but it produces one of the greatest separations imaginable. This separation is between the two great orders into which reality is divided, that of nature and spirit, concerning whose heterogeneity something has already been said and which will be treated extensively in the following pages.

The great distance—a truly unbridgeable abyss—open between nature and spirit, however, does not hinder our attempt to understand the motive for the appearance of the latter, with the former serving as a foundation. The meaning of that appearance will be discussed when we attempt to establish the relation between spirit and transcendence.

Removed as spirituality may be from natural intentionality, basic though the novelty be that it introduces into the picture of totality, one must recognize that it was already present as a possibility, even as a seed, in the first intentional attitude. What we have referred to as mere intentionality is an imperfect intentionality. In the light of spiritual demands it even appears as frustrated because the subjective return does not emerge as a *plus,* but rather as a decrease in the objectifying intention. In general, intentionality characteristically constructs objectivities, perceives them, thinks them, and directs itself toward them in emotional and volitional movements. The objective direction is thus inherent in intentionality. What happens before the appearance of the spirit is that the objective direction, not entirely fulfilled, is delayed by a ballast that hinders its free advance. That ballast is the structure of the self as a sheaf of individual interests. Mere intentionality, therefore, is revealed to us as something incomplete and mutilated, as an impetus of the subject toward what he is not—an impetus that later weakens and returns to the subject, bringing to it, one might say, the usable spoils of the object. Basically, the intention of the subjective return, the "vested or interested interest," constitutes the purely intentional act and defines it from the beginning, although this return may indicate an obstruction of the objectifying impulse. The naturalness of the nonspiritualized intentionality is rooted specifically in the final reference or the redirecting of the acts toward the self as a particular center, whereby it shares the particularism that, as we shall soon see, characterizes everything natural in contradistinction to the radical universalism of the spirit. With its vested interests in the world, the nonspiritualized subject shares in its own way the condition of the organic entity, which is only interested organically in its surroundings, for its own specific and individual goals. The attitude is the same, although the actors and the stage may change. One must admit, however, that although particularism is the general law of nature, its forms allow for degrees of extension and dignity, and that intentional particularism at times approaches spiritual universalism, as when the objectified world is enlarged and the self broadens into a 'we' which may come to include all humanity and even elements in addition to man which are accepted for purposes of an interpenetrating sympathy. Many times, no doubt, the self is enlarged and ennobled when it is broadened into a 'we,' but any act ultimately referred to that 'we' is purely intentional—though of a superior intentionality—because the open and cleanly objective direction is basic to the spiritual act, a projection toward something as "other."

Thus mere intentionality, which in itself is on a high level in the scale of reality, on occasions comes to border on the spirit through the broadening of the subject into a 'we'—to which, for all practical purposes, the subject's acts are referred. The 'we' of which we speak here is not the social complex to which the primitive refers his behavior before he has lived as a true and individualized subject. Rather, it is the 'we' that is constituted after there has been an actual subject; it is the 'we' that presupposes the self. Yet this bordering with the spirit does not suppress the enormous difference in level between the two. One need only keep in mind that with the self broadened into a 'we' the subjective return is the same as it was before, except that the center to which the action is directed has changed. The particularism acquires a much broader base, but it does not cease to be particularism.

What defines the spiritual act is not that the subject swells and is enlarged, but that it gives up the subjective return of the act. The notion of the 'we' is always relative: we, the living human beings, Americans, those of our class, our family, the doctors, the athletes, the contributors, the pipe smokers—we, who now agree in something and feel bound by that tie, which can be fundamental or accidental, permanent or temporary. The notion of pure objectivism, however, which is the mark of the spiritual state, is absolute. It is the absolute projection toward the other, conditioned only by the mode of being and of the other (and of the objectified subject itself as an other). In the spiritual state, as well, the subject has become larger, but in a special sense that is not akin to the broadening of the circle of concrete interests of the 'we.' The subject has become larger because he has turned loose of his battery of individual interests and has converted otherness as such into his own interests. He has not evaporated as a subject, as one might imagine; he has only annulled himself as a subject who functions as a single unit, which, for all practical purposes, redirects every existing thing toward himself. The purely intentional subject works naturally. Nothing is more *natural* than this: that each one work according to, and as a function of, what he is with intentions that terminate in himself because he is a self. The spiritual subject is no longer a natural entity. It is not *natural* that a self yield itself definitely to the other. The spiritual state is freedom, it is evasion. This freedom, this evasion, is above all the destruction of the walls of particularism that enclose each self in a private enclosure and, generally speaking, enclose every natural instance in the special regulation that pertains to it. For every consciousness, the natural state consists in spontaneously or reflexively living as a privileged and incomparable existential reality; as an entity infinitely superior to any other, which places all else at its service; as an instance closed and centered on itself, regardless of its openings toward the outside. The spirit conquers precisely when this enclosure is broken and the soul is freely and generously distributed throughout the world. Thereby the natural order is overcome and a new order is implanted.

If we fall into the temptation of classifying the appearance of the spirit as mysterious, we should not forget that it is as mysterious or more so that anything at all exists. For just as mysterious as the appearance of the spirit is that of life and of intentionality itself. We neither believe that, given intentionality, it is impossible to explain the birth of spirit, nor that the possibility of that explanation diminishes the originality and the value of the spiritual act.

The merely intentional act is characterized by its two moments: its objective projection and its subjective return (or the subjective intention which adheres to the objectivist projection). The main thing in the act, its founding element, is the objective projection, which is attenuated and limited by the subjective intention adhering to it. That projection does not exist in preintentional psychism, in which the agent does not have objectivities before it but rather feels the external environment as a series of influences decidedly conditioned by his organic constitution. The intentional subject depends on a world whose autonomous existence he recognizes and which surpasses his practical interests in many ways. Even if he focuses on his world in terms of his interests, he is never able to forget completely that it is a reality which remains foreign to him. It may be presumed that the continued presence of objects, their habitual handling, creates that radicalizing of objectivity of which the spiritual attitude consists. Since the self is accustomed to its objective world, a permanent citizen of it, it comes to recognize the reality of each object as existing in itself and for itself. It may come to feel, somewhat vaguely, that in practically referring these objectivities to itself, it is partly denying them, ignoring their meaning of being in and for themselves, which is implicit from the beginning so far as they are objective instances, entities subsisting for themselves. We might say that the exercise of mere intentionality is what makes possible this strange *tour de force* of leaping toward the object and remaining with it. It is as if the frequent handling of objects brought about in the subject such a fascination that it makes him forget himself as a living being, as an existential center of reference. So that one need not be surprised by the broad support that spirituality provides to otherness, it is convenient to keep in mind that what is imposed with the spirit is only the fulfilling and the perfection of the objective direction inherent in intentionality. It is undoubtedly *natural* that the subjective center should work according to its natural particularism, but it is in the nature of the merely intentional act that it should eventually overcome its naturalness and impose its native objectivist condition. There is recognition here of the fullness of the being and of the right of each objective instance, a recognition that on the one hand lifts the self to the greatest imaginable heights and on the other inflicts upon it a practical-existential relativization, because it brings about its descent from that pedestal from which it exercised a tyrannical dominion over all existing things.

In the psychic life of man, ordinary intentionality and spiritualized intentionality follow each other and are interwoven in many ways. There may be, for example, pure acts of one and of the other as well as intentional acts which retain their subjective return, yet within certain limits imposed by the demand of the spirit. The coexistence of the two instances brings about an abundance of problems. Something will be said about this in Chapter VIII. Let us point out here, however, that the duality does not give rise to a strict duplicity in the self, although it occasions divisions and conflicts which at times seem to split the one self and cast one half against the other. Regarding continuity, identity, self-consciousness, and memory, the self is one; but within this oneness, sometimes the duality of attitudes is almost equivalent to the existence of two opposed subjective instances. In producing spiritual acts, the self gets rid of that sentient background which demands the subjective return; it denies its particularity and lifts itself above its strict, concrete situation. In projecting itself disinterestedly on its objects, it is as if it participated in them. It apprehends them in dimensions that necessarily eluded the individual's sight when it was practically conditioned by mere intentionality. It contains them without warping or diminishing them in a modifying grasp. The subject of the spiritual act is not a 'we' but a self—a self leaning toward totality.

SPIRIT AND NATURE

Totality

"Totality" refers to everything that exists, regardless of its type of existence, all that is given, thinkable, and imaginable, without exception and even with the supposition of unknown existents. The so-called theory of objects and recent ontological formulations have attempted to make a completely neutral inventory of totality —without preferences for any kind of object—by including everything that is, pointing out the various modes of being, including those of ideals and values, so that the picture would be truly complete. Ancient ontology was a section of metaphysics, and it was seriously concerned only with absolute reality or reality-in-itself, a reality whose characteristic depended on the accepted philosophical point of view. However, it would be exaggerated and unjust to say that a neutral and complete ontology is entirely new. Since the time of the Greeks, philosophy has been accumulating abundant material for an ontological recapitulation of reality. What is recent is the intent to order and relate these materials so as to arrange the ontological picture of totality systematically. As with other philosophical questions, one must distinguish here between the problem and that lucid awareness of the problem that brings the decision to isolate it and set it forth separately and rigorously, to investigate all its aspects and prepare an adequate solution. The many, dispersed elements are then extracted from the situations in which they appear and are brought together and adequately arranged in the light of a new criterion, which affords them unity and a new meaning.

Such ontological tasks require an analysis of totality and a characterization of its major areas. Just as the sciences—in the broadest sense—attempt to know what is, so the ontological divisions appear at times as attempts at a philosophical classification of the sciences.

Searching through the history of philosophy, one finds here and there sketches of the ordering of objects, but none are done with the intention of carrying through a total ontological classification for its own sake. Usually such a sketch is found on the fringes of other tasks. In Schopenhauer,[3] for example, the investigation of the principle of sufficient reason and the specification of its forms leads to a classification of objects as known, as subservient to the given principle. There are four resulting classes: that of sensible or empirical representations; of concepts or thought objects; of space and time; and the class which has as its only object the subject of the will as it is grasped from within. If to these objectivities we add that which eludes the principle of reason and is reached through a metaphysical means, we will have a complete picture, according to Schopenhauer's interpretation.

The first attempt at a formal ontology we owe to Meinong[4] in his theory of objects (*Gegenstandstheorie*). For him the concept of object is of maximum generality. His definition falters, therefore, on the inconvenience that since everything that is or is given is in this sense an object, it lacks a proximate gender and an ultimate

[3] *Ueber the vierfache Wurzel des Satzes vom zureichnenden Grunde* in *Sämtliche Werke* (Wiesbaden: E. Brockhaus, 1946–1950), Vol. VII. Also in *The World as Will and Idea* (London: Routledge & Kegan Paul, 1957), chap. xii, in which the classification of the sciences is discussed, using the criterion indicated.

[4] *Gesammelte Abhandlungen* (Leipzig: J. A. Barth, 1914–   ) II.

difference. That is to say, it lacks the subtle characteristic found in the etymology of the German word (the *Gegenstehen* or "standing over against," presupposed in the *Gegenstand* or object) ; there is no reference to the intuition grasping the object; it does not point to something constitutive of the object itself. The theory of objects is a rational discipline that considers objects *a priori,* neglecting the moment of existence. On its own level, its extent is greater than that of metaphysics, since it also includes what is unreal, the possible as well as the impossible—matters which the sciences confront only when they are of concern to knowledge of the real. Since, with some exceptions, the determination of the large objective groups must be in keeping with their respective modes of apprehension, Meinong establishes his four fundamental classes according to the faculties to apprehend, to think, to feel (*Fühlen*) and to desire (*Begehren*) . The demand for a systematic ordering and recognition of the objectivities, as essences, distributed in regional ontologies, appears also in the phenomenology of Husserl.

At present we are not concerned with the problems arising from an exhaustive classification of objectivities, a matter fraught with difficulties, many of which are only beginning to be examined. It will be sufficient for us to adhere to a classification which has the advantage of rather common use, though, to be sure, it should be considered as imperfect and provisional. It is as follows:

$$
\text{objects (totality)} \begin{cases} \text{real (temporal)} \\ \quad \text{(sensible)} \begin{cases} \text{spatial} \\ \text{nonspatial} \end{cases} \\[1ex] \text{ideal (mathematical objects, essences,} \\ \quad \text{relations)} \\[1ex] \text{metaphysical} \\ \text{values} \end{cases}
$$

The relations between these objects are many and complicated, and often arguable. For example, the relation between metaphysical objects and real-emprical objects varies considerably from philosopher to philosopher. One rather widespread interpretation holds that perceived reality is a repercussion of metaphysical reality on the senses (thus stated by Democritus, Descartes, and others) or on our total cognitive structure (Kant). Yet there are other solutions, such as the empirical world standing in the relation of participation or imitation to the metaphysical world (Plato), and there is Aristotelian realism as well as the reduction of the metaphysical order to divinity. The relation between being and value has also been conceived rather diversely. Value has been attributed to being as an intrinsic note of perfection; it has been limited to what is human, and even to a certain aspect of human life. As for ideal objects, some—such as number—assume a partial universality, since nothing can elude enumeration, not even the absolute one. The same occurs with some relations, such as comparison, which is inevitable as soon as something is conceivable, since to conceive something presupposes the subject-object duality, which is an instance of a relation of difference.

In the outline of totality we find first the section of reality made up of entities that we grasp originally through our senses and which have temporality as their most general and significant characteristic.

Reality. Nature and spirit

Reality is the continuous and interwoven whole of real objects. These objects are of two kinds: spatial-temporal (physical bodies and living beings); and merely temporal (psychical intentionality and the spirit). Let us consider preintentional psychism as an inherent function of the living body, as inseparable from its vitality as any physical or chemical property is from a physical entity.

For reality to be composed of the objects which we call real does not mean that the remaining objects in the picture of totality are completely alien to it. On the contrary, all these objects are involved with the real objects or related to them in some way.

The relations between reality and ideality are multiple. Spatial reality comes under the ideal principles of space in two ways: intrinsically, since every body contains an internal space that defines its limits; and extrinsically, since it occupies a position that locates it among other bodies. All bodies, as has been stated, are numerable and therefore subject to the operations stemming from that quality. For each there is a corresponding essence. All maintain some relation to the others, and some of these, as has been indicated, take on a universal character, as for example comparison.[5] More than once an attempt has been made to reduce all reality or a part of it to the ideal elements, either metaphysically (Pythagoreanism) or scientifically (mechanism). Besides, the relation between mathematics and reality has not yet been clearly defined. This relation is sometimes one of an obvious correspondence (the quality of being numerable) and sometimes it is approximate, as in the relation of pure geometrical forms to the spatial objects in reality. Mechanics, on the other hand, presents the problem of the irrational element in continuity, which is equally evident in the other mathematical implications of reality, as in the mathematical itself (the continuum, the theory of wholes). The field of mathematics, and perhaps that of all ideality, surpasses that of reality, because the ideal can be identified in a certain sense with possibility, whereas the real is only a small island in the ocean of the possible.

The relation between the real object and the metaphysical object is different. The metaphysical object is either distinct from the real object in the sense that the latter is an unfaithful manifestation of the metaphysical object for the subject; or it is identified with the real, given object and thus disappears as a special kind of object. The objects of the so-called external experience (or spatial-temporal objects) are commonly held to be phenomenal, that is, they correspond to a metaphysical object distinct from them in the manner already indicated. Those of inner experience (merely temporal objects) have been interpreted as phenomenal (Kant) and noumenal, as manifestations in accord with the cognitive activity of the subject, or as absolute and ultimate realities which are given to us in their actual being and do not presuppose another, more profound and true reality, that is revealed through them. This difference in appraisal of psychospiritual reality stems primarily from what is thought about time. Since, for Kant, time is a cognitive form, something that the subject imposes on the known, the psychospiritual must be phenomenal, since it appears in terms of an essentially temporal reality. For some later philosophers, who explicitly or implicitly introduce time into ultimate

[5] See Romero, "Contribución al estudio de las relaciones de comparación" in *Papeles para una filosofía.*

being, or convert it into the very heart of ultimate being, psycho-spiritual reality is immediately apprehended in its metaphysical being.

The relation of reality to values has been conceived in a variety of ways. Only in contemporary philosophy—with the isolation of the notion of value—has the problem of this relation been seriously confronted. In general, the predominant concept seems to be that values constitute an autonomous realm with its own hierarchy and principles, and that values are incorporated into certain real entities as notes or qualities of a special kind. For Scheler, values are irrational essences, and they are grasped through the emotions. For others, values are relative, with a psychic root. Our own interpretation of value proceeds along another line; it is presented briefly later, to the extent that it seems necessary for the purposes of this work. A complete examination is left for another occasion.

These relations and implications, and many others that we cannot delay to mention—some established and proved and others subject to controversy—do not prevent the definition of the whole body of reality as a complex of temporal entities. Temporality bestows on reality its most general and important character. Everything real is temporal, though it is not valid to say, for our own purposes, that everything temporal is real, since there may be temporal instances in totality that are foreign to the real complex and there may be a reality completely separated from our own.

For our purposes, the reality of which we may speak is the whole of actual and possible experience accessible through a means that is itself real. By real means, we understand one that lacks nonreal instances; that is, instances which are separate and subsistent on their own. We insist, however, although it may seem superfluous to say in the light of what has already been asserted, that every real instance is interwoven with nonreal elements. It is through real means that what is recognized as having its source in external and inner perception comes to us. Through the former, we obtain a knowledge of external reality, which, so far as it passes through a cognitive structure of which the sense organs are a part, is knowledge of phenomenal reality. Through the latter we come to a knowledge of our own inner reality, which is absolute so far as it is based on what is perceived and on what is rigorously founded on this perception. The note of phenomenism is not essential to the notion of reality. The only undoubtedly phenomenal knowledge is of the so-called external reality, given the manner in which it is manifest to us.

Reality, therefore, presupposes a continuous interweaving in which the subject and the real means of knowledge are also included. Any instance foreign to this interweaving, independent and cut off from it, would be prevented from being an object of real experience. There are other modes of sure, direct knowledge —certainly those of ideal entities, and perhaps, also, those of values. On the other hand, we maintain that knowledge of what external reality is in itself is necessarily problematical, since we lack an incontrovertible experience that would present it to us. The roads of access to this metaphysical foundation are never certain.

The ties within reality presuppose not only a contact but the action of some parts on others. A pure contact without action would be equivalent to a separation, an isolation. There do not cease to be inconveniences in conceiving the actual interaction between the parts or elements of reality. Yet these difficulties are much more pronounced for an exceedingly demanding rationalism, and in this day and age we are far from granting an undisputed right to a rationalism of this kind. Further, when an attempt has been made to eliminate interaction, it has been to assume a decidedly agnostic position (Hume) or to revert to hypotheses that are much riskier and more gratuitous than the thesis which was doubted, as is true of the "preëstablished harmony" of Leibniz. The hypothesis of interaction appears to us as one of those that is inevitable and justified if we do not wish to immobilize thought. For us, then, reality is a unit of action, a great body functioning as a whole because of continuous interchanges. The experience that the subject has of it appears to us as one instance, no doubt privileged, of that general, active connection, as a special resonance and elaboration of the pressure of reality on the subject. Even the most elevated knowledge of the real, when seen 'realistically,' is produced in this manner. For example, in order for essences to serve as means for knowing reality, the event perceived through a sensible channel must allow us to intuit the essence of the event, and the recognized presence of other similar events authorizes us to rely on the events in which that essence is pluralized, since it is individualized in them. Without a real transaction, no knowledge of essences would serve for knowing reality.

Real entities are foci of action: they act in accordance with what they are; or, more adequately stated, to be and to act is for them the same thing. The major part of them, in acting, affirm their particularity, their singularity, so far as they are strictly defined moments of partiality. What they manifest in their acting, the influence they exert, is only the expression of their own particularity, of their special mode of being, which is exhausted in the present or latent action. Their "field" is a diffusion of their own substance: it is the vibration, projected afar, of their inner turmoil or the awakening of latencies that are transformed into centrifugal movements akin to the latencies. Each of these entities produces a resonance stemming from the unique modulation—which may be complex at times—with which each is gifted. We refer to the whole of these entities, which are subject to a rule of particularism, as *nature*. Nature, therefore, is the section of reality whose components act with reference to themselves, as centers whose actions, originally and in principle, are determined by their own differential character and not by something external or foreign to them. What is "natural" is for "each one" to act and work itself out in accordance with what that "one" is, and this is the way natural entities behave. To proceed in any other fashion is antinatural. The spirit, which is what works itself out in another fashion, is radical antinaturalness.

The spiritual act, as has been stated on other occasions, is defined by its disinterestedness, by its unhindered objective projection. The subject of these acts does not attempt to affirm himself as a particular center, but to affirm what is or what is valuable. He turns with cognitive interest toward totality to see what it is like, as if the fact that something should be implies for him the obligation of taking it into cognitive consideration. If he discovers an ethical order, he does not limit himself to mere assent, but he feels duty-bound to contribute effectively to the triumph of that order and its implantation within reality, even though this may be to his own detriment. In contradistinction to the particularism of the natural entity, spirituality is clearly defined by its universalist vocation or intention. *Spirit*, therefore, refers to those subjects and acts totally projected toward objectivities with no other motive on the part of the subjects than to yield themselves toward the other (toward what exists or what is valuable).

One of the current ways of conceiving the natural order is to consider it as including the physically and organically real, while completely excluding man and the products of his specific activity (culture). The latter are placed under the classification of the spiritual, sometimes with the restriction that what is purely organic in man is nature. We have turned away from this way of looking at the matter, since we maintain that it is not justified. In the total realm of reality, the only distinction capable of separating two fundamentally diverse parts seems to be the one we have adopted as the criterion: particularism and universalism, which, according to our conviction, characterize nature and spirit respectively. This distinction is evidently given in reality, and it cannot be surpassed in its scope by any other. In the following section, in order to indicate our objections, we will examine some of the more widely accepted statements about this issue.

The distribution of the sections of reality, as we make it, is indicated in this sketch:

$$
\text{Reality} \begin{cases} \text{Nature} \begin{cases} \text{inorganic} \\ \text{organic} \\ \text{intentional} \ldots \ldots \end{cases} \\ \\ \text{Spirit} \ldots \ldots \ldots \ldots \ldots \ldots \end{cases} \Bigg\} \text{man and culture}
$$

Contrary to what is usually admitted, we consider that mere intentionality—the intentional subject with his acts and his world—constitutes a special order or group within nature for the same reason that the inorganic and organic are special orders: that is, because of its basic features and characteristics, and because of its structural and functional irreducibility to the group closest to it, the organic. The inclusion of intentionality in the natural order seems fully justified because the purely intentional act shows that same concrete reference to the agent, the bond in fact and purpose between the act and the acting entity that we have judged to be decisive in defining natural activity.

It is not necessary to clarify the particularism of physical activity.

Each inorganic instance evidently functions without reference to any support other than its own differentiating nature. In the following passage some difficulties are mentioned that can be solved through a brief analysis. The act of the animal, for example, seems frequently to be characterized by a notable generosity, because it does not revert to the interest of the agent, but rather to his offspring, at times at the sacrifice of the agent himself. One might be tempted to compare this act to the spiritual act because of the condition the acts seem to have in common: that of being governed by an extraindividual interest. An examination of the situation persuades us that such a comparison does not exist. With regard to the goal of the act, the agent of the organic act and the one who is helped by it (the offspring, for example) form a single entity, outside of which the act lacks a meaning. Within that concrete unity, bound by the strongest vital bonds, the particularism of the act is not belied. Its enclosure within the special, actual nature of the agent is radically unlike the universalism of the spiritual act, which is determined by pure motives of being or value. The same may be said for merely intentional acts when the interest of the act does not coincide with the strict interest of the subject. In such instances it is a matter of complex units (for example, family) constituted by *de facto* ties (affection, solidarity of interests), where the agent, in producing his act, serves as a representative even to the extent that in some situations the agent is no more than the figurehead of the unit with which he is identified. The particularism of such acts is seen, above all, if we take into consideration the reality that is foreign to the reality which these acts serve and to which they are subdued, even when the reality is most akin and closest to the agent. We are able to observe how the agent ignores or even contradicts, more or less openly, purposes and interests of this reality. The inorganic, the organic, and the intentional entity possess closed and partial "fields." Only the spiritual entity has an open and universal "field," because spiritual activity is a universalizing intention that asserts itself or struggles to do so.

In attributing reality to the spirit—subject and acts—we assign to it temporality and effectiveness. We will not introduce here, nor in any other part of this study, the much-discussed notion of causality, because we would thereby be constrained to assume a position with regard to a very obscure and much-debated matter. We subscribe to the notion of action or influence in its current sense without presupposing anything with regard to its ultimate nature. We maintain that spirit—in being a special mode of action and in this instance of psychical action—is subject to the general condition of reality. It has already been stated that in their structure spiritual acts do not enjoy a condition or articulation proper to them. An act of knowledge that is merely intentional and another that is spiritual may have the same content. The different intention or projection, which in the former refers ultimately to the subject and in the latter to the object, suffices for definition of the act as of one kind or another. The same happens in noncognitive activities. For example, the practical act of one who, on seeing some delicious fruit on a tree in his garden, plucks it and eats it, is no different in its steps than the act of one who, when confronted with an abuse or an injustice perpetrated against his neighbor, intervenes to restore the violated moral order. In both events a situation is perceived and a subject acts to bring about another situation that strikes him as desirable—the enjoyment of the fruit and the restitution of a violated moral order. The difference consists in that the enjoyment of the fruit pertains to the subject as an individual; it is the appropriation of something by the agent to draw it in to his own private sphere. On the other hand, the energetic reaction to the violence or the injustice inflicted upon one's neighbor and the active reaction against it presupposes the objective direction of the act, its final projection toward the victim of the abuse and toward an order that is considered valuable and worthy of the effort to maintain and restore it. The only thing that distinguishes the spiritual act, and by the same token the subject of such an act, is its meaning, and in no sense is it what we could call the material condition or consistence of one or the other. This special meaning is sufficient to grant to both an incomparable and preëminent dignity, because by means of it they break the iron-clad natural particularism and the kind of slavery that reality had thus far endured within each of its forms, in order to liberate it and spread it out over a horizon that aspires to totality. The spiritual subject is the subject that has freed himself from the enclosures within the redoubt of his own individuality and then enters a limitless expanse. His constitutive and essential judging capacity is now projected toward all that is in order to decide whether each instance is of one kind or another—whether it accords or disagrees with what it should be.

Let us turn now to man's place in this scheme of reality. As has been shown, we accept the possibility of natural man, but this man is nascent and in the making. We exclude the possibility of a purely spiritual man. In his fullness, man is a dual, composite being. His integrity demands the confluence of mere intentionality and of the spirit, and there is no true humanity without the mixture of these two components and the tension that grows between them, even to the point that the most characteristic aspect of man does not stem from one or the other of these elements, but from their dual indwelling within the human unity. In due time we hope to clarify the articulation and the reactions that these two constituent principles of man manifest with respect to each other. At this point, we are concerned solely with establishing that we do not eliminate the organic component in man, an impression that might be received from a superficial interpretation of what has been said. When one speaks of the organic, one does not forget that the living being is still a complex of physical substance, no matter how much one concentrates on its rightful condition as a living being, or how much one sets aside the physical processes that it shares with inorganic entities. Under merely intentional being, or within it, is organic individuality, although it is absorbed by the intentional structure, so that the organic messages are received in it with an intentional meaning or as an informed substance molded in intentional channels. When we decide that one of the components of man is naked intentionality, we come, in some way, to say, therefore, that this component is the whole of nature—not in a confused amalgamation of three natural levels, but rather written into the level of greater hierarchy, which receives and transforms the substance of the two inferior levels according to its own principles. This must be strictly distinguished from the simultaneous existence in man of the physical and organic; of forces, such as gravity, to which the human body is subject as much as any other, or of the functions of nutrition and reproduction which are found in him as in any other living being, since all this does not affect man's distinctness, which is our concern in these pages.

A critique of other divisions of reality

The consistency of the division of reality to which we have committed ourselves will stand out better if we bring to mind some of the other divisions of reality which have been proposed and point out some of their weak aspects. We are neither concerned with a thorough criticism of these points of view, nor is one to deduce from their rejection, the certainty of the judgment set forth in the preceding pages, since its strength or weakness can be appreciated primarily through an inspection of the judgment itself. All in all, a review of the other criteria claiming to support the separation will aid in deciding if another principle capable of providing the ground for a strict distinction has appeared.

The most elemental form of a dualism in the midst of reality is that formulated in the *nature-man* duality. It seems to be the clearest solution and, at first sight, the most satisfactory. It separates two groups of entities that are perfectly identifiable, one of which—the human group—enjoys a special prerogative that is unhesitatingly conceded to it. But the difficulties appear as soon as one gives it a little thought. The experience of the duality within man is ancient and common. It even finds doctrinal expression in religion. Common sense is aware of it and regularly distinguishes between spiritual attitudes and those which are not, and this distinction is refined in the philosophical attempts to define the spirituality. Vague and comprehensive as one may imagine the notion of spirit to be, no one will accept that man is only spirit. The distinction between nature and man is admissible only if one grants, as we have done, that man is a composite being and that the spirit is one of the components. But the character of the other component remains to be established, and since there is no other alternative than nature, it falls into our arrangement, for then what is actually opposed to nature is the spirit and not man as a whole.

The distinction between *nature* and *culture* as the two realms of reality has been much commended during recent times in keeping with the growing interest in the philosophy of culture. Such a distinction, used with undoubted advantage in the theory of science and in the main by Rickert, takes the problem out of its narrow methodological formulation and shows it forth in all its complexities, above all in the detailed examination that Rickert gives to the matter.[6] To those who separate reality into nature and culture—the former understood as reality that is spontaneous and existing in itself; the latter understood as the result of man's activity—one may well ask in the first place where man is to be located, since he is not comfortably included in either of the two sections. If one adheres literally to this division, one would have to consider man as a natural being and thereby forego, to begin with, the understanding of the novelty that is introduced with him into the cosmos. Here one falls back into a naturalism which even the men of science have abandoned or tend to abandon. On the other hand, if man is a natural being, culture, which is his product, not only should be included in nature but subordinated to spontaneous nature as one of its manifestations. One might argue that culture opens up a new section because of the values that occur in it, but then one would have to go back to the creator of the culture, to man, and recognize that he is the one who introduces a *novum* into nature, a novum that, on the basis of its originality and import, is sufficient to separate it from nature. One recognizes man as the one who introduces this novelty so far as he is an entity capable of access to the realm of value and capable of activity which is polarized by values. It is therefore unnecessary to add that one cannot count on man as being within the realm of culture on the basis of the definition of it. The separation between nature and culture, which has been so useful in the theory of science, has left the special problem of the nature of man untouched.

The distinction between *nature* and *spirit*, such as follows from the separation between the sciences of nature and the sciences of spirit (Dilthey), is related to the previous classification, but does not coincide with it. This present distinction, however, should not be likened to the distinction that we propose, in spite of the identity of the terms. If the spirit is the topic treated in the sciences of the spirit, as they are referred to at present, including all the psychospiritual reality of man and culture, such a reality does not appear to be neatly defined, and it includes what we refer to as mere intentionality and spirit. Although it is not rare to find in

[6] Heinrich Rickert, *Die Grenzen der naturwissenschaftlichen Begriffsbildung* (Tübingen: Mohr, 1921).

philosophy this extended use of the word "spirit," one should recognize that it contradicts an experience not only philosophical and reflective but also traditional and common, as mentioned earlier. For it is repugnant to anyone to refer to the man whose habitual behavior is of an obvious and brutal egoism as a spiritual being, and to a spiritual act as that directed to fulfilling man's elementary needs. Given this distinction, the sciences referred to as those of nature, strictly speaking, are of inorganic and organic nature, and those referred to as sciences of the spirit are concerned with a reality in which nature and spirit are interwoven. To be sure, each of these two groups of sciences constitutes a well-defined complex, not only in that one refers to corporeal realities and the other to incorporeal realities (or realities whose essential content is incorporeal), but in that they obey different methodological principles and involve different, cognitive attitudes. But if the so-called sciences of the spirit actually make up a single group with a single great theme, this theme is man together with his culture, and not pure spirit which, in man as much as in culture, is not the only element, but one alongside the natural element, much though it may dominate and prevail in some instances.

The distinction between *nature* and *history* is likewise unwieldy for an adequate division of reality. In a Cartesian context, it would undoubtedly be justified. If nature is essentially a mechanism, if there is only mass and movement in it and the quantity of both remains invariable throughout all the processes, then nature is fundamentally nonhistorical. One might parallel the historicism of man to this evaluation, although the Cartesian mind does not follow in this direction. In the extreme developments of mechanism, when it is generalized and converted—as in the presuppositions of a scientific materialism—into an ontological vision of the whole of reality, no historicist consideration can go beyond a superficial level. Its reach is minimal or at least secondary when confronted with the fundamental nonhistoricism of an ultimate mechanical foundation, from which, it is supposed, everything proceeds and in which everything is resolved.

In the present, such interpretations of reality are laid aside, and as the mechanical interpretation is almost abandoned even in its own, natural domain—that of physics—the historical conception of man and of everything human is being continually affirmed, not so much as a more or less superficial phenomenon, but as a fundamental fact. Simultaneously, the historical interpretation of organic nature continues to gain strength, with organic nature conceived as the outcome of a vast process which grows and is diversified with time. The historicist conception of inorganic nature finds more opposition, above all from the mechanistic remains that have been solidified in a mental habit which continues to concede the primacy in the constitution of inorganic entities to the mathematical elements, the model of all nontemporality. A gratifying step toward complete historicism is Leibniz's *Monadology*, which should be considered as the source of any generalized historicism. In our opinion, historicity, far from differentially characterizing a sector of reality, is the general and fundamental law for all of it. But even if this opinion is not shared, it is still true that historicity is an extremely fragile criterion with which to open up an area of reality before and in opposition to the area of nature.

The subordination of the idea of nature to that of history does not occur solely through the introduction of historicity to the whole of reality, that is, on the ontological level. More than once it has occurred in modern philosophy on other terms. If one accepts that every thesis of a scientific or philosophical order is formed and constituted in the midst of, and on the foundation of, the world view which inspires it and provides it with substance and meaning, the subordination of the concepts of nature to the general world view is obvious, and obvious also is its unavoidable historicity, since world views are historical structures. This type of subordination appears in Spengler. In his opinion, "the producing is always the foundation of the product. If, then, history represents an ordering of the cosmic image in the sense of its being produced, then history is the primitive form of the world." The sciences, with respect to history, are derived instances, products—something that happens in history and is historically determined, something that must be interpreted and understood historically. Scientific knowledge is thus decidedly subordinated to historical knowledge, and, in the morphology of universal history which historical knowledge permits one to detect, scientific conceptions enter as moments. In the presence of the morphology of culture, the mathematical and natural sciences appear as secondary disciplines. Everything that is scientifically knowable, what we refer to as nature, "stems from something historical—the world as a reality for a subject, as a possibility which develops in him." [7] A similar implication can be seen in the conclusions of Collingwood, in his penetrating examination of the philosophical problem of nature. Nature, for him, depends on something else, a form of thought that depends for its existence on another form of thought, which is no other than history.

> A scientific theory not only rests on certain historical facts and is verified or disproved by certain other historical facts; it is itself a historical fact, namely, the fact that someone has propounded or accepted, verified or disproved, that theory. . . . I conclude that natural science as a form of thought exists and always has existed in a context of history, and depends on historical thought for its existence. From this I venture to infer that no one can understand natural science unless he understands history; and that no one can answer the question what nature is unless he knows what history is.[8]

The notion of nature, which possibly falls under that of history from the point of view of ontology, is also subordinate to it, and for tenable reasons from the point of view of the theory of knowledge.

Neither is the distinction between *nature* and *society* adequate, in our view, for indicating a dividing line within the realm of reality. Animal societies are doubtlessly natural. If, in proposing this distinction, one has in mind an exclusively human society, then one must search for a criterion that will permit one to distinguish this kind of society from that of the animals, and such a criterion will no longer be social. We believe we have found this criterion in the intersubjective functioning of intentionality which refers back to individual intentionality and, therefore, to something logically preceding the social fact, although in its actual genesis it may coincide with it. If one accepts our characterization of human society, while maintaining, against our thesis, that

---

[7] *Decline of the West* (New York: A. A. Knopf, 1926–1929) .
[8] Collingwood, *op. cit.,* p. 177.

human society presupposes an original separation from nature, one would need to define nature as opposed to intentionality to begin with and to establish a separation between them on the basis of principle. However, we have already attempted to establish that mere intentionality is a natural instance. If society functions exclusively on natural resources, it will be nature. If it extends beyond the natural, it will be through the intervention of non-natural motives, which can only be spiritual; and the distinction will fall back onto the spiritual element and not the social element.

The opposition between nature and society has been studied by Kelsen in an important book; his investigation is supported by a vast, principally ethnographic, documentation.[9] According to Kelsen, nature has been conceived primarily according to the principle of retribution and therefore as a part of society, within the system of sanctions and punishable acts. It is only later, when interest is extended to facts not directly related to the interests of man, that one conceives in nature the objective relation of cause and effect. When causality is emancipated from retribution, and when the law of nature is distinguished from social norm, nature and society are conceived as two completely different systems. This dualism of nature and society, however, is in no way definitive in the evolution of science, and it becomes problematic when the nature of the norm is submitted to a critical analysis. From the point of view of science—Kelsen concludes—society is a part of nature, because there is no inconvenience in applying to society the same kind of laws that are now considered to be in force in nature. Kelsen's argument, therefore, leads to the conviction that the mere idea of a norm is not sufficient to open up, in contrast to the natural domain, another domain that would be opposed to it. In this conclusion we agree with him, although our reasons do not coincide with his; there is also the reservation that something radically distinguished and separated from nature exists, namely spirit, whether it appears in the acts of a subject or is materialized in a norm or some other product of culture.

[9] *Sociedad y naturaleza.* Spanish trans. by J. Perriaux (Buenos Aires: Depalma, 1945).

VI

THE UNIQUENESS AND SIGNIFICANCE OF THE SPIRIT

TRAITS OF THE SPIRIT

The central, founding event of the spiritual act—the projection in this act of the subject toward the object—has certain consequences and is manifest in certain modes that can be considered as the principal traits of the spirit. These traits, however, are not to be considered as independent properties that meet in the spiritual act, as something added to it, forming part of it, or making it complex; rather they are to be considered as different expressions of its most genuine and profound character, as diverse aspects of a single reality.

The first of these traits is *absolute objectivity,* which is the fundamental condition of this kind of act. The merely intentional act is also of objective scope because it gives form to objectivities and manipulates them in various ways; all intentionality is a working with objectivities. But this objectivity is not absolute. In it the subject functions with the particularism of a living, intentional being, keeping continuously in mind his particular concrete being; and this gives a highly subjective quality to his act. The subjective interest imposes its direction on the intentional glance: heightening some aspects of the object and darkening others, it circumscribes the realm of objectivities according to its own standard. In addition, the object is given in a modified form because the practical intention of the subject is included in it. It is understood as "something for the subject," and to the extent that this occurs, it diminishes or annuls the autonomous condition of the object, which is an undeniable part of it and on occasion the fundamental aspect, since the object can signify its own unchangeable meaning, its very heart. In spiritual or absolute objectivity, the *whole* object is objectified, without its being altered with subjective innovations, and without neglecting the ultimate and independent significance of anything that is not the object itself. Knowledge of a spiritual kind is concerned with what is only because it is; the interest thus projected toward the object deserves the characterization "disinterested," because it is not governed by any interest peculiar to the agent, but rather by an interest engendered in the agent by the mere fact of the object's existing or by its being given. In ethical behavior, a given objective situation may be disvalued in a moral judgment, or the attempt may be made to correct it through actual intervention. But this is not equivalent to an interference of subjective particularism in the objective situation; rather the subject, facing a complex situation characterized by a conflict or an encounter with something given as real and something considered as an objective value or duty, decides for the latter—that is, for an order he recognizes as justified and valuable above the given reality.

Absolute spiritual objectivity does not permit the elimination of the subject as the terminal for its acts, but it does permit the elimination of the subject as a complex of subjective interests. The spiritual subject does not deny itself; rather it recognizes in itself an objectivity parallel to others. It is doubtlessly concerned with itself, but only as its being and meaning are conceived objectively.

Universality is another trait of the spirit; it has already served to distinguish the spirit from nature because of the particularism that is akin to everything natural. The spirit is universal in various ways, and all these stem from total objective projection. The subject, deprived of actual reference to itself, of the intention of redirecting everything to its own concrete being, feels universalized, cleansed from any existential particularism. This universality does not mean self-denial, as was indicated previously; on the contrary, the subject lives with a new intensity in this new situation, which, at the same time that it opens him to reality, in a sense brings the whole of reality to him. Universalism takes on a special characteristic in the attempts at fusion, in mystical union. The subject, in being projected toward reality, attempts to empty himself into it, to be assimilated in it, but in the attempt he is shipwrecked by reality and disappears as a subject. Hereby the spiritual instance, which is absolute transcendence, is annulled; it becomes one with a reality lifted above natural particularism only through spirituality. In the order of reality, universality is obtained only by the spiritual subject; and when his thrust is exhausted in the identifying purpose, he is annulled as spirit, and reality is deprived of the universal moment that the spirit alone brings to it.

Another aspect of universalism is the spirit's aspiration to totality in all directions in which objective projection is possible: cognitive, ethic, aesthetic, and so on. It is inherent for the spirit to aspire to know everything, to bring about a perfect ethical order everywhere. In principle, every limitation of knowledge stems from the fact that the subject restricts himself to what is of interest to him from the point of view of his natural particularism. On the other hand, in spiritual cognitive acts, every given or anticipated instance, in all its aspects and connections, attracts the attention and the inevitable limitation of knowledge, for each subject and each occasion depend only on circumstantial conditions. On the ethical level, also, reigns a universality of projection that is not restricted on the basis of principle but by the necessary relativity of all human behavior. In all, with the spirit characterized by its objectivist calling, it is sought by the whole realm of the objectified and the objectifiable, and any restriction is indicative of a restraint in its impulse—an impulse that is innate to it.

The *freedom* characteristic of the spirit, which Max Scheler considers to be one of the three traits that define it, is only the evasion of natural particularism; it is autonomy with regard to the interests and incentives of the living human being as a single concrete entity. Freedom, therefore, is absolute objectivism and universalism as viewed from the relation of the spiritual subject to the nonspiritual subject that sustains it and with which it lives. One should keep in mind that, properly speaking, it is not a matter of the spirit's independence from "life" in the biological sense— from the strictly organic and animal complex—because the section of nature most closely related to the spirit is not organic nature, but intentional nature. The freedom of the spirit is affirmed against the propensities and attitudes of what we have called the natural man—the man subject to intentional, nonspiritualized acts. It is not opposed to some animal-man who does not exist in the human race. The essential duality of man is rooted precisely in the difference and the frequent conflict between the natural conditioning of what is merely intentional and the freedom of the spirit or, what amounts to the same thing, between full subjectivism and full objectivism, between particularism and universalism. This spiritual freedom, however, is not total or metaphysical, a freedom concerning which we do not commit ourselves at this point. It is a freedom or, better said, a setting free, with respect to a determined constriction, that of the requirements of the natural order. With the autocratic rule of the spirit conceived in this manner, however, we do not pass judgment whether, within its own sphere, it is determined by a rigorous necessity; or whether it eludes all strict determination and whether everything in it is spontaneous and contingent; or whether necessity and contingency are combined; or whether we must decide to accept the solution of Spinoza, or Kant, or Bergson on this point.

From this radical objectivism also stems a *unity* of the spirit, which is primarily perceivable in the most general and consolidated spiritual attitudes, such as the cognitive and the ethical attitudes. To the extent that they are ultimately governed by their practical interests, which in each instance make up a complex different in the quality and quantity of its ingredients, the nonspiritual subjective centers maintain a fundamental divergence among themselves aside from the divergence, which is also sometimes in conflict with others, that occurs when each refers his own intentions to himself. Facing this diversified plurality there is, in the spiritual acts, an identical tone which, from afar, points to the total unity of the spirit without detriment to the multiplicity of the centers in which it is embodied. The subjects whose acts are accompanied by the subjective return can never come together and feel completely linked together except when they form a 'we' to which the final intention of the act is referred. But this 'we' functions in effect as a center of particularized interests that are opposed to those of other possible or existing 'we's.' In the spiritual act, or at least in many spiritual acts, the impression of unity or identity is obvious—as, for example, when the objective demands of reason, the strict rules of logic, the incontrovertible evidence of mathematics are obeyed, or when fundamental ethical postulates are recognized. In such cases, the subjects, compelled by objectivity, feel as if they are identical, as if they coincide completely in their acts.

The unity of the spirit has been upheld since ancient times and constitutes a common experience that has led to a number of interpretations. Let us review some of these. In spite of all uncertainties concerning the foundation and the nature of Socratic teaching, it seems quite likely that the enterprise of Socrates consisted primarily in showing the identity of the concepts and the norms grasped by reason (which for him is identified with the spirit). That is, since man is a spiritual being, Socrates sought to defend the unity of man's fundamental existence, a unity found underneath the irreducible diversity of men—a diversity upheld by the sophistic skeptics. The unity of the spirit is supported in Plato through contemplation of the immutable world of ideas; the souls are identical in that they are equally capable of perceiving this ideal world and that they then harbor in their minds, though in concealed fashion, this awareness which occurs before life on earth. The surprising experiment with the slave, in the *Meno*, is the demonstration, through a case that is all the more convincing since it is deliberately extreme, of the unity of the human spirit conceived in keeping with that kind of thought, that is to say, as reason. This unity is also upheld in Aristotle, especially in his notion of the active intellect. It is a unity distributed in a plurality of centers, but such that it provides the ground or pretext for the Averroist thesis of literal or numerical unity in the conception of the one intellect, a single spiritual entity that hovers above individuals and makes possible in them the superior forms of knowledge. The vision of the ideas which God has in some of the developments of Christian speculation brings with it also the identity of the spirit, so far as it apprehends and holds within itself identical content. In modern philosophy, the instrument *par excellence* for giving account of unity has been the aprioristic apparatus. One might say that in Kant one can conceive of the one subject, a supra-individual complex of forms or norms that is imposed on individual subjects and is a central part of each one.

It is important to point out that the unity of the spirit does not destroy or minimize the spiritual individuality in the subjects. The fundamental principle of that individuality is the plurality of the subjects and their effectiveness as the agents of their acts. The acts give rise to a spiritual experience that enriches the subject in his achievements and strengthens him through practice, structuring habit in him. In addition, this individuality takes on a markedly different character because each subject is oriented in his own manner to the unlimited horizon open before him, preferring one sector to another and taking on this task or that within each sector.

Spiritual unity appears at times as fulfilled and at other times as an imperative or a demand, but in any case it is implicit in the nature of spirituality. With regard to the metaphysical significance of this unity, one might risk the following hypothesis. Reality, which is one with respect to logical or historical priority, is divided and diversified in a process of particularization. The partial instances, as they increase in their particularism, at the same time gradually open up to totality, leaning toward it without neglecting the individual foci that are being constituted, in such a way that simultaneously the individuality is purified and the striving for totality is intensified. An animal, for example, is more an individual than a plant, and it is also more open to reality. In the spiritual individual this double process comes to a close because it achieves maximum individuation, and correspondingly it becomes completely open to totality. In the spirit, totality experiences a reëncounter and a recognition of itself, coming to possess itself in terms of consciousness. Suppositions of this kind are not rare in the history of philosophy; and with adequate modification, they serve as different interpretations of the whole.

The *historicity* of the spirit has been previously discussed. The spirit has a historical source; it emerges in a determined season, probably when the merely intentional function has been consolidated. Spiritual acts are absolute—that is, they either have the distinctive features or they are not spiritual acts. But their "habitualness," their frequency, is undoubtedly a historical conquest. One must allow for the genius of the spirit, the gift of certain individuals, groups, or peoples to initiate spiritual attitudes unknown before and sometimes to exercise these attitudes—which for others are exceptional or infrequent—in a current, normal way. The spiritually gifted thus take upon themselves the mission of spiritually educating the others. On the other hand, as the treasure of cultural achievement increases, the corresponding spiritual activities find their means of functioning more accessible through the example and the stimulation of what has already been achieved, which also serves as a model. It is evident, for example, that the superior cognitive activities are easier for one who lives in a community that has enjoyed a long philosophical and scientific tradition than they are for one who can count only on his own personal desire for knowledge. Likewise, the acts of aesthetic creation or contemplation will have considerable support for one who has access to and takes advantage of works of art of great value. With these brief notations we wish only to assert the historicity of the spirit, the actual introduction of time into its appearance and continuation, without entering into a discussion of the modes and directions of spiritual progress or increase.

Respect and interest (the "disinterested interest") are the secondary traits of the spirit. The spirit respects everything and is interested in everything, and obvious signs of the absence of spirit are lack of respect and indifference with regard to beings and things. The pragmatic stamp that mere intentional consciousness imposes on its objectifications is a lack of respect for what they are in themselves and a lack of interest in their own, nontransferable character. From a certain point of view, to behave spiritually is to be aware that everything is worthy of respect and everything is interesting. Philosophy, pure science, and art are born of a disinterested interest in things, of a respect for what is and for what is imagined. It is not difficult to discover in the moral attitude the confluence of the high potential of interest and respect. For common eyes the only hierarchy of beings and things is that given by reasons which pertain to the practical order. Art tends to regain possession of what is abject and humiliated in daily life by setting it apart with a halo which interest and respect together place around it. Thus we have modest household utensils in Dutch painting, or the common rustic whom Cervantes lifts momentarily to worthy and moving levels of human action, as if to compensate for so many jests and blows; thus also the "divine swineherd Eumaeus" in the verses of the *Odyssey*, and the poor savage Tastego in Melville's brilliant novel. The spirit is always redemption. It redeems through that mixture of interest and respect which is inherent in it and in many other ways that need not be examined here.

Responsibility is a trait of the spirit that has received little attention. There is a feeling of responsibility that tends to reach very elevated forms and, though not belonging to the sphere of the spirit, almost borders on it. We do not refer to the responsibility that primitive man experiences toward his group, for he is hardly individualized; rather it is that felt by the subject when he lives as an identical and continuous self. This responsibility to one's own individuality, to one's own life as reality, whether as fictionally imagined or as projected, at times reaches the heroic and the sacrificial. The same is true of responsibility with respect to others when a solid nexus of interests and affection exists. Spiritual responsibility has special characteristics. The responsibility of the subject to himself as a spiritual subject, as a person, presupposes responsibility to other persons conceived as entities of equal worth. The spirit, as we have repeatedly stated, is an absolutely objective projection, and it feels, as an intimate obligation, that it must act as such. It feels clearly responsible for any fault or detriment in its functioning. This is seen, for example, when the subject feels impelled to extend the boundaries of knowledge and then feels ashamed for having advanced insufficiently, or when he feels at fault in not having completely fulfilled a distasteful ethical obligation. Examples can be easily multiplied. More difficult and interesting is another problem—that vague and universal uneasiness that seems to be the constant companion of the spirit, as if in every instance it felt responsible for all stupidity and evil in the world, present, past, and future. It is as if every violation of spiritual demands is the subject's fault, remote though the violation may be from the subject who experiences this feeling. The spiritual subject feels himself to be the bearer of a supreme and universal principle that he accepts as justified and responsible, and he suffers when he ascertains that this principle has not succeeded. In every spiritual attitude there is the impression of an unlimited responsibility, because the command to take charge of totality, to be the meaning of totality, and to carry out complete spiritual colonization, is inherent in the spirit.

Self-consciousness has been considered by Max Scheler as one of **the** three principal traits of the spirit. But self-consciousness is not an exclusive attribute of the spirit. In nonspiritualized intentionality, self-consciousness is to be found as soon as the subject is firmly constituted as a self. An unprecedented intensification of subjective interests tends to reënforce self-consciousness without taking into account that there are more or less morbid psychic dispositions that turn the subject toward himself and stir up a watchful and even exasperated self-consciousness. In general, the adolescent, the timid person, and the introvert turn toward their own inner reality. There is also a frankly pathological complacency in self-contemplation in some psychic types (the one who analyzes himself, the one who feels sorry for himself, the one who suffers from an excess of intense scruples, the one who feels inferior) that leads to a constant probing and, as a result, an exaggerated self-consciousness which abounds in erroneous interpretations and a defective appreciation of the context in reality in which the self is found. It is undeniable that sometimes an authentic spiritual consciousness may arise from such conditions, but in itself, the spiritual consciousness is something different. The spirit is—or tends to be—the consciousness of totality; spiritual self-consciousness must work with that universalized consciousness and be at its command. Spiritual self-consciousness, then, is the consciousness of the subject so far as he is the agent of such acts; it is consciousness of a self in spiritual relation to the whole. It is not the look merely directed inwardly, toward an inner reality that can well be an unventilated enclosure with a foul atmosphere or even seething with corruption; rather it is the self-possession of the center of objectively directed acts, understood as a focus whose incomparable value derives not from the more or less suspicious secrets of the so-called "inner life" but from the clean spiritual life that is a generous acceptance of all that is. From this comes the material for an intimacy in which the objective and the subjective are two sides of the same coin.

Finally, we hold *absolute transcendence* to be the essential trait of the spirit.

SPIRIT AS ABSOLUTE TRANSCENDING

As we have repeatedly asserted, the fundamental difference between the spiritual act and the merely intentional act consists in the fact that the former is directed toward its object without a subjective return, whereas the latter has a subjective intent, a subordination of the object to the particular goals of the subject. Such a difference may also be expressed by saying that the non-spiritual act is transcendent to the extent that it has an undeniable, objective direction inseparable from its intentional character. Yet it partly denies or shifts its transcendence by referring the object, in one way or another, to the interests of the subject. The spiritual act, however, is absolutely transcendent because it goes out to the object and remains with it, in no way actually referring the object to the existential uniqueness of the subject.

The spiritual act thus achieves pure transcendence. Its reference to the subject is only the inevitable connection between the subject and his act. Undoubtedly, the transcendent movements of the spiritual subject—his cognitive, ethical, and aesthetic acts—gradually organize in him a background of experience, forming habits that might be interpreted as immanent acquisitions. Yet such an interpretation would be in error. This enriching of the subject is completely contained within the understanding of transcendence, for it is only the accumulation and the functioning of moments of transcendence that are sustained in consciousness without change in its nature. As accumulation, it is only of transcendent instances; and as habit, it is only the propensity to persevere in the transcendent attitude. Immanence is the enclosure in one's own particular reality. The private interests of the subject (and by the same token those of any concrete 'we') make up an immanence to which the object is referred and redirected in the merely intentional attitude. There is nothing similar in the spiritual attitude. What the subject harbors, he holds without trimming or modification, without referring it to himself, rather referring himself, as a subject, to the content of his own experience. To speak of immanent activity at this point would be a contradiction, because here the transcendent intent has unlimited jurisdiction. The special manner in which it could be said that the subject "possesses" the results of his acts is not actually a possessing in the current sense of appropriation; it is rather a new and unique situation, exclusive to spiritual transcending, for which it is just as valid to say that the subject possesses the acts as it is to say that he is possessed by them. When we understand the unconditional value of an ethical axiom and in our conscience hold it to be such, it is just as important to say that we have it as it is to say that it has us. It is well to keep in mind that transcendence is always a going out from oneself, a spilling over, and a seeking of the other; but the center that transcends must be maintained, since otherwise there is no transcendence, but evaporation or dissolution. Transcendence consists in a transcending being and not in ceasing to be when the transcendence is accomplished. Seeking the other for its own sake presupposes the agent of that seeking, and this very seeking ceases to be when the being who seeks the other disappears. Spiritual transcendence requires the presence and the permanence of the spiritual subject who converts his objects into his own intentional possession without making them immanent, because he recognizes in them the complete transcendence of being, purpose, and meaning.

We believe that the attribution of total transcendence to spiritual acts cannot be called into question, since it is concerned with a characteristic of these acts that has always been recognized in them. In the everyday use of language this characteristic has been identified when the acts are set up as "disinterested acts" or "altruistic acts" in opposition to intentional acts linked to the practical interest of the agent, which, in their turn, are referred to as "interested" or "egoistical." These terms indicate, respectively, the absence or the presence of a direct subjective interest, the full projection toward the other or that which is accompanied by the return to the subject, the final transcendent or immanent significance of the act.

The absolute transcendence and the full objectivism of the spiritual act come to be the same thing. But the introduction of the notions of transcendence and immanence makes possible the sounding of the spiritual act to its very depths, the placing of it in relation to metaphysical hypotheses that help in understanding its place and meaning in totality. It also offers a new interpretation of values that recognizes their objectivity without falling into the error of disconnecting the realm of values from that of being, an error incurred by most axiological systems of an objectivist bent.

Although, as we have indicated, absolute transcendence and complete objectivism come to be the same thing, strictly speaking they are not identical. In our opinion, absolute transcendence is primary, basic, and original in the spiritual act. Thus, one should not say that an act is fully transcendent and objective, rather that it is completely transcendent; and, as a consequence, it is completely objective, because absolute transcendence is what provides the foundation for complete objectivity. In the merely intentional act the transcending toward the object is accompanied by the domination of the subject as a cluster of interests which leads to the modification of the object, its practical subordination to the subject. The transcendence is, therefore, weak and incomplete, and it is ultimately defeated by the subjective demands. In the spiritual act, transcendence works without obstacles or limitations; its strength yields to no opposition. The spiritual subject is the one who is identified and the one who coincides with the transcending impulse of the act. The objectivity is a direct expression of that transcendence, of the lack of subjective return; and all other qualities of the spiritual act, as they have been previously set forth, can be equally understood as manifestations or consequences of absolute transcendence.

Something will be said later concerning transcendence in general and freedom. Transcendence is always a setting free and, in its turn, freedom is a mode or an aspect of transcendence. The constitution of the intentional order undoubtedly points to the appearance of a regime that is much freer than the organic order. The intentional individual enjoys an autonomy superior to that of the animal; his realm is an objectified world, with many given, foreseeable situations, with a vast temporal and spatial perspective. For the organic individual, however, the situations are immediate and rigid, single or limited in number, and capable of exercising on the individual an attraction or a rejection that diminishes in the extreme the possibility of selection. All told, the freedom of action of the intentional individual is held within specific limits, which depend on his natural character, on the fact of his being a solidification in nature, and on his submission to natural restrictions. The parallelism between freedom and transcendence is evident: to the partial transcendence of the merely intentional act corresponds a partial freedom; and to the absolute transcendence of the spiritual act corresponds an obviously greater freedom, because all natural compulsions have been suppressed. We do not wish to designate this freedom as absolute, since, as we have seen previously, we have no desire to include in this discussion the difficult topic of freedom in its ultimate metaphysical reaches.

As for self-consciousness, lived though its content may be, it is only conceivable through "reflection," by the return of the subject to itself. The subject goes out of itself in order to fall back on itself; it is the point of departure and the destination of the act. Self-possession confers on the self a dual role, as possessor and as possession. However it occurs, it presupposes that the subject steps out of himself in order to return again to himself. This going out of oneself is a transcending of oneself. And in the same manner as we have already done for freedom, we must distinguish here between restricted and total transcendence, between a transcendence that later becomes immanent and a pure or spiritual transcendence. There is a transcendence accompanied by a tendency to immanence when the reflection which grants the self-consciousness does not take the subject out of the natural level; when in it and through it the subject continues to live, in an absolute sense, as the supreme reality to which everything else, for all practical purposes, must be subjected. There is spiritual self-consciousness when the subject, as he transcends in his reflection of himself, perceives himself in full objectivity—which is close yet at the same time distant—and therefore can possibly refer to himself with that "disinterested interest" of which full objectivity consists. The reflective transcendence that this self-consciousness affords is obviously absolute.[1]

SPIRIT IN THE CONTEXT OF A METAPHYSICS OF TRANSCENDENCE

To affirm that total transcendence is the fundamental characteristic of spiritual acts and of the subject of such acts seems to us to be sufficiently justified, not requiring the additional support from new arguments. However, we still need to examine how this transcendence functions in particular things—that is, in each kind of act. We will dwell particularly on cognitive and ethical acts whose nature seems relatively clear and will not demand a spelling out of minor details, since such a task is properly undertaken in the

[1] In connection with the topic of this section and the next, see Romero, "Programa de una filosofía" in *Papeles para una filosofía* (Buenos Aires: Editorial Losada, 1945) .

theory of knowledge and in ethics rather than in a general theory of man. Little will be said regarding aesthetic acts, since the multiplicity of the reasons proposed for understanding them has not yet jelled into sure and widely accepted criteria. The harmonious organization of the principal themes into a solid whole has not been achieved, nor has any one of them been designated as dominant and capable of arranging the others around it.

Before turning to that task, which will sketch the first lines of a theory of value, we will be concerned with tracing a general theory of reality, within which the theses we have been developing will be systematically arranged. We believe that these theses can be supported on their own and that they find their justification in the reasoning that has been given in each case. The general hypotheses that we now add are not intended to provide additional justification. Yet they offer perspectives for a broader interpretation, thereby fulfilling the philosophical prerequisite of not keeping any particular problem isolated from the concepts concerning the whole. One might decide that any evaluation of the whole, since its validity is inevitably hypothetical, would carry this relative fragility over to the special theses brought together in it as subordinate parts. One might also conclude that the result of these present reflections will be to contaminate with uncertainty what has been previously established or at least expose it to the risk of rejection that is the lot of every metaphysical hypothesis. However, these hypotheses share in this trait through the innate condition of being plausible and nothing more, since even in the most favorable cases one can never come to a definitive proof, regardless of the number of conjectures that may be listed in its favor. In spite of these unfavorable arguments, we have decided to introduce at this point the following considerations, since we are persuaded that other plausible arguments support them. The ideas concerning man defended in this work, and the metaphysical principles stated below, were born at the same time in the mind of the author. A desire for intellectual honesty encourages him to present the complex of ideas to which those concepts of man belong, since to present these thoughts in isolated fashion, without the living connection that they maintain with the other notions of reality, would be to misrepresent his thought. To this reason, which is perhaps a little personal, there may be added another that is not personal and that is of greater import. Philosophically, it is impossible to state the idea of the human without presenting some thought concerning the place and significance of man with respect to the whole. More strongly, this last concern is the basic issue in the problem of man, resting at its very center and affecting all its parts to such an extent that, if it were not confronted, the problem would be left up in the air, far from any convincing and satisfactory solution. With respect to this point, however, one should keep in mind that what is said regarding the spirit does not apply in exactly the same sense to man, a being who is defined not by the spirit but by the nature-spirit duality that occurs in him.

The positive element of reality, that which gives it dynamism and perhaps its very being, is transcendence. Two notions have come to be inevitable for thinking about reality: structure, and evolution or development. Both, properly understood, presuppose transcendence; both reveal the entity as moving beyond itself, as transcending. Structure is a whole that implies novelty with respect to its parts; such a novelty cannot be conceived without admitting that the parts transcend themselves when they form part of a structure, as they overflow and become welded into an original synthesis. Development, evolution so far as it is a complete unfolding, is a transcending in the direction of time, in which the entity pours itself out into the future. Everything real is acting, and in every case to act is to transcend. The mechanistic conception, which has achieved such an exalted and entrenched prestige in science and philosophy, not only ignores the transcendental impetus that gives form to all of reality but has eagerly set itself to prove the illusion—the fictitious and superficial character—of all transcending. Any change that is full and true, any actual mutation, implies transcendence, a moving beyond oneself. The mechanistic interpretation, as is known, reduces all change to the act of moving—that is, the mere changing of place—which is a pseudochange since it assumes that the nature of the being remains identical and that the only thing that is altered is the mutual arrangement of the entities or of their elements, that is, their spatial distribution. This attitude bestows a special importance on space, since distribution in space determines all transformation. All significance is taken away from time since there is no true change, and temporality slides over the surface of entities without settling into them, without affecting them. The mechanistic conception has arisen in modern philosophy and, inspired mainly by rationalism, has prospered throughout its development; at its root, mechanism is an embodiment, an outgrowth of rationalism. Extreme rationalism attempts to discover in reality a structure akin to a strict reason, founded on identity. As Meyerson has shown, the causal explanation seeks to establish a substance that is identical with itself, that is immutable even in becoming. That is to say, this rationalism, which is most evident in the mechanistic interpretation of reality, affirms an absolute immanence, condemning all transcendence as illusory and reducible to an actual immanence. The principle of identity is also a principle of immanence; it affirms that an entity is exhausted in its own inner reality, in its being immanent. It ignores, therefore, the true mode of being of reality, which is its going beyond itself, its transcending itself. Strict, identifying rationality does not coincide, therefore, with reality. Intelligence—much more comprehensive and elastic than strict or Eleatic reason—recognizes this lack of accord and is able both to judge the real and the rational, separately and as they confront each other, and to inquire wherein they coincide and wherein they differ. A considerable part of the philosophical work of our own day consists in a critique of reason on the basis of the conclusions established along this line.

In passing, we have referred to the predominant role of space and the elimination of time in the mechanistic interpretations. This is because space is closely connected with immanence and time with transcendence; and these connections depend ultimately on the frigid neutrality and passivity of immanence and the vibrant flowing of transcendence which can neither be stopped nor reversed.

Reality is arranged on four different levels or orders: the physical or inorganic level; the level of life; the level of intentional psychism; and the level of the spirit. Each is the foundation of the level that follows it, emerges from it, feeds on it, and surpasses it. A notable increase in transcendence is evident in this succession of levels. One can best imagine a pure immanence on the physical level here, transcendence is least visible. It is at this point that the attempts at a strict rationalist interpretation have felt the preference for "downward explanations," that is, for the idea that the physical order is the only one with substantial or metaphysical worth and that all the rest is a manifestation of the physical, a mere accidental result of the interplay of matter. Transcendence is quite evident in life. Living beings are active centers of transcendence, not only as individuals and species but, above all, as they make up the whole current of life, multiplying on the inorganic level as they colonize it. Living beings succeed and reproduce through the series of generations in which the progenitors transcend themselves and seem to continue to transcend themselves, even after they have disappeared, through the continuity of a vital message entrusted to the farthest reaches of time. In intentional psychism transcendence is even more evident: intentionality consists precisely in the transcendence toward the object. The subject is the point of departure of innumerable, continuous transcending acts, and the horizon for such acts is practically unlimited because everything is objectifiable—everything is or may be the target of intentions. The whole of reality with all its elements, real and nonreal, has been converted into a stage where the intentional individual acts out his role, which consists of nothing other than acts of intentionality, of transcendence. This transcendence, however, is not complete. The intentional individual refers his acts to himself; as an existing individual, he holds himself to be the ultimate concern to whom all his acts are tied by the bonds of his own interest. Such a limitation or relativization of transcendence disappears in the spiritual attitude, so that all actual reference of the act to the subject is severed—except that the act still remains that of the subject. The subject, we might say, is the point of departure of the act but not its goal; this is true, however, of the purely intentional act, because of the concrete and individual interest in the purpose of the act. The spiritual subject, therefore, is a focus of pure transcendences; in him transcendence reaches its highest possible attainment. The animating thrust of the whole of reality thereby achieves its triumph and functions with total autonomy, free from any remainder of immanence. This functioning consists in reaching out to the whole of reality, unhindered by bonds or compulsions; it consists in turning in a special way toward oneself as the informing principle of reality, in cognitively apprehending oneself and in achieving an ethical wholeness with oneself.

A thorough discussion of the foregoing statements is not called for at this juncture. The considerations that follow are presented merely as some indications, which, of course, should be considerably amplified and more solidly grounded, and perhaps in part corrected. In modern times, notions of a decidedly immanent leaning had their golden age during the seventeenth and eighteenth centuries, when the dominating thought was rationalist in the extreme; and they reappeared temporarily in Positivism. Romanticism was a veritable insurrection against an intellectualism that was strongly immanent. In many ways and in countless instances there arise in Romanticism intuitions of a transcendent kind, convictions or premonitions that reality does not consist in immanent solidifications, but in foci of transcendence, in creative movements, in full and true changes. The subject in Fichte is not only pure action, pure transcendence in his acts, but he produces the world, the nonself, in an unconscious going beyond himself. Evolution, as continuous creation and development, is one of the principal channels of transcendence; and it is quite understandable that, since that time, interpretations of reality in keeping with evolutionist schemes should have recurred, although with different intentions and content. The first one in a grand style is found in Schelling: nature is a teleological process whose destiny is the production of the spiritual being. In Hegel, the Becoming of the Ideas occurs through a dialectical process that culminates in absolute spirit. In Positivism, in keeping with the general tendencies of the historical moment, philosophy rejects interpretations of transcendence with a cosmic scope. Natural positivistic evolutionism is mechanical and leads to immanence, but with regard to man it tacitly affirms a progressivism that, in its own way, makes room for transcendence. After Positivism's loss of influence, these insights, which broke through for the first time during the romantic period, were resurrected, seeking new formulae, more critical, rigorous, and in accord with facts and in harmony with the findings of the sciences. They find expression in the metaphysical systems of our own day, as in those of Bergson and Whitehead.

Thus far the principles proposed in philosophy to give an account of the development and growth of reality do not include all the events with which real instances confront us. These instances overflow, go beyond themselves, radiating in ever enlarging circles, until in spiritual operations they reach an activity of absolute transcendence with an outreach and a meaning that are clearly universal. Only with great difficulty could our own age condescend to interpretations that are originally centered in a spiritual principle, like those of Fichte and Hegel or to interpretations that require a complete acceptance of final causes like that of Schelling. In Bergsonian metaphysics, where time is first taken in to the very midst of being, the informing principle, the *élan vital*, gives shape to a vitalist monism at the expense of other aspects of reality whose autonomy and distinctness should not be dismissed. The hypothesis of transcendence—along much broader lines than those proposed by Simmel—seems to side step accusations of partiality and to have the indispensable breadth needed to include all events that are being accepted since the necessity for giving up schemes of immanence has been recognized. Transcendence is one, to the extent that it is the general tendency of entities to go beyond themselves, to launch out in diverse directions from a given center, yet it is multiple in its forms, in keeping with the different levels of reality. The monism of transcendence is diversified in the pluralism of the different rules of transcendence, according to the four orders of reality, and, within these orders, in special ways—as for example cognitive, ethical, or aesthetic transcendence in the realm of the spirit. A reality composed of purely immanent instances would lack the attributes that we feel obligated to admit in what is real; it would be like a cadaver of reality, or its skeleton. The function of immanence would seem to be the formation of the centers of transcendence, or perhaps the storing of latent transcendent activity that becomes actual when given adequate expression. The immanent center decreases and tends to resolve itself in transcendence as it rises in the scale of entities. Perhaps at one extreme mass is the focus of gravitational transcendence and at the other the spirit, in which immanence is a mere point, a center without dimension that is completely identified with its transcending.

The three orders of reality that form an echelon above the physical level reveal a gradual increase in transcendence. There is more transcending on the organic than on the physical level, on the intentional than the organic level, and on the spiritual than the merely intentional level. Spiritual transcendence indicates the apex and does not allow for a higher level; it is absolute and total transcendence. Spiritual acts are defined by their completely objective direction, and the spiritual focus—the subject—is immediately identified with his acts. As self-consciousness, the subject is constituted through acts of pure, reflected transcendence, which do not form kernels of immanence. Spiritual self-consciousness is fully objective, and the only 'lived' factor found in it is the direct impression of transcendence, which is the specific feeling that accompanies every spiritual act. One might conclude from this that when the concretely immanent disappears from the subject, all effective individuation also disappears. But we have already made clear that transcendence is not the annulling of the center that transcends, rather it is action that stems from that center, a going beyond oneself without ceasing to be that self. Spiritual individuality is assured by the unity and continuity of the subject, by its reflexive reference to itself, and by the distinctness of the spiritual processes, so far as they form an organic complex that constitutes the activity and experience appropriate to each self. This complex, undoubtedly, is different for each spiritual unity— among other reasons, because of the limitation of the powers of each one, and the infinitude and difficulty of the task of the colonization of totality, a task that the spirit sets for itself and from which stems the distinctness or specialization of the spiritual realm of each unit.

VII

VALUES

Concerning Value in General

As has been asserted, the positive element of reality is transcendence, and just as Hegel states that the truth of being is essence, we might propose another affirmation: the truth of being is transcendence. Actually, from our point of view, transcendence is being itself in its truth, in its life. Immanence can be considered as that kernel of transcendent acts which have not been actualized and are held in reserve. The different levels of reality, from the physical to the spiritual, show an awakening, a growth of transcendence; and the echelons that rise above the physical level may be interpreted as the series of successive and ever more complete ways of transcending which reality creates in order to fulfill its truth.[1] It is like the progressive liberation of the transcending impulse that is inherent in being and that reaches its final stage in the spirit.

For us, value is not a special quality superimposed on acts, nor is it something exclusively subjective in that it is determined by the value-giving attitudes of the subject, whether this be the individual subject in his uniqueness or the universal subject. Value is the degree of transcendence and therefore the degree of the actual reality of being. In each instance, whether entity or activity, it is

[1] See what was stated in this regard on pp. 59–70.

the dignity that belongs to it in accord with the transcendence it embodies. The evaluating subject apprehends this dignity by means of special emotional acts. We therefore accept the objectivity of value yet restrict its reference to the metaphysical structure of what is, and, likewise, we accept the apprehension of value through feeling and not through the intellect, a position taken by many eminent writers on value.

As will be seen, our point of view on value is intimately linked to the anthropological thesis presented in this work, and it completes the picture of reality that was sketched in the preceding section. It would be rather uncalled for and somewhat disproportionate to develop, at this point, a complete theory of values, in all its aspects and details, even were we in a position to do so. Hence, we will limit ourselves to summary statements. As a total doctrine, the problem should be confronted independently, in a special investigation, and it is in this manner that recent philosophy tends to proceed. But if we avoid the problem, our thought on man would not be adequately understood. The reasons for introducing these thoughts are the same as those that led us to include the sketch of reality in the previous section, though here they are justified still more, because we feel that an interpretation of spirit which dispenses with an explanation of its relation to value must necessarily be mutilated and unsatisfactory.

We divide values into spiritual and nonspiritual. The former we call absolute, since higher values are not to be found, and the latter relative. This relativity of nonspiritual values should not be understood in the sense of subjectivity or mere accident, or variability arising from circumstantial considerations. The relativity means that the values allow for degrees and nuances in magnitude and dignity that, regardless of the grade they attain, never equal the magnitude and dignity of absolute values.

Spiritual values are absolute because it is only in the spirit that absolute transcendence is found. Absolute values are achieved and apprehended by the spiritual subject in spiritual acts, that is, in absolutely valuable acts. The spiritual subject also apprehends the relative values in absolutely valuable acts. In special situations, which will be referred to later, the nonspiritual subject may give rise to spiritual creations. That is to say that the act, without being purely spiritual, may obtain spiritual ends, and, by the same token, the spiritual act may obtain nonspiritual ends. This apparent incongruity arises from the difference between subject and culture. Transcendence for the subject consists in the nature of the intent and not in the quality of the result, whereas the cultural product is a result that subsists in itself and is valid apart from the subjective intentions which produced it.

Relative values are embodied in the whole of reality, to the extent that transcendence is manifest throughout it. It is the magnitude of this transcending that determines the dignity of the value in each situation. The organic is more valuable than the physical, and the intentional more than the organic, because the respective levels are like platforms that make possible the new and more active forms of transcendence. The merely intentional subject appreciates and normally achieves relative values, and he is also able to make a comparative evaluation of them. But he does not apprehend absolute values because in so doing he would *ipso facto* become a spiritual subject. Neither is he capable of comparative evaluations of relative and absolute values, an ability which is found only in the spiritual subject.

Transcendence, taken in itself, is always absolutely valuable. When one speaks of acts of partial transcendence, one actually speaks of the situations in which the transcendence occurs on a foundation of immanence or with an immanently directed return. Consequently, relative value corresponds to those entities or acts in which the transcendence is incomplete and not to the transcendence itself that is found in them. The merely intentional subject grasps the (relative) value of the total situation in which transcendence and immanence are mixed. The spiritual subject, besides apprehending and achieving the absolute value that belongs to the complete transcendence of the spirit, also apprehends, as has been said, the relative values as well as the absolute value of the moment of transcendence that appears in every entity or act.

The constitution of the inner center of every entity is a particularly interesting result of transcendence. It is a transcendence that is reflective and self-directed, which gives birth to a center, a new reality, by the mere act of transcendence, and the particular dignity of such centers stems from this act. The first and most obscure is that of the inner reality in plants and animals, a mere regulative center that is raised in the zoölogical ascent to a diffused focus of consciousness, capable of pain and pleasure and, later, of more complicated physical processes. This should be taken into consideration from the point of view of value. In spite of the subjective return that characterizes merely intentional consciousness, it is here that transcendence takes on a tremendous intensity. There corresponds to it, therefore, a very high value, though it does not attain absolute value, which is reserved for the spirit; the spirit is the only form of reality in which transcendence functions without any vestige of immanence.

Since we are not presenting a complete theory of value but limiting ourselves to providing the rudiments that we consider a necessary foundation for the concept of man, we do not feel obliged to examine all kinds of value. Neither do we find ourselves in a position to confront the problem in all its ramifications, although we are accumulating material for such a presentation. So, for these reasons, we will be limited in the following pages to considering cognitive and ethical values, values that it is not well to ignore.

Concerning Cognitive Value

Theoretical or cognitive value pertains to every act that concerns knowledge in the proper sense, that is, objective apprehension. Relative cognitive value is given in merely intentional acts. Absolute cognitive value belongs to spiritual acts of knowledge. Spirit, which is absolute transcendence, transcends cognitively through these acts toward everything that can be apprehended in terms of objectivity.

Inevitably, cognitive apprehending is knowledge of an object by a subject. No aspiration to some ultimate and pure knowledge, some supreme knowledge free of imperfection, should guide us or lead us to imagine that the subject-object contraposition is a situation that can be surpassed. The essence of knowledge is that it should neither be an actual appropriation of the object nor a fusion with it, but a cognitive appropriation, and that this appropriation should be intended and carried out by the subject of the knowledge. As soon as one takes away their functions from the subject and the object, knowledge is suppressed and becomes impossible. Frequently, it is supposed that the perfection of knowledge is achieved through the identification of the subject with the object. Not only does this full, mystical identification, if it is possible, annul knowledge, but at the same time it annuls a part of the only spiritual reality of which we have an experience that is certain.

Spiritual cognitive transcending unreservedly demands knowing all that is objectifiable, all that we have included in the word "totality." Any restriction would be equivalent to curtailing the absolutism of that transcendence, which is inherent in it as a spiritual attitude. An inborn demand of the spirit, therefore, is to know all there is to know to its very depths. This demand based on principle is not denied, even though, actually, spiritual knowledge is specialized and restricted in each subject. For one thing, each man embodies a certain fraction of the spirit, which is incorporated in a concrete human situation that prescribes the orientation and sets down the limits of spiritual activity. For another, cognitive spiritual absolutism, as was stated, demands the total exploration of totality, that is to say, a complete search of it, reaching to ultimate limits in extension and depth. From this arises the conviction that the investigation in depth is feasible only in especially absorbing tasks carried out at the expense of the investigation in breadth. The latter investigation becomes valid as the results of many lesser tasks are brought together. From the rigorous point of view of spiritual requirements, these requirements demand, on the one hand, the totality of knowledge and, on the other, the dividing up of active knowledge for each subject without exception, since any individual pursuit that seems to incline toward the totality of knowledge is also a dividing up. This is true because it must invariably leave aside the foundations and the detailed implementation inherent in absolute and complete knowledge.

In many sections of totality, study in depth is possible only through scientific investigation. The distinction between what is scientific and what is philosophical is presented in various ways. All agree in referring to scientific investigation as handling objects in a so-called material way: visual recognition, measurement, observation of phenomena, experimentation, authentification and deciphering of documents, and so on. In some instances the use of the label may be questionable. Thus, there is no particular reason for mathematics to be considered a science and the theory of relations to be placed within the confines of philosophy, since the natures of both are so much alike. Perhaps the only justifiable distinction is that which maintains that science is knowledge with presuppositions and philosophy knowledge without presuppositions, since the latter takes as its task the discussion of every presupposition, including those of the sciences. This criterion takes into consideration the need to attend to totality, a demand that is proper to philosophy. Actually, the investigation of every presupposition is nothing other than the imperative to consider totality from one of its aspects, the aspect that provides depth. What we of the West call philosophy is ultimate and perfect knowledge; it is the complete knowledge of totality, in theory and also in practice, to the extent that it uncovers for us what is fundamental and moves us to assent to it, primarily from the ethical point of view. The principle of totality is implicit in the philosophical attitude, and when this attitude is maintained but totality is not covered, there is a tendency to proceed in this way for special reasons that presuppose a direct or indirect recognition of the imperative to the totality of knowledge. Perhaps this is due to the emphasis on what is *basic,* leaving aside what is not judged to be so, an emphasis which presupposes a previous consideration of totality—even though it be in rather sketchy terms—and, from the point of view of value, raising certain aspects and problems to the foreground. Or it may be that a part of totality is declared to be fundamentally unknowable, and the investigation is restricted to what is judged to be knowable, which likewise requires an evaluation of the whole in order to decide what is available and what is not available to knowledge. Thus one finds in philosophy the ultimate expression of the goal of complete knowledge, which, in its fullness, cannot be separated from the spiritual cognitive attitude, and whose impulse to transcend cognitively to all there is does not seem to need further justification. But if the philosophical attitude is the end and the culmination of the spiritual cognitive attitude, it is manifest wherever there is free knowledge, partial and limited though it be. However, it is not found where knowledge is subordinated to concrete subjective ends, although it may crystallize in a most imposing philosophical system.

Implicit in the inherent absolutism of spiritual knowledge are the demands that it be knowledge of everything and knowledge of the ultimate foundations. These demands reinforce each other. Because of the bonds and the constant influences between each member of the whole and all of the others, and the infinite implications among the parts of the whole, no one thing can be fathomed if all the rest is ignored: the knowledge of any one thing presupposes knowledge of the remaining matters. To know oneself is also an undeniable imperative. It is a knowledge of one of the parts of the whole, which cannot be disregarded; but it is also a knowledge of the one who knows, and therefore it is a knowledge that affects the focus of all knowing—indeed, its very source. Thus it provides the indispensable resources for a critique and purification of all knowledge as it throws light on the activities that produce knowledge. To know oneself exhaustively not only demands that one penetrate intimately into what one is oneself, but also that one inquire into the place and the significance of the subject within totality.

Thus it is that spiritual acts of knowing take on absolute cognitive value. This value stems solely from the pure transcendence of the act, from its completely objective intention. If it has anything to do with truth, it is indirectly, since the act does not tend toward truth, but toward the object. If it faithfully apprehends the object, the knowledge is true, but the apprehension can be deceptive and erroneous without affecting the value of the act, because the value is with respect to the act and not to its result, since the result sometimes coincides with the intention and sometimes does not. The same object can be the occasion of a spiritual act of knowledge in one subject and to a nonspiritual act of knowledge in another; and even if the result were false in the first act and true in the second, the first would not lose its absolute cognitive value, nor would the second have more than relative value.

When it is a matter of the acts of a subject, absolute cognitive value depends on the intention of the act and not on its truth. However, when it is a matter of objectified knowledge it does depend on the truth. An important qualification needs to be made at this point. Objectified knowledge, for example a series of propositions that we read in a book, can be understood in two ways: as a living, direct expression of the author, the immediate echo of his acts; or as a series of fully objective propositions whose substantial significance depends only on what they explicitly express. In the first case we listen to a man, we evaluate the results he presents, but we do not detach them from the author himself, and we evaluate his acts, his intentions, the tense projection toward the matter or perhaps the mixture of other nontheoretical interests that we discover in him. Quite different is the case for knowing that we accept as fully objective, in which we ignore who set it forth and adhere to the express significance of the ideas. Here value falls on the truth and not on intentions, for these are not taken into consideration. The general principle that value depends on transcendence is not thereby denied, because for an impersonal thesis transcendence consists in the projection toward the objective situation that it attempts to reflect, which is fulfilled absolutely if the propositions are true and is fulfilled relatively if they approximate truth without reaching it. The totally erroneous thesis is immanent within itself and does not succeed in going beyond itself and becoming bound up with the situation to which it should refer. Thus it lacks cognitive value.

As can be seen, instead of identifying absolute cognitive value with truth without qualification and assigning to this an autonomous meaning, we make that value depend on absolute cognitive transcendence. For a subject, this consists in the full transcendence of his acts, independently of the truth that they attain; whereas for objectified knowledge, the value depends on the transcendence of the theses, a transcendence that is here identified with truth.

An interesting consequence of this distinction is that not all spiritual acts crystallize in an objectified spirituality, nor does all objectified spirituality stem from spiritual acts. Many acts of a purely transcendent intention, and therefore absolutely valuable, fail, whereas acts which themselves stem from motives that are not strictly spiritual and on which only relative values fall may attain results that are absolutely valuable. There is no enigma here if one remembers that the important thing in the act from the point of view of value is the intention; and the important thing in what is produced and objectified is the proper consistency of the product and not the intentions of the producer, since his intentions are necessarily set aside when there is complete objectification and when the product takes on its own meaning. This does not happen only in the cognitive or theoretical aspect of spirituality, but in all spirituality, and it should be kept in mind in order to understand how the accumulation of objective spirituality grows in the complex of culture.

Aside from and underlying the absolute cognitive value that is written into spiritual cognitive acts, there is a relative cognitive value in every nonspiritual cognitive attitude, and in every objectification of that kind which approaches truth or in some way stimulates or promotes it. We need not enter into any specifications about the resulting hierarchy, or the gradation of values that arises. Let us point out, however, that if some intentional acts are linked to others and if the latter are subordinated, the value of the subordinate acts depends on that of the subordinating act. For example, if a cognitive act does not tend freely to the recognition of the object but is dependent on an absolute ethical intention, it will not reveal an absolute cognitive value, but is a part of the ethical act to whose intention it is subordinate and, therefore, it will take on the value of the ethical act.

The elementary acts of cognitive intentionality, through which objects are given, do not presuppose a special interest by the subject for the objects, but a mere indifferent functioning of the subject, who is necessarily an intentional subject. Once the objects are apprehended, they enter into the makeup of the natural world of a natural subject, that is, of a subject who is part of the complex referred to as nature. All intelligent handling of those objects, all knowledge of them stored up by the individual subject or the intentional community, is also included in the realm of nature, if the concrete interests have not been overcome. These concrete interests may be of an applied nature as well as any other that is linked to the actual needs, conveniences, or desires of the individuals or groups. All of this area is undoubtedly cognitive, for any kind of knowledge, lowly as it may be, must be true in order to be knowledge. The demand for truth is inseparable from knowledge, and it forms one body with it. Such a demand coincides with the transcendence toward the object, and if absolute value does clothe an act that does not attain truth—provided it is fully transcendent—it is because transcendence is primary and demands truth, even though occasionally it may not obtain it. The demand for truth is obvious even where it is apparently denied. When the convenience or usefulness of certain false assertions is proclaimed, one falls back on the argument that *it is true* that these false assertions are useful or convenient. That is, one accepts a true assertion that is judged to be fundamental, primary, and adequate in its truth and importance in order to authorize certain subordinate false assertions, which even in their falseness receive, in a sense, justification and prestige from the radiance of the truth that gives them authority.

From its lowest levels, therefore, knowledge is subject to and governed by truth. Thus it is not simply the reference to the truth that separates merely intentional knowledge from spiritual knowledge, and natural cognition from pure cognition. The difference between one sphere and the other is that, in the former, truth (the correct apprehension of the object) is not sought for its own sake but for other reasons which are connected to the natural order, whereas in the latter there is interest in the truth merely because it is true. In the first case truth is the servant, and in the second it is lord. In the former, cognition is subordinate to factors that are foreign to it, whereas in the latter there is pure cognition with no admixture.

The only prerequisite, therefore, for spiritual knowledge is that it be constituted on the free consideration of the object. This is equivalent to saying that it must be knowledge according to truth and nothing more, and it is equivalent at the same time to asserting that it must be knowledge acquired through a fully transcendent act. Total objectivity, obedience to the truth as the final instance, and absolute transcendence of the act are one single thing, indeed, the only thing necessary for a cognitive act to be classified as a spiritual act.

All remaining conditions and characteristics that occur in knowledge lack the scope either to confer or to deny any spiritual significance to knowledge. Knowledge of facts and of essences, interest in the phenomenal and aspiration to apprehend the metaphysical, investigation of ideal entities and research into values are of a spiritual quality when they are obedient to the demand that has been indicated, and they are not when they do not obey it. Therefore, in any area or on any occasion, with respect to any object, there can be knowledge of a spiritual character, which, in principle, can be achieved in single or discontinued acts as well as in continued and regular activities when they are directed according to the methods and purposes of scientific and philosophical investigation.

However, even though *in principle* it is immaterial to the quality of a spiritual act whether it occurs in isolation or in an articulated and organic series, the normal exercise of spiritual knowledge carries as a consequence the ordering of that knowledge into areas arranged according to an objective systematization, that is, it reflects and interprets the nature and the relations of the objects. In general, spiritual knowledge orders its divisions according to the objects themselves, and nonspiritual knowledge arranges them according to interests that are not objective. For example, the physicist, the chemist, the botanist, and the zoölogist, when their sight is fixed on pure knowledge, order their knowledge so that it leads to the various theories according to the standard that the facts themselves show and with the sole purpose of reflecting cognitively the corresponding sections of reality. The technician, on the other hand, takes this knowledge and orders it in a different manner, dispensing with what is not useful to his practical purposes and ordering what is helpful, in keeping with the applied purpose he pursues. His systematization is not objective; it is not governed by the mode of being or the behavior of the objects, rather by what he desires from them, by that special interest of his to whose service he subordinates them. Thus one sees that pure knowledge, and it alone, manifests that objective systematic quality to which we have referred and which allows for a correspondence or a parallelism between the divisions of knowledge and those of known reality. It is a correspondence or a parallelism that, in the long run, includes the condition that the classification be complete, that it not exclude any instance of that reality—an exclusion which occurs, however, in any ordering of knowledge for practical purposes. In addition, each division or section of pure knowledge is, in principle, unique, or, better said, it tends toward unity to the extent that it approximates perfection because it aspires to be the true and neutral version of a sector of reality, and its peaceful coexistence with other different versions would indicate a defect in one or another. Naturally, this unity is an ideal that may be unattainable; as a *desideratum,* however, it cannot be dismissed since that dismissal would imply assenting to a definitive relativism of knowledge that contradicts the idea itself.

In the cognitive-spiritual attitude, it is clear that any actual knowledge is relative, but we strive to diminish that relativity and to approximate the unconditioned knowledge. Only in this sense does knowledge as a superior function of the spirit have meaning.

Having clarified that pure theoretical knowledge, in its conscious and normal exercise, has a systematic objectivity and tends to perfect itself in sections that are unique for each division of objects, it is well to add a few words concerning the demand that these sections be complete. This is not an accidental condition of spiritual knowledge, but an indispensable prerequisite. Since the acts of absolute transcendence are those that provide this knowledge, and since these acts are determined only by the possibility of discovering or designating presences or existences, everything that exists as given or presumed figures in principle as the consignee of such acts. But what exists reveals a structure that can be referred to as logical, as uncovering recurrences, likenesses, and relations which the intelligence grasps. Things make up species and genera. To subsume individual entities or processes under specific or generic objects is not an expedient of the mind, but a recognition of a certain structure of reality, that consistent structure whose major and most important consequence is that totality should be a cosmos and not a chaos. In subsuming individual instances under specific and generic groups, as the natural sciences habitually do, we do not dispense with these individualities, because the species is conceived necessarily as a species of individuals. What we do is to dispense with the examination of the individual variations when there is no special reason to record them, since our cognitive capacity is incapable of including all of them in the vast sections of systematized knowledge. An intelligence infinitely more powerful than ours, whose cognitive function is of a spiritual type, could not elude the particularized knowledge of the whole of natural reality, of the innumerable entities and processes that make up nature. But this knowledge of individuals would not exempt such an intelligence from that other knowledge exercised by our natural sciences—the condensing into species, genera, and laws—because these collective objects, since they also look to emphasizing what is identical and repeated with each individual, are not limited to the comfortable grouping of single entities. This condition denotes an objectivity of a special kind—the objectivity of certain instances, notes, agents, or principles which are operative in many individualities and, perhaps, in their highest expression, constitutive of them. Historical knowledge, for an infinite spirit, could not legitimately evade any single instance, any fragment of the actual stream of history, any individuality or episode, regardless of how minute they might be. This would not release such an unlimited spirit from taking full consideration of the historical entities of a much greater volume than human knowledge can hope to understand, such as nations, ages, cultures, and the great collective movements, both peaceful and warlike, which are not mere aggregates or resumes of individual events, but integrated wholes with their own content and meaning. When human intelligence confronts the task of knowing history, with its resources that are very limited compared to the prodigious quantity of historical material, it must choose, establish thresholds of historicity, and set out boundaries beyond which are the events that seem to be less necessary components of the area that has been conceived. The imperative of complete knowledge constantly enters into conflict with the possibilities of human knowledge, and the contrast leads to a *modus vivendi* in which this demand is kept ever present and in which the attempt is made to hold the distortion to a minimum.

Intelligence is the only instrument of knowledge. This is true in two senses: first, all cognitive operations depend upon it, from the first objectifications that supply perceived objects to the highest intellectual operations; and second, intelligence is the same in the merely intentional and in the spiritual order.

In Part One [2] we attempted to show the uniformity of the cognitive processes, all moved by one supporting force— objectification. The homogeneity of these processes is explained and corroborated if one keeps in mind that behind or within objectification is judgment, whose decisive role in the very fact of the appearance of any objective instance has been emphasized, for it brings the primary cognitive processes closer to the higher processes and even causes them to be assimilated. One of the most

[2] Pp. 44–59.

important consequences is the continuity of knowledge, which we have discussed in pages 51–59.

The capacity to focus on objective situations, these being understood in a broad sense, is essential in intellectual activity. The so-called laws of association and the psychology that rests principally upon them are in error, even though they rest on true facts. It is true that intelligence in its most spontaneous and unguarded moves is governed by associations accounted for in the mentioned laws, but this happens because the associations are presented to the intelligence, though somewhat vaguely, as objective relations. As soon as the intelligence begins to work seriously, it corrects the results of such spontaneous associations, imposing upon them connections based on the objective situation. Stated in other words, an initial false and superficial objectification is corrected and replaced by a superior objectivity, founded on the object itself that is apprehended under the guidance of the dominating purpose. If, when occupied with a particular matter, we come in contact with a certain person, we may be led to recall another acquaintance who is like the one just met. This is spontaneous, and it cannot be denied that the relation of similarity is an objectivity. But if the intelligence functions with more rigor, one will turn away from the image of the second person as though it were a parasite and think about it no more. That is, one will recognize that objectively there is no reason for the latter person to come into the present situation. If, on the other hand, we have set out to classify our acquaintances in terms of their physiognomy and bodily appearance, the relation of similarity comes to be the only objective instance that is of concern for establishing the groups. Thus we purposely pursue the relation and even point out likenesses we had not noticed before, and all other relations among the persons considered are set aside. Intelligence rigorously follows only one law—that of objectivity—but this objectivity turns to the superficial and the most apparent connections when the intelligence operates vaguely and carelessly. On the other hand, in its normal function, intelligence always pursues a definite purpose, and in keeping with it attends to some objective moments and leaves others aside.

A singularly important aspect of the objective function of the intelligence is its recognition of and obedience to the ideal orders, as for example to mathematics and logic. This topic leads to another of extraordinary importance that we will only be able to state summarily the relation between intelligence and reason. The notion of intelligence is broader than that of reason. We cannot attempt a portrayal of reason at this point, though one might venture to say that by reason one understands a certain ideal order implanted within the area of intelligence, a rigid system of boundaries or norms that constrains the intelligence and would stand as its perfect and rightful expression. For the ancient mind, the matter presented no problem—intelligence was justified as being reason, and in classical rationalism reason was converted into the criterion of ultimate existence. The most notable example is afforded by the Eleatics with their resounding negations in the name of the principle of absolute intelligibility. This reason, the Eleatic reason of identity, gradually comes to be problematic, partly because of the idea of continuity and its many aspects, though perhaps principally because of the admission of continuous physical processes. Other significant factors are not to be ignored, however. For our purposes it suffices to point out that intelligence includes reason and is capable of thinking of it, criticizing it, viewing it problematically, and proposing models of reason that differ from the classical one, completing this classical model or perhaps, to a certain extent, replacing it. The most comprehensive constructive attempt—that of Hegel—remains a sketch. The whole problem is one of the most urgent and difficult confronting philosophy. Perhaps the most solid ground on which modern thought can depend to state the problem adequately are two negative considerations: the discarding of the old attitude of suppression and proud rejection of all irrationality and the forsaking of a certain complacency, or morbid delight, in the irrational that has been pursued by well-known thinkers of recent times. The problem consists in discovering the order in which certain facts should be included—facts that do not fit comfortably into the traditional logical order. That order should exist stems from the fact that everything that is, is ordered because totality is a cosmos and not a chaos.

The unity of intelligence, as we stated, holds also in the sense that intelligence is only one whether it functions in the natural or

the spiritual order. The difference between the intelligent be
havior in one realm and in the other is a matter external to
intelligence itself, and it depends on the use to which it is applied,
the purposes and goals that direct it. Under the direction of
subjective particularism, intelligence is embedded in nature, but
once it is emancipated and directed to the task of free knowledge,
it becomes an aspect of the spirit. The existence of different
cognitive faculties has often been presupposed when the diverse
nature of the tasks has been taken as a guide. But the distinction of
the tasks corresponds to the order of the objectivities and not to
the variety of the potential of the knower. If in its natural function
intelligence does not surpass the bounds of what is interesting
from a practical point of view, it is because it is ultimately tied to
subjective requirements. Free from these requirements it projects
toward totality in a campaign for knowledge that is complete and
unlimited. The ability that presents and recognizes objectivities
suffices as an account of intelligence in its natural function, that is,
as a theoretical transcendence toward objects which terminates in
an immanentization, in a subjective return. The suppression of
this return, the attitude of absolute transcendence, is sufficient for
understanding how that same intelligence, without the addition of
any support or any other special capacity, is able to fulfill the
highest cognitive functions.

CONCERNING ETHICAL VALUE

Cognitive value is achieved through turning to what is. It does
not presuppose taking sides with respect to what is, rather admitting it as it is, accepting and recognizing it in terms of knowledge. Through knowledge, the spirit fulfills its intrinsic demand
for universality in one of its dimensions, the theoretical dimension,
in turning toward what is and accepting it in its totality; for, as we
have seen, the spiritual vocation to know strives necessarily toward
knowledge that is complete in its depth and extension. Through
the work of knowledge—through its highest achievement, the
spirit—reality turns toward itself and includes everything in terms
of consciousness, in terms of knowing. It is a kind of reëncounter
of totality with itself.

The positive element of reality is transcendence. In the presence of universal transcendence, the spirit, which is pure transcendence, cannot be satisfied with the cognitive attitude that terminates with the cognitive admission of what is, which is limited to the neutral recognition of the knowable environment. This attitude is not affected by the difference of value between the distinct grades of transcendence that it discovers on the different levels of reality. The positive quality of the transcendence that is recognized as valuable impels the spirit to side with transcendence, to give it special, active attention, to collaborate with it. This practical assent to transcendence is ethical activity. Those acts which explicitly adhere to transcendence reveal an ethical value.

Absolute ethical value exists only in the absolutely transcendent act, in the spiritual act. This act, in turn, is directed only toward transcendence, regardless of where it is found or of the extent to which it occurs. Full ethical activity, therefore, is personal because only a person is capable of fully transcendent acts; and it is universal—with respect to the object of the act—because transcendence gives life to the whole of reality.

The extent of the duty or the obligation depends on the magnitude of the transcendence recognized in each case. There is a partial obligation toward every partial manifestation of transcendence that is noticed. Any center capable of sensation—pain and pleasure—is constituted by a reflex transcendent movement that is particularly powerful, and it is the focus of vibrant acts of transcendence. For the spiritual subject, this implies an obligation much superior to the transcendence that has not become organized in centers of this kind. Greater yet is the obligation to mere intentionality in which transcendence is much superior. At this point, however, one must distinguish between the merely intentional act and the subject of these acts, who is potentially a spiritual subject. Strictly speaking, absolute obligation is toward a spiritual subject, toward the spiritual face of man, which is where transcendence functions in its perfection and purity. In all intentionality, as was indicated, the spiritual attitude is found latently and potentially. This attitude is assumed when intentionality sets free its internal objectivist propensity, when it is projected in a clean thrust toward the goals that its own nature points out to it. The spirit, therefore, is a vocation of the intentional being—of man—even when it is not an actual reality in him; hence the legitimacy and the convenience of considering, in principle, that every man is a person. However, this does not mean assenting to the details of his behavior that might contradict the spiritual imperative. We maintain that it is legitimate to consider every man as a person because the spirit is not a mere possibility in intentionality, but a potentiality that is actualized when certain prerequisites are fulfilled; and we maintain that it is convenient to do so because in this way one assists and encourages the appearance of spiritual activity that is kindled by each one's most convincing experience: the example of spiritual activity in another which is directed toward oneself.

Sociability and ethical behavior must be strictly separated, even though there may be much that links them together. Sociability, in itself, precedes ethical behavior and even man himself. In man, sociability takes on special characteristics, which stem, primarily, from mere intentionality, and which, since they stem exclusively from it lead to a sociability that is peculiarly human although "natural." When, however, the social relation becomes close and warm, when it changes the "other," toward whom we are indifferent at first, into a "thou" bound to us through a tie that can be intimate and fraternal, we can extend toward the "thou" the relationship felt with a "him." That is to say, we are aware that he is an "I" in himself independent of any relation that he may have with us. Absolute ethical value falls on acts of absolute transcendence, and when these acts are directed toward human beings, when they are directed toward the other spiritual centers with no regard to the relationship these acts may bear to the subject of the act, they create an absolute obligation. Any special connection between the subject of the act and an "other" leads to a "thou," who for the subject of the act is "his thou," and an "I" that incites a particular interest because he is in some way "his," in a positive or negative bond, as an ally or as an opponent. There is thus an element of subjective return that opposes complete transcendence. The latter occurs only when the act is directed toward a "him." Pure ethical activity, in the fullness of its obligation, functions only, therefore, when an "I" is assented to, but as a "him"; that is, as an "I" that is not related to our own self in any particular concrete relation. The affirmation of our "I," the active support of ourselves, is equally ethical, in the absolute sense, when we turn to our own "I" in the same way as we would to a "him." The mere changing from the "other" to the "thou" probably presupposes the appearance of a relative ethical value, but the spiritual or absolute ethical quality demands the changing of the "other," of the "thou," of "myself" to "him." It is probable that the discovery of the "him" as the objective of absolute ethical intentions is habitually practiced above the experience of the "thou," though it may not necessarily have to come through it. It may also be realized above the experience of the "other" or above that of one's own "I."

It seems almost unnecessary to point out that the ethical projection is intrinsic to the spirit, inherent in it. The spirit is pure transcendence, and if it hesitated before any given possibility of transcendence, it would deny itself, at least in part. Ethical projection, the practical adherence to transcendence, is a spontaneous and necessary activity of spirituality, but it takes on a special meaning in addition. This is the reëncounter of reality with itself, not in terms of a neutral, epistemological recognition, in the sense of a consciousness of totality, but in terms of involvement, of an actual assent to the positive moment that reality contains, of a collaboration with the ascending movement that we discover in reality, of a participation in its fundamental task. If one accepts the thesis with which Bergson concludes his last great book, that the universe is essentially "une machine a faire des dieux," ethical activity is the conscious collaboration with this machinery in order to accelerate its rhythm and to assist it in the production of the divine.

As with respect to the sphere of knowledge, one must distinguish here between the ethical value of the act and the value of the cultural objectification of an ethical kind. The act is defined as ethical in the light of its intention and not of its achievement. It retains its value even though it fails in its purpose if the intention is transcendent, and if the intention is not transcendent it will not be an ethical act, even if the achievement itself carries the seal of ethical activity, of the collaboration with transcendence. The value of ethical objectifications—norms, institutions, and the like —does not depend on the intentions that created them, but on their inherent structure and meaning, on their objective insertion in the ethical order, on their ethical adequacy and efficiency. The reason for the difference is the diverse mode of the transcendence of each. The act transcends in accord with its intention and the objectification transcends to the extent that it is adequate to its purpose. For if this objectification proclaims itself to be ethical, pretending to justify itself in this way, but does not work in keeping with ethical activity, it does not transcend itself and remains immanent within itself.

We believe that with this characterization we have not only defined the special nature and ultimate significance of ethical activity, but we are also in a position to resolve some conflicts that arise in ethical doctrines. We will now consider those which seem to be most important.

According to Schopenhauer, there are no duties except those toward others; for Otto Weininger, however, there are duties only with respect to oneself. From our point of view the two affirmations are compatible. It is true, as Schopenhauer asserts, that every duty is toward an "other," because the ethical duty toward oneself is toward the "I" itself as a "he" that is respected because it is an "I" and not because it is "my I." It is equally true, as Weininger believes, that there are no duties except toward oneself, because the "oneself" that is taken into consideration is the spiritual "I" whose essence consists precisely in transcending toward the other, so that, for him, to be and to be directed toward the other are the same thing; and when the "I," who is the subject of the acts, is accepted and affirmed, then the other "I's" are also accepted and affirmed. All of this stems from the identity of duty and right on the level of the spirit. On this level, the rights of each one are inalienable and amount to duties. We have the right, for example, to be recognized and respected for our own worth, and at the same time we have the moral duty to demand that this right be recognized.

There is a well-known discrepancy between the point of view of Kant, according to which ethics must be formal, that is, it should establish the general form or foundation of the ethical act—the only way, in his opinion, to found an *a priori* ethic—and that of other philosophers who inquire into the content or the purposes of the ethical act. In many contemporary philosophers, the ethical act is defined in accordance with value, an approach that sees ethics as "material" and not formal in that it proposes concrete goals for ethical activity. The interpretation we uphold is both material and formal. It is material in that it assigns a concrete goal to ethical activity, the projection toward transcendence and its collaboration with the projection. It is formal in that the basic ethical precept may be formulated thus: "Act in such a way that the direction of your act accords with the essential direction of reality." Note that the act could be transcendent in itself although it might not be directed toward transcendence, but in the end it would enter into a contradiction with itself since it would collaborate with the element of immanence in reality. It would be a transcendence at the service of immanence, and it would tend toward a direction that is opposite to the essential march of reality. This march is recognized as valuable because it is the growth of transcendence.

The contraposition between the ethic of effort and that which might be called of grace is suppressed in the concept we propose. For the first, ethical activity must be governed by the mere consciousness of duty, and any introduction of other elements mars the purity of the act and may even annul its ethical quality. It is presupposed that the ethical posture is not spontaneous, but disciplined, a self-constraining directed to overcome some anticipated difficulties. For the second, ethical activity is genuine only when there is spontaneity, when it springs forth as a direct manifestation of an ethical nature. In our opinion, the only thing that is decisive is the intention clearly supporting transcendence. The ways by which one comes to this are of secondary importance, because they depend on circumstantial motives. What is important is that transcendence be grasped and assented to in a practical manner. As for the duty toward persons, recognizing the suggestions of some recent thinkers,[3] it would not be difficult to accept that the ethic of works has taken certain masculine traits into consideration and the ethic of grace certain feminine traits. We would even accept the biological root of both traits. Yet it would still be solely a matter of different types of "occasions," of different vital situations, that would facilitate diverse ways of reaching an

[3] See Ernst Bergmann, *Erkenntnisgeist und Muttergeist* (Breslau: F. Hirt, 1932). For an exposition of his ideas, see Romero, *Filosofía de ayer y de hoy* (Buenos Aires: Argos, 1947).

identical end. Neither one nor the other of these ways has any decided advantage; for if the masculine tendency must overcome some powerful natural impulses in order to achieve an ethical stand, it does not stumble across the excess of biological and emotional egoism that, in maternalism, sharply defines the family "we," crudely isolating it from everything else. We insist that the radical experience of the "other" as an "I" can be achieved in various ways, and that the important thing is not the itinerary, but the destination. The transition from nonspiritual to spiritual interest is a "conversion" in the full sense of the word, it is a change of direction promoted by the discovery of a goal that is judged to be superior to the goal previously held in mind, a change which may occur in many different ways.

The absolutism of the obligation toward spiritual centers is founded on the fact that to assent to them is also to assent to one's own "self," since the essence of the spiritual "self" is to seek after the other. When instances of partial transcendence are confronted, the subject has no reason to subordinate his own degree of immanence to that of others. The specification of duties according to particular circumstances falls outside the purpose of these thoughts, which pertain to matters of greater generality.

PART THREE: MAN

VIII

DUALITY

Duality is the constitutive event of the complete man. The being we properly refer to as man, who has a destiny, who develops historically and is determined by individual and group motivations—yet he also obeys certain demands that are foreign to these motivations which shape an ideal order—this being, we say, is fundamentally a dual entity. In principle we have maintained that man is created when the intentional function is normally organized, bringing with it the appearance of the subject, the constitution of an objective world for him, and the elaboration of culture with the indispensable, objectified creations. All this carries with it something new with respect to the animal kingdom, and it is sufficient to provide for man's separation from the zoölogical scale, justifying that a new section within the bounds of reality be marked out for him. If what is human rested solely on intentionality,[1] as defined in Part One of this book, that special section kept apart for man would be within the natural sphere. When intentionality is dispossessed of spiritual demands, it is no more than the highest expression of natural activity. From his beginning, however, man is capable of spirit, and he seems to be

---

[1] Personal spirituality is always intentionality. For the sake of convenience, when we use the word intentionality by itself, we are referring to what at other times we have called mere intentionality—that is, an intentionality not spiritualized.

gifted with spirituality from the first stages of history. Perhaps what we currently call history is the human process beginning with the emergence of the spirit. The man we know, and the one to whom we attribute the characteristics which define the species, is man with the spirit, though we do not absolutely exclude the existence of men lacking in spirituality. The complete, finished man, not some fiction or idealized image, but a historical reality, is he who comes to us as a complex in which mere intentionality and spirit alternate and are joined together. Man permanently deprived of the spirit may subsist in the lowest levels of the species, in the midst of embryonic cultures or even sporadically located in middle and high cultures. In any case, at least in some degree, the spirit is indispensable if we are to recognize what it is in man that we call human in the full sense.

Without spirit, man is already something more—rather, much more—than an animal. He is a subject who through his continued, subjective activity is converted into a self; he contemplates and conceives a world of objectivities which is extended in space and time and which leads him to live, taking into consideration what is present, what has happened, and what is foreseen, and is thus in keeping with the past and the future. He makes use of the rich accumulation of objectifications of the community, which he receives through significant language, and he creates and uses culture, which in its elemental forms does not necessarily presuppose the spirit. There is nothing similar to this in the animal kingdom. Natural man, or man without spirit, is, then, a being different from any organic entity, because he encloses his organic life in, and makes it conform to, intentional lines, in keeping with the general situation traced by the enumerated elements whose extraorganic character seems quite evident. Demanding as the biological requirements may be for natural man, they echo throughout a structure which imposes its own special mode of being upon them. Preintentional psychism comes to be an echo or a psychical modulation of the organic realm. Intentional psychism responds to its own laws and is governed by them, strong as the organic ingredients may be that are introduced in it.

As was stated, spiritual projection is latent in intentionality. Intentionality perceives objectively, it recognizes what is perceived as subsisting. The spirit radically strengthens the objectification, showing that what is objectified enjoys a fullness of being and autonomy when confronting the objectifying subject, making it possible for the latter to act without the subjective return. In order to understand the significance and scope of spirituality in man, one must keep in mind that it does not consist of a principle completely alien to his primitive nature. It does not consist of an element which comes to primitive human reality from the outside and is inserted into it in some mysterious manner. We might say that it is the fulfillment of the promises contained in the most unpretentious intentional attitudes; it is the completion of what was already present as a seed in the first objectifying acts.

However, this does not set aside the radical difference between mere intentionality and spirituality, for this difference points to a profound break between the spirit and all natural reality. With the spirit, a new order in reality is established; the enclosure of each part of reality within itself, which is characteristic of nature, is broken, and centers heedful of totality are organized, centers which lean toward totality, receiving it in keeping with their universality. Stated in another way, they are centers which transcend themselves and radiate to every horizon, giving wholehearted attention to whatever is, through different spiritual attitudes yet without being dissolved or even weakened thereby, but rather purifying and strengthening their condition as personal centers. Spirituality, as we have already seen, imposes a complete inversion in the direction of the interest of the subject, whose behavior changes, through the work of the spirit, from subjectivism to full objectivism, from particularism to universalism, from partial to absolute transcendence.

The duality of man is a fact widely recognized in religious and philosophical concepts. One might say that there is a common experience of this duality, and that it receives different expressions and is an important part of the concepts of reality. The extreme form of the interpretation of dualism seems to appear in the affirmation of two great superhuman principles which are embodied in Good and Evil, as given in some religions. Stated in another way, a duality is admitted or presupposed in the idea of salvation, which is basic in many religious beliefs and which, from the human side, asserts the necessity of redeeming man from his natural state and promoting him to a superior order in which he achieves perfection. The nonspiritual attitude cannot be identified in an unqualified manner with brute evil. Subjectivist particularism, however, many times is interpreted as relative or total evil, when it is viewed or judged by other subjects whose interests it contradicts and whose ultimate reality it ignores. In many instances, this same judgment is exercised by the supreme court of the spirit which condemns particularism, above all when it violates the ethical imperatives, which frequently happens.

Duality appears yet more clearly in the habitual philosophical distinctions between the various principles or components of the human complex. When more than two components are accepted, one of these, conceived as the spirit, is usually opposed to the others. This is true, for example, in Aristotelian anthropology, which was influential for such a long time, as well as in the three-fold division of vitality, soul, and spirit proposed by Ortega y Gasset. When attention is called to life, as in contemporary biologism, the opposition is usually set between life and spirit, as in Nietzsche, his follower Klages, and many others.

This opposition between life and spirit has a special interest. When spirit is in contrast to matter in general or the human body in particular in religious or philosophical positions which have decreed beforehand the incomparable sublimity of the spirit and the lesser worth or even the lowliness of what is material and corporal, the question of the duality is considerably less problematical and its tension is relaxed in favor of the undisputed primacy of the spiritual element. One does not fight against a dead and buried enemy and, on the theoretical level at least, what was contrasted to the spirit in man appeared to be in this state. This problem was summarily solved in its theoretical formulation, even though in the area of actual events it retained all its seriousness. An important outgrowth was that it was not considered necessary to probe deeper into the nature of the spirit, its characteristics and modes. It was sufficient to affirm it reverently. Traditional religious and philosophical spiritualism has not contributed very many clear statements about the essence of the spirit. One does well to note that something similar has happened with regard to the problem of reason. The convinced rationalists have been those who, spontaneously, have taught us the least concerning rational activity. The foundations, tendencies, and limits of reason have been more clearly defined through the attacks of the skeptics, the empiricists, and the irrationalists, and the strengthening has come as a direct result of these attacks. Clarification has also come from rationalists who have defended their convictions, seeking sturdier foundations in order to resist these attacks. There is nothing surprising in this if it is carefully examined. For the believer, for someone who is absolutely persuaded of something at the outset, the justification of his belief and its critical exposition lack meaning. The spiritualism dominant in religion and philosophy, therefore, has been the cause of the situation in which the problem of the spirit and the duality of man have not been examined in the depth and detail desired. The problem has been stated adequately for the first time when an adversary to the spirit has been raised up; an adversary which energetically claims for itself a positive value and which, thus, introduced a crisis in a habitually placid spiritualism. Needless to say, this adversary is life. Among the contributions of Friedrich Nietzsche,[2] the most impassioned and eloquent champion of life over the spirit, there is one that is important, even though it is indirect and, of course, unintended. This contribution was to stimulate, through reaction, a new interest in spirituality, encouraging investigations that would rigorously define it and throw light on the conflict between spirit and life which he solved by crowning life and condemning the spirit.

The introduction of the notion of life to the debate causes frequent confusion. Several things may be understood by the word "life," but usually two meanings come to mind: organic life, in the strict sense, as found in animals; and life as it occurs in man—the whole aggregate of his attitudes and processes. As notions destined to set apart a realm in man distinct from spirituality, that is to say, a realm juxtaposed to the spirit, the first instance errs by defect and the second by excess. Organic life is not everything in man that differs from the spirit. It does not seem necessary to support this affirmation with argument after what has already been said. And if by life we understand the aggregate of human attitudes and

---

[2] Concerning Nietzsche, see "Nietzsche a lo lejos" in Romero, *Filosofía de ayer y de hoy* (Buenos Aires: Argos, 1947) and "Nietzsche" in *Cuadernos Americanos,* VI (México: Jan.–Feb., 1947) .

acts, then spiritual functions become a part of the aggregate, and the opposition would be between the whole and the part. The contrast should stipulate that life refers to what is specifically human about man's life while excluding the decidedly spiritual attitudes. Roughly at this point we would find ourselves holding to the distinction which we proposed, for we have referred to mere intentionality as the sum of the typically human acts in which spiritual behavior is not included. Our position has the advantage of avoiding the ambiguities which the notion of life tends to have; for this notion has a blurred profile, which encourages the seductive halo surrounding it in contemporary philosophical vitalism as well as its literary and popular expansions, for in these the word "life" has become a magic word. It is not out of place to comment that in this widespread prestige of the vital, there is secretly at work a tacit courting of the concept which is often antagonistically opposed to the concept of life: the concept of death. The word "life" carries with it such notions as strength, impetus, activity, creation, health, efficacy, and so forth. That is, it carries with it a host of positive meanings which seem to be denied by everything that is distinct from life or is placed above it. Nietzsche said, "Long live life and may truth perish," whereby he indirectly condemned the spirit, since truth is an unavoidable spiritual demand. Yet this had already been stated more decisively in a text which is one of the forerunners of pragmatism: "Only error is life—knowledge is death," [3] an assertion in which the intentions or overtones to which we have just referred are laid bare.

Human dualism has posed the problem of which of the two elements is the most powerful and energetic. For Max Scheler, who places the nonspiritual component of man on the vital or psychophysical level, the spirit lacks any force of its own. (For him there is no life without psychism, and he disregards the absolute originality of intentional psychism.) He maintains that the spirit must be satisfied with channeling vital energies, using them to its advantage, and providing new purposes for them. One should keep in mind that somewhat the same could be said of life: a large part

---

[3] These are lines from Schiller's poem "Kassandra": "Nur das Irrtum ist das Leben . . . Und das Wissen ist der Tod." Hans Vaihinger whose philosophy is of a completely pragmatic bent has mentioned in his autobiographical memoirs the profound impression these lines made on him.

of vital functioning is physical and chemical functioning, stimulated and directed by life in keeping with its own vital purposes. However, there is no contradiction in admitting that every vital activity is so constituted, even though life is a new and original principle, because the important thing is the structural and functional moment, and not the component elements which take on a new meaning and a new ontological condition as they give rise to entities with a form and being which is irreducible and characteristic of them. In touching on this point, Nicolai Hartmann exercises his usual wisdom: it is evident for him that the spirit uses up life; one might say that it introduces into it a degenerating ferment and even a disintegration. Yet the spirit is new in the cosmos, and its existence dates from a recent yesterday if it is compared with the other levels of real being, the physical and organic levels. The relative inconsistency or vulnerability of the spirit would be a consequence of having arrived recently, still somewhat ill at ease with neighbors who are more settled and better established. It comes also from a condition in keeping with a basic ontological law, which states that the lower the level of being, the stronger and more stable it will be. Yet, one must point out that while maintaining that the spirit consumes and destroys life, Hartmann would seem to have primarily in mind a restricted aspect of spirituality. This aspect we might refer to as a professional spirituality which is normally dedicated to the superior tasks of a reflective culture and perhaps influenced by the example of the German specialist, who is often indifferent to every-day life, absent-minded, and distant. With this one exception, which attenuates his arguments without making them invalid, his observations seem justified. The greater resistance and strength of the physical when compared to life is evident, and, with reference to our own point of view, the same can be said of the organic with respect to the intentional and of the intentional with respect to the spiritual. What is more primitive and crude is more solid than a more recent arrival. But one must not derive any hurried conclusions to the effect that the more stable and rough principle will always be the victor in a struggle. The rock that falls on a plant and crushes it undoubtedly destroys it, but the plant that grows on the rock disintegrates and transforms it into living substance. The most crude and stable element is also the blindest and least resourceful, and, in the long run, is at a disadvantage when confronted by a superior principle. Intentionality receives the vital impact and frequently yields to it, but it also shows itself capable of directing life according to its own molds. Spirit is implanted upon mere intentionality and to some extent subdues and conditions it. This problem should be dealt with in all its extent and complexity. Perhaps it is a permanent characteristic of the spirit to consume life to the extent that it restrains life in subjecting it to its own demands, depriving it of its inherent spontaneity. On the other hand, however, spontaneous life is a struggle—it is also fierce competition and intentionality to the extent that it is a free play among individual centers moved by their private interests, is frequently a conflict between individuals, is a hostility in which enormous amounts of energy are wasted. In itself and in principle, although it may not always be true in fact, the spirit is order and harmony, a universality which tends to include particulars and to coördinate them harmoniously, suppressing the friction between them. In the final balance of gains and losses for life and mere intentionality, we cannot be limited to determining the wear which stems directly from spiritual activity. Human life, which is our concern at this point, has shown tremendous growth through the centuries. There are many reasons for this, but among them the spiritual element must be recognized as of great importance, for it includes scientific discoveries and the gradual recognition of human rights. Even from a merely quantitative point of view, this growth of human life compensates with increases for the reduction which spirituality may have brought about on the vital and intentional levels where it became established. When the situation is viewed as a whole, life and intentionality gain with spiritual control, because this control tends to impose a superior order which diminishes useless waste, and a blind competition abounding in pain and failure. The problem of the respective dominion of the spirit and of the nonspiritual in man should be confronted in the same broad manner in keeping with the comments made earlier. In a rough, spontaneous conflict, the nonspiritual, or the more crude and solid, tends to triumph; for in evenly matched conflict the physical triumphs over the organic and the organic triumphs over intentionality. But in the long run, just as the organic level prospers and becomes master of the physical level and as intentionality subdues the organic level, bringing it into its own streams, so the spirit imposes itself on mere intentionality and gradually accumulates a positive balance in the historical progression.

Let us reëxamine Scheler's thesis, according to which the spirit lacks strength of its own and is mobilized only by channeling vital energies. This thesis tends to be superficially and erroneously interpreted to mean that life has its own powers and that the spirit lacks them, so that it would be something of a parasite of life—even though of exceptional quality. This is not Scheler's interpretation, at least in his most explicit passages. He says, for example:

> Every superior form of being is relatively inert in relation to inferior forms, and it does not *develop* through its *own* power but through the power of the inferior forms. The process of life is in itself a process in time, with its own form and structure, but it *develops* exclusively through the matter and strength of the *inorganic* world. The relation between spirit and life is wholly analogous to this one.[4]

This passage maintains that spirit lacks strength of its own, even as life does. For if the spirit takes its borrowed strength from life, it is because life previously had taken its own strength, also on loan, from the inorganic level. One could conclude that the only level with its own intrinsic force is the material level, a vast reservoir which would provide energy to the superior levels of reality. Regardless of the original source of the energy of the nonmaterial levels—life, intentional psychism, and spirit—it would be legitimate to attribute ontological autonomy to them; for what is determining and basic in them is not the obscure impulse of which they make use, but the form and structure of each one which gives shape to that impulse in a manner that is peculiar and incomparable in each—whether life, intentionality, or spirituality. But that is not all. The identification of the primary impulse with the one given in the material level, the equating of that impulse with physical forces, does not seem justified. Just as that impulse

---

[4] *El puesto del hombre en el cosmos* (Buenos Aires: Editorial Losada, 1943), p. 98. The English translation of this work by Hans Meyerhoff is published under the title *Man's Place in Nature* (Boston: Beacon Press, 1961).

acquires special traits in keeping with the structures and forms of what is vital, intentional, or spiritual, we believe that its prior condition as physical power also depends on certain structures and forms and in no way stems from its primitive and original character. That is to say that the physical impulse is already a specialization or conformation—the most simple and elemental—of the original impetus. In itself, this impetus is foreign to any special form it may take on, even if it does achieve its most genuine purposes in the highest and final form which it assumes after having passed through the others, this final form being in the spiritual level. As we have previously affirmed, in our view this impulse is transcendence, which in a certain sense would coincide with that foundation which is ultimate and common to everything of which Scheler speaks. According to him, two distinct and irreducible branches emerge from this foundation—the psychophysical order and the spiritual order. For our own part, spirituality does not take root directly in the ultimate foundation, rather it is the highest branch on the great trunk through which transcendence ascends and is diversified. In addition however, the spirit introduces a change—fundamental both in character and meaning—which we have attempted to make clear and which is opposed to any naturalistic interpretation of spirit and, therefore, of totality.

As life constructs and arranges the inorganic materials and movements to its own satisfaction, it enters into conflict with the physic order, subduing it and consuming it for its own benefit. But it does not break the rigid natural law of particularism which prevents nature from producing acts of total transcendence. With mere intentionality, transcendence is expanded and the particularism is broadened in that a world is present to a subject. However, it does not cross over the border that separates this from universalism, from complete transcendence, for this occurs only in the spiritual attitude. The merely intentional subject, whose distinction from the organic has not been touched by Scheler, behaves toward organic life just as the latter behaves toward the physical level. The spiritual subject, in his turn, behaves with respect to mere intentionality just as the latter does with respect to organic life. The difference here consists in that the orders of life and intentionality, although they introduce new and higher forms and thereby, in each case, new ontological levels, do not go beyond the natural level (particularism, partial transcendence). However, the constitution of the spiritual order breaks or surpasses all naturalism with its universal projection and its absolute transcendence. We find no reason at present to deny an inherent force to the spirit; what it has is as much its own, on its own level, as what mere intentionality, life, and even matter have on their respective levels. Spiritual acts are intentional acts of a special kind, characterized by total objective projection. When the subject is capable of such projection, when he recognizes the fullness of being of the other and actualizes this recognition in the various types of acts in the spiritual realm, his projection is equally as energetic as that of the purely intentional subject in his own acts. Error may arise from the relative infrequency of spiritual acts in relation to nonspiritual acts, which are more habitual and frequent in regard to the ordinary behavior of a subject.[5] This infrequency receives its compensation with the constitution and eventual strengthening of the spiritual realm. This occurs through the tendency of the spirit to accumulate and to persist in objectified, impersonal achievements. At every instant, the sum of the nonspiritual acts of mankind is infinitely greater to that of the spiritual acts. This same disparity, however, does not exist in what remains of the one and of the other, for in the spirit one finds a propensity to endure and to accumulate which is inherent to it because of the elements of meaning and value which distinguish and characterize it.

The most immediate and visible manner of the encounter of pure intentionality with the spiritual principle is that which occurs within each human being. In the quantitative aspect, the intentional moments are notably preponderant, except in personalities of outstanding spiritual stature. But one must keep in mind that the exalted quality of the spirit prevents any computation from being established by a comparison of quantities. In the final results, above all, small quantities of spirituality balance and even surpass very large quantities of nonspiritual intentionality.

[5] In many instances the spiritual element is hardly perceptible at first glance; it is not one act among others, but an ordering or a regulating; it is the domain within which the merely intentional acts operate.

One must also keep in mind that the distinction in principle between what is merely intentional and what is spiritual (self-reference and particularism in the former, and other-directedness and universalism in the latter) does not mean conflict which is continuous and applicable in every case. This occurs only when the one is actually opposed to the other. The foundations of human life are intentional, and the negation of mere intentionality would mean to deprive the spirit itself of its natural setting, leaving it in the air and thus annihilating it. Given man's condition, a community of pure spirits is unimaginable. The desirable harmony of the two moments demands, first, the suppression or domestication of what is directly opposed to the spirit and, second, the prudent organization of the rest, according to norms and standards which concur with the spiritual demands.

The clash of the two components does not occur in simple terms. We are able to offer only a few incomplete and scattered indications with the understanding that a laborious gathering of information would be necessary to present the problem in its true light. Above all, one must keep in mind that the visible predominance of one component or the other does not provide the last word concerning the meaning of personality, because the intensity of the respective forces must also be considered. A weak intentionality can coexist with a strong or a lax spirituality and, in the same way, a robust intentionality may coexist with one kind or the other of the forms of spirituality. It is easy to see immediately that the four resulting types of these modes of encounter are only useful sketches for a first draft, because the real situation is a gradation of the respective potentials of energy that come in exceedingly varied proportions. On the other hand, one must keep in mind the relativity or partiality of the intentional as well as the spiritual instance. In both one and the other, and for each human individual, many elements enter which are distinct in number and potentiality. In intentionality, organic requirements, ambition, and the whole range of the affections lead to rather diverse constellations. In spirituality, however, the preëminence, in fact almost the exclusiveness, of certain dimensions is normal, even though there would seem to be some incompatibility between these dimensions, at least so far as they are strongly felt and practiced with resolution. The articulation or the clash of the two phases of an individual is the same as that of two complexes which are uniquely shaped with singular characteristics, not only in their potentiality but in their structure. The resultant whole is probably unique and could not recur.

It is frequent in adolescence and youth that these two phases should not be congenial. On the intentional side, overpowering demands, which have not as yet been subdued by social discipline, make themselves present. On the spiritual side, it is a source of constant wonder that those values whose worth and preëminence are deeply felt, and are even recognized as normally admitted by others, are not, as a whole, effectively carried out in life. The situation is doubly uncomfortable, for not only is there a lack of adjustment between the two phases of one's own inner life, but there is a lack of adjustment to the social reality, with which, as yet, one has not been able to work out an acceptable *modus vivendi*. Some of the more sensitive adolescents, pulled between awakening sexual drives and the simultaneous longing for that pure affection which idealizes the beloved, alternate between one extreme and the other and are late in finding a reconciliation of the two principles. Sometimes, however, they fall into a cynical naturalism or continue in the duplicity in which the flesh and the spirit are hardly associated. One might say in passing that a careful phenomenology of the relations between man and woman, which as yet has not been pursued with the necessary breadth and strictness, probably will be the kind of investigation most fruitful in providing evidence helpful for properly evaluating the general fact of human duality. Considering the situation of the adolescent in its totality and not only in reference to love, one can see a double maladjustment—internal and external—which is a struggle with oneself and with one's environment. Undoubtedly, this confronts the educator with the important task of wisely guiding toward a resolution of the crisis and a reconciliation of the conflicting forces which will lead to a full and harmonious life, under the inspiration of superior interests. It is obvious that for work of this delicate quality, official teaching certificates are not sufficient; rather that other title is necessary, which is conferred only by the "love for leading the young," as it is often referred to.

Maturity, from the point of view that concerns us here, affords a settlement of the conflict—a more or less stable agreement between the two aspects of man. Many experiences have become a part of life, many possibilities have been explored, and the two principles have tested their strength repeatedly and each knows what is to be found within the other. In this way, each human being fashions a formula of his own, a comparative estimate of his own different spiritual and intentional dimensions, with a certain assured fundamental equilibrium which never suppresses the fluctuations arising from different situations, above all when the situations vary from what is current and expected. For ordinary situations, previous behavior tends to afford a ready standard, but in new and unexpected situations a conflict frequently emerges, though ordinarily it is resolved through assimilation to what has already been practiced. The unique formula for each individuality is not only the internal structure. It is also a special way of articulating with the whole, of tying into the social and cultural complex; it is a system of interchange which is complicated, which outlines for each individuality the adequate external environment, which establishes the nature and magniture of what it gives and of what it receives or demands. Therefore, the individual formula signifies not only a relative inner equilibrium, but also a certain normality in the relations with the surrounding community and culture. This normality is not merely equivalent to a comfortable implanting within these areas, but is due to the fact that, in general, the tensions between a given person and his environment come to have a constancy and permanence, lacking great modifications or excessive fluctuations. Each unity is defined in its own context and in its relations with others. But this dynamic equilibrium, which does have fluctuations, is broken on occasions when especially serious circumstances cause a man's foundations to tremble. This results in temporary or permanent mutations, which can be extensive, in his individual formula, bringing about the weakening of certain ingredients and the intensification of others. So-called "conversions" are extreme examples of these transformations, and their function is probably to bring into the open a mode of being more authentic than the one which was replaced, to uncover the true countenance of each one, since it had been obscured up to this time through an accumulation of pressures, habits, and compromises which prevented a genuine manifestation.

In each person's relationship to others, duality performs an important role with a multitude of aspects of keen interest. We can examine only a few. In what we have referred to as the individual formula, that is, the more or less consolidated structure made up of the various elements in each human individual, the fluctuation which predominates at one moment or another, depends largely on the demand of the circumstances. One of these is the presence of other men, each having his own individual structure and his own field of forces radiating from that structure. Each human being present automatically affects the others through stimulating certain dimensions and repressing others, inviting support or polemical opposition. Many motives determine a change in attitude—a transitory change in the formula—and these are in accord with the character of the individuals who come face to face. As anyone may demonstrate, there are depressing presences who pull us below our normal level, and others who are encouraging, lifting us above it. Both situations exhibit a great diversity in energy as well as in their qualitative characteristics. In reference to the sublimating action, there are well-known instances of imposing personalities who exercised a strong, almost overpowering, influence. This must be interpreted as an alteration of the normal formula in those who experienced the influence. It could be said that the formula of each individual undergoes a mutation—from an imperceptible change to a basic alteration—with each human presence whom he actually takes into consideration.

In collective situations, many phenomena are connected with this matter. We cannot make distinctions and analyses which would unduly lengthen this chapter; we will be limited to what is essential. Human groups may or may not form a mob; that is, they may or may not attenuate or even suppress the individuality of each human unit in favor of mob unity. The group which has not been made into a mob, especially one that is not too large, tends to stimulate dimensions of superior quality in each individual and to suppress the inferior aspects, because of a plural control. On the other hand, the group that has been made into a mob, in which the control is negative and in the hands of the one who would seem to elude being absorbed into the mob, ordinarily stirs up inferior dimensions, even those of a very base nature, because the mob minimizes individualization and dilutes each unit into the irresponsibility of anonymity. Such a mob favors the satisfaction of desires which, normally, are governed by a discipline leading eventually to spiritual standards. This does not exclude the possibility that mob polarization sometimes may be carried out for reasons of a spiritual quality. But even then it may happen that the legitimate motivation serves as a pretext for the discharge of primitive impulses that are all the more violent when they are felt to be justified beforehand. By way of summary—otherwise one would need to discuss situations of many different kinds—one could assert: the group that has not been made into a mob transforms the individual formula in the direction of the predominance of spiritual factors, and the one that has been made into a mob leads in the opposite direction.

Spiritual progress depends on an exceedingly interesting factor, which is one of the most important and successful influences in human relationships. In a given situation, anyone feels in himself certain impulses or requirements stemming from the intentional aspect of his being and others, opposed to these, stemming from the spiritual aspect. Frequently the former are more energetically at work than the latter, and the person inclines toward the former with a relative ease of conscience. In any case, however, if he feels at fault, he provides the excuse in his favor of having yielded to the constraining of powerful inner forces of almost insurmountable appetites. But if, as a disinterested spectator, he observes another in a similar situation and the other person behaves as he did or would have, his evaluation of the event changes and he will heap sharp censure on the individual who violates the spiritual principle. The element of intentional particularism is private and different for each one, hidden within his own conscience. The spiritual element, however, is universal, dwelling within individuals and at the same time hovering above them. For the average person, who has little concern for the motives and the import of his acts, or who imposes false, justifying motives upon them, the violation of the spiritual mandate in his own conduct is rarely noticed at first, even though he tends to be aware of it in the conduct of others. This creates a vigilance which each one exercises on the others and everyone exercises on the individual, so that anyone knows that the reproaches and sanctions he would be unable to apply to himself will automatically be applied to him by others. This external spiritual control works on everyone; each subject is constrained to take it into consideration to begin with, and its sanctions, even when ignored, do not cease to be important to him. In the most fortunate cases the foreseeing of these judgments from the outside makes clear to the subject, by reflection, the true significance of his purposes, obliging him to reconsider them and to direct his acts along proper paths—not because he bends slavishly to the whims of others, but because he comes to see himself from the outside. Thus he strives to align his conduct with the accepted standard, as when we see ourselves in a mirror, and, in the presence of our own reflections, without condescension, we lift our stooped shoulders, straighten our ties, or change the sour expressions on our faces. This is a special case of duality in which the conflict is not found inside the individual, but between the subject and the collective consensus of opinion, whether this is expressed or presumed. This is a form of coercion, but it would be superficial to accuse someone who responded spontaneously to this verdict of being weak or hypocritical, because every triumph of the spirit is a compulsion exercised on nature. When correctly viewed, the situation as a whole presupposes imposing the spiritual element onto the natural element, though this occurs in a special way—in the form of censure or as a stimulation of the spirituality of all with reference to the natural inclinations of each. Depending on the circumstances, each individual may be a part of the body which proclaims the consensus of opinion or, in turn, may be a subject who receives it and takes advantage of it. Sometimes he accepts it and takes part in it with a good disposition and at other times, unwillingly. But as he yields, he also contributes to the increase of the spiritual order.

Just as there are these aspects of duality which occur within the realm of social intercourse, that is, in human interrelations, there are others which occur in the relation between man and objective culture. As we have pointed out, the whole of culture is not to be found within the realm of the spirit. Frequently, the spiritual purpose of a man or of a group is to fight against a cultural objectification which is opposed to spiritual demands or does not satisfy them to the desired degree. Every human advance demands the creation of cultural complexes which become increasingly spiritual, and in many instances this arouses the opposition of the existing cultural realities which seek to remain established and are resistant to change. Every attempt to surpass a given cultural reality rests upon that culture and—in the long run—on the whole cultural tradition, and only in this way can the attempt surpass it. For example, the reformer, who seeks a more perfect judicial system and rejects the existing system as unjust, does not embody a sense of justice which belongs to him alone or which has come down to him from the clouds. He represents, rather, a given moment in the long struggle whose successive triumphs have been incorporated in judicial objectifications. These have educated and, as it were, fed the feeling which serves him as impulse and guide in attempting to surpass these objectifications. For every man, even the one who brings to the accumulated culture a personal contribution of incomparable magnitude and brilliance, the debt to culture is infinitely greater than what he brings to it. This is because the human capacities of intentionality and spirituality have themselves been formed in the tasks of the creation and use of culture; they are inseparable from it, and as a whole their level depends, in each instance, upon reaching the level of the surrounding culture, even though the individual may tend to surpass it.

The struggle between man (taken individually or collectively) and objectified culture generates a complicated situation. A few observations will be sufficient to indicate the complexity. The primary and most common situation is that of the foundation or support provided by culture, by which man lifts himself to the cultural level of his environment. Once the individual has become a citizen of a given culture, he does not relate to all of its aspects in the same way: some satisfy him; others disgust him, and he feels they are below his standards; still others are so far above him that perhaps they strike him as incomprehensible or useless. If the resulting tensions occur in energetic persons, they may take concrete form in movements of opposition or reform. In some cultural orders, the innovating forces are embodied in the whole social group or in large groups. In other systems, the majority may find itself so much in accord with the status quo that the renovating zeal and its actual advance have as their agents restricted minorities or a few outstanding personalities. The negative tensions—that is, those that occur between the constituted culture and an individual below this level—are of various kinds. All education is but a process planned to raise individuals from a lower level to some given cultural level. In general, the negative tensions in themselves are advantageous for the individual, just as the positive tensions are for the culture, because ordinarily they are educative and elevating. The culture present in each segment and stage of history is the great and universal school in which all learn, and those who find themselves below the average cultural level experience a continuous demand to raise themselves to this level, a demand in which the influence of the actual presence within the culture is reinforced by diverse regulations and sanctions. If the usual procedure by the individual is the more or less sincere obedience to that in the cultural environment which is above him, quiet resistance or open rebellion are nevertheless frequent. Normally this resistance is expressed in practical conduct though sometimes it takes the form of arguments and even theoretical formulations.

Innovating activity is exercised in all cultural domains, and it always finds some resistance in the cultural realities which it would modify or substitute. This resistance is much more evident in the collateral aspects of culture than it is in areas directly related to the cultural fact itself. Cultural activity, in any of its expressions, becomes *custom;* it is habitual for men to abide by it in each time and place in such a way that it tends to perpetuate itself, to become fixed and organized in a body of norms which are supposedly valid for all times and places. There comes the decree that anything done henceforth must adhere to the pattern of what has been done thus far. From this point of view, the innovation does not struggle against the established culture, but rather against the unjustified pretension of assimilating and reducing all possible future culture to this one. The creative forces thus have to struggle against artificial normative systems, against rules that are not founded on the nature of the corresponding values but on the particular structure of the immediately present cultural entities. Grammatical purism, for example, attempts to restrain every effort at linguistic innovation. Another important aspect is this: around every cultural activity a conglomeration of *practical interests* is inevitably constituted, and it is linked to the current practice of this cultural activity which, indeed, would be seriously handicapped by any innovation. The major resistance on this side comes from complexes of an institutional kind, which are the most capable of unifying and consolidating their interests as well as adequately providing for their defense.

Passing from one section of duality to the other is similar to this, though it is actually different. This occurs primarily when expressed purposes, which were achieved in their purity in the initial stages, are obscured and become little more than nominal goals—even though the external cultural structure is maintained and serves interests of another kind, which are usually of a utilitarian nature. For example, a political group or a charitable institution, which began by serving their specific purposes, are falsified and converted into instruments for the vanity and private gain of those who direct them. This example differs from the previous one because of the notorious descent here from one level to one below it, while the appearances of the upper level are kept up and the prestige is turned to profit. In the situation described previously, however, the proposed cultural activity is maintained while the practical interests developed around it do not hinder it but are prescribed to guide this activity in its accustomed direction and meaning because it would deteriorate with any alteration.

Duality, a fundamental fact in man and culture, is thus present in most human activity. We will find it in the phenomena of wearing a mask and of justification, in social relations, in the historical structure and projection of man, and in the problems of the meaning of human existence.

IX

WEARING A MASK, JUSTIFI-
CATION, SELF-CONSCIOUSNESS

Animals in the pure state of nature are at peace and thus manifest a compactness and unity in keeping with their character. Their acts emerge naturally, conditioned by a specific organic makeup, instincts, and needs, within given circumstances. Animals do not recognize any situation in which they must justify themselves; there is no subject who desires to persist and to make himself known. Their only past is stored in their organic constitution and in actual experiences. Any anticipation of the future is equally organic and is actualized through physical development, instincts, and procreative functions. Therefore, animals are unconscious of the past and of the future, and neither of these is related to the backward and forward intentional glances which man casts in recapitulating the past and in constantly anticipating the future, both being characteristics of the self. Animals present themselves candidly for what they are, neither aspiring to anything better nor pretending to be different. When instances of hiding or dissimulation occur, they are tactical or functional, stemming from instinct or from self-training. Thus, for example, they will hide in the face of danger or guard against premature detection while preparing to bring down some skittish prey. Except in these circumstances, an animal is unconscious of itself, and has no reason for hiding or dissimulating.

In man, however, there are numerous instances of wearing a mask, of disguising in relation to oneself and to others. These instances depend upon the intentional structure and the possession of the spirit. Acts of masking are related to resentment, self-justification, and meaning as well as to self-consciousness. These matters are discussed not because they are important or interesting from a psychological point of view, but because they are typically human to the extent that they stem directly from elements that are limited to and constitutive of man, and serve to define and to particularize him.

The acts of masking considered here are not all of those involving a hiding or a disfiguring of the self, or of one's attitudes or behavior. Deliberate and tactical falsification, straightforward mendacious acts in which covering up or disfiguration is used in attempting to obtain some clearly defined purpose are excluded. This occurs, for example, when one feigns friendship or love for the purpose of material gain or of seduction or merely to get some satisfying benevolence from the deceived. Such acts may be exclusively human but are not typically such, and their examination is the task of psychology and not philosophical anthropology. Also excluded are acts in which the organic or intentional phase has been successfully molded or modified, hidden or sublimated by the superior element, either intentionality or the spirit. Such masking does not represent true hiding but rather a conquest and a cleansing. Thus it is with good manners, the refining of customs, the physical training of the body, the normal controls over impulses, and every process of improvement. Many of these acts, bordering on those of immediate interest, may be distinguished from them by the following criterion: if the inferior element is shaped and is habitually subservient (except in occasional rebellion) to the superior, then we are confronted with instances such as those mentioned above. If, however, the inferior element is set free, retaining its original character, while we cover it with a different appearance and temporarily hide it in order to appear to ourselves and to others in a more favorable light, then the situation is the kind referred to below. The molding or the control of what is on lower levels by what is above, is not set aside as nonessential. It is a fundamental act, inseparable from man as an intentional being normally endowed with the spirit. In general this is manifested in the subjection of what is organic to the intentional disposition, and in the control over the latter, exercised by the spirit. It is, therefore, an event of wider implications and which, in one form or another, appears in several themes treated in this work. Our immediate concern is much more special and limited. Briefly, the acts of premeditated and mendacious disguise are set aside since they are more psychological than anthropological in nature. Those of actual conquest or molding of the inferior by the superior are also omitted in this chapter because they are the processes of culturalization or spiritualization. These were discussed earlier and, because of their broad implications, will be encountered again. In what follows, the principal concerns are acts of a much more limited scope, although they are basic or anthropological and shall be referred to as phenomena of masking.

Masking is characterized by concealing a reality which remains intact below the mask and by the good faith with which the reality is unconsciously or consciously disguised, because of the subject's conviction that what is hidden should be repressed or denied. The masking is unconscious and self-deceiving when one attributes false motives to one's actions. The masking is conscious when one represses some crude exclamation or modestly covers some part of the body.

Even without the influence of the spirit, the self performs acts of masking. It is not necessary to refer to the spiritual element to recognize that the self needs to affirm its self-respect, not only in its own eyes, but in the eyes of others. In the attitudes of self-affirmation and in the demands for outward prestige a multitude of motives intervene which do not belong to the spiritual level, when this level is understood as set forth in chapters v and vi. The intentional self masks certain aspects of the organic order as well as certain intentional movements not in harmony with the idea or the image which one has of oneself or with the tradition and standard inherent in any mature, well-established self. The spiritual element also represses the organic and the intentional when they appear to be in obvious violation of its demands and principles. It is not always practicable to discover if the mandate for masking stems from the intentional or the spiritual side, because of the intricacy of human duality and of the character of the acts themselves.

Acts which tend to conceal organic nature constitute the lowest level of masking. These include clothing the body, hiding physio-logical functions, and disguising the more intense biological ap-petites (sex, hunger, the need for violent action, bodily comfort). Much of this can be accredited to the domestication, culturali-zation, or spiritualization of human corporality. Actually, what we have in mind is not some refinement stabilized into a habit and deeply implanted in the organism, but the repressions or con-cealments which may or may not be carried out and which are similar to a confrontation of the original act with a certain 'ought to be.' In this confrontation, the tendency is to deny or, at least ideally, to eliminate what should be. In extreme situations, when the duality has been decidedly affirmed as the opposition between soul and body, and when a desire is present to live a purely spiritual life, the repression of the biological aspect has sometimes been pushed to the limit through mortification such as wearing hair shirts or even mutilating the body.

Just as one conceals or crushes organic nature, so one disguises or hides intentional nature when it seems to go against the standards of the spirit. Censure falls primarily on the emotional and volitional movements in which the subjectivist tendency is to be energetic, yet, because of its radical particularism, is adverse to spiritual universalism. For example, a mother will say that, for her, all her children are equal, while she hides her preferences and even attempts to be equally loving to them all. Linguistic usage curiously masks acts of the open, acting will actually expressed, as they ought to be expressed, in the first person of the present indicative ("I want," "I wish"). Many times these expressions are attenuated or falsified to improper conditional expressions ("I would like") because the direct show of the will appears im-pudent, and the correct grammatical form would give the impres-sion of being rude. It would not be difficult to find other verbal phenomena of the same kind. In general, we tend to soften or suppress the crude externalization of intense feelings or desires when they are recognized as conflicting with spiritual universal-ism, especially when they are impulses of appropriation, avarice, envy, hatred, and anger.

In most instances mentioned, what is hidden or reshaped is the open manifestation of an organic or intentional act. The impulse or movement is censured and its expression is thwarted though not destroyed because the censure does not completely suppress it, though it may temporarily overcome it. The censure denounces its inconvenience or immorality and modestly covers it up. Hereby one recognizes the difference between masking and effective cultural development. In the latter, the natural state has been molded and subjected to a discipline which becomes a deeply rooted and permanent second nature. Thus it is unnecessary to insist that this disguising also differs profoundly from tactical or interested dissimulation, because the former is done in good faith and without underhanded purposes or ulterior motives. There is no attempt to gain advantage; rather, the masked act is scorned, either in a spontaneous reaction or in a reflective evaluation which recognizes its source as an external consensus to which the person is loyally subject. More important are the acts of justification, in which the subject does not mask an impulse whose true character is clear to him, but unconsciously masks the act itself, its motives and intentions. He deceives himself concerning the nature of the act through a shift in his view of the act so that it accords with the idea he has of himself and with the principles to which he desires to remain faithful. The better-known acts of this kind that have attracted attention are those related to resentment. In our opinion, the acts of resentment that produce masking are only a part of the self-deceiving acts of masking, and this part is a special form of masking in general. As has been shown, a kind of masking exists in which the subject is not mistaken about the real character of his attitudes and impulses so that he attempts intentionally and successfully to check them.

The importance which Nietzsche assigned to the phenomena of resentment in the emergence of moral acts and in the role they play in his interpretation of Christian morality is well known. Max Scheler, in a widely read book, refuted Nietzsche's conclusions, denying the role of resentment in authentic moral feeling. Nevertheless he recognized the insight and the originality of Nietzsche's affirmations, his unquestionable discovery of profound levels of conscience which were unexplored until that time. For Scheler, "the point of beginning that is most important in the formation of resentment is the impulse for vengeance." To result in resentment, the desire for revenge must have been repressed; it must have been encysted through inability to find release in direct and effective acts of vengeance. Other antecedents or producers of resentment are envy, jealousy, and competition. Resentment "is a psychical *autointoxication* with well-defined causes and consequences. It is a permanent psychical attitude that emerges when the expression of certain emotions and feelings, which in themselves are normal and basic to human nature, are systematically repressed. As a consequence, there arise certain constant propensities toward determined kinds of evaluational deceit with their corresponding value judgments. The emotions and feelings which must be considered as primary are: the feeling of and impulse to revenge, hatred, wickedness, envy, spite, treachery." [1]

Our concern at this point is the deceit provoked by resentment. The impression of weakness and impotence which resentment engenders tends to produce a feeling of inferiority and insignificance in the subject which he cannot endure. He escapes from it through a craftily negative estimation of the values of which he is deprived and feels incapable of reaching. Scheler describes the situation in these terms:

> The phenomenal character of evaluative deceit caused by resentment, that is what is distinctive in a man who "rails" against alien values which are oppressive to him, does not consist, therefore, in that the alien values do not strike him as "positive," or "high" values, or as "not existing" for him. In such a case one could not speak of "deception." Yet neither does this character consist in the formulation and expression of false judgments, that is, those contrary to what is lived. This would be an "error" or a lie. If we wish to describe this attitude, we could only say: Values continue to exist for him as positive and lofty, but they are, so to speak, *covered over* with illusive values through which the real values may be vaguely distinguished. Stated in another way, the real values "reflect through." This "reflecting through" of the true objective values in spite of the apparent values which are opposed to them by the illusion of resentment, this obscure awareness of living in an *apocryphal world of appearance,* without the strength to overcome it and

[1] Max Scheler, *El resentimiento en la moral* (Madrid: Revista de Occidente, 1927); the two quotations from Scheler which follow come from the same book.

see what it is, constitutes an immovable component of this complex psychical phenomenon."

The deceptive evaluations which are crystallized through resentment revert back to the resentful individual, detracting from the dignity of what becomes unattainable for him in such a way that the individual may be presented to himself in a favorable position. They constitute, therefore, a defense mechanism and belong to the area which includes the acts of self-justification.

In keeping with what has been previously stated, we do not maintain that all phenomena of self-justification should be explained through the contraposition of the two elements in man, that is, the indwelling of mere intentionality and spirit in man. Even for a merely intentional being, the beginning of self-justifying processes is quite conceivable because the intentional individual is a self, and as such he affirms his subjectivity, his own lived being as seen from within and centered in himself. It is inherent in the self to feel that he is a self, to desire to persist in his being, and to long to be something more. The impulses of material appropriation are naturally expressed in tendencies to acquire power, authority, and prestige by the mere fact that man lives in a community of his own peers. From this point it is often only a step to that illusory feeling that one is deserving and capable of such privileges. Excepting absolute and spiritual values, social existence may be the first stimulation for many phenomena of self-justification. The higher values have little to do with the desire that others revere or fear us, that they recognize our property as private, or that they believe us to be stong, able, and intelligent. The desire that these dispositional attitudes toward us be found in others is a mode of desiring power, because these attitudes are concrete goods for each individual; they are real elements, which enter into the positive circle which enlarges the self, for they rest on those borders of subjectivity which each one feels to be a part of "what is his." Subjective reference, unassisted by the spirit, is therefore sufficient to account for all this. If the subject finds that he does not measure up to these requirements, if the ability and capacity requisite to stir up feelings of subjection and fear in others are not found in him, and, in addition, if he has a vague impression of his own deficiency, it is probable that a false consciousness of his powers and abilities will arise, but which is in keeping with what his desires demand and is also a justification of himself. Undoubtedly, however, many acts of self-justification depend on man's duality and can be explained through the effect of the censure of the spirit, stemming from within the subject or from the repercussion on him of the general consensus.

A basic fact in self-justifying processes is masking the motives of one's acts. The norm in phenomena of resentment, for example, is to criticize a person severely and, if possible, to inflict personal injury, while sincerely believing that one is obeying a feeling of strict justice, although in reality one's acts are governed by resentment. Not only does resentment result in masking of this kind; so does any active function of one's soul which requires justification. Sometimes, those who are cruel or violent, even though they are not resentful, are misled by the belief that they act justly when in fact they are only giving a loose rein to their evil inclinations. The miser sometimes believes he is wisely saving for his children, when the true motive for his conduct is his stinginess. An ambitious person, zealous for power and command, tends to imagine that his entire motivation is disinterested and that his sole aim is the public good.

It is evident in these examples that the desire for justification causes a twisting of the act in order to show that it is justified, a shifting done through masking the motives. In other situations, justification occurs in different ways so that seemingly there is no masking because the subject is aware and admits that his acts are more or less as they really are. But it is probable that masking arises also in these situations when an excessive importance and dignity is attributed to the situation which is external to the act itself yet is referred to for justification. For example, there is the justification, in the light of the past, by an individual who believes that what might be called his spiritual accumulation, that is, his prior achievements under the banner of supreme values, amounts to such a magnitude that any future not-too-serious transgression is automatically justified. This type of self-justification might be called "on interest." But there is also a justification "on credit" by an individual who forgives himself and feels that his base acts are justified because of the excellent quality and nobility of the acts which he is sure to carry out in the future, "when the occasion arises."

Man conceives of himself and passes judgment on himself in three different ways: in each of his acts, taken separately; in his being as a whole, as a person; and in the complete development of his life, his entire existence including its termination. To these three ways of confronting oneself correspond three ways of justification: the justification of the act, of the personality, and of the life. Most of the preceding comments dwell on the justification of acts. The justification of the whole person may result from the partial justifications of the acts, but it may be achieved by other, sometimes rather bizarre, means. For example, some practice of curious self-justifying procedure, which consists in being a "true" person over and above their acts. In a sense, they feel separated from their acts and even depreciate them as functions of a "trivial" reality, to which one can haughtily make concessions without harming what is held to be the profound and authentic person. This kind of personal justification implies an indirect justification of the acts. The feelings of cynicism and pride are closely connected with the justification of the person. "Pride," writes Scheller, "always rests on a waning of spontaneous self-consciousness. . . . Pride is the conduct which stems directly from having experienced a *diminution* of that genuine awareness of one's own value; it is an act of reflexive apprehension and 'defense' of one's value." The justification of the whole life is of concern primarily to one who feels it has come to an end, either because he considers the active period of his life to have ceased or because he is confronted with death. Frequently memoirs and autobiographical accounts, when written late in life, stem from some self-justifying purpose, and it is rather idle to add that though this purpose may not have been the original motivation, self-justification tends to be present throughout works of this kind. Matters that are closely related to these, so much so that they are often identified with them, will be dealt with later in the discussion of the problem of meaning.

The previous discussions throw some light, by way of reflection, on the obscure and perhaps, to a large extent, insoluble problem of self-knowledge. It is a light which, unfortunately, tends to focus on the difficulties of the problem.

The strange situation with respect to the image of our own body serves to put us on the alert. After some association we know what to expect with regard to any outward human characteristic. Undoubtedly, association is indispensable, because a human body is not a statue but a dynamic complex, which is not only rich in changing expressions, but is principally defined by the whole of these expressions. We all know how the understanding of an acquaintance varies until it stabilizes after a number of experiences. There is always the possibility of coming to some more or less stable image of someone else's physical appearance describing it as beautiful or ugly, serene or disturbed, active or passive, fresh or worn, vital or decadent. But we never are clear in our own mind about these matters with respect to ourselves, regardless of how much we consult the mirror. The same thing happens with our voice. We believe that we know our voice well, because we hear ourselves speak. But if we hear it from outside—as on a recording—it usually surprises us, as if it were foreign and unknown. Perhaps the closest that we come to knowing our own appearance is what we are told by others, either voluntarily or involuntarily, for they see us as strangers, just as we see them.

Schopenhauer has left some interesting observations along this line. He writes:

> Why, in spite of all the mirrors, does everyone really ignore what he looks like and is not able to visualize himself in his own imagination even though he is able to visualize others? This is a difficulty which is confronted in the very first step toward *nosce te ipsum*. Undoubtedly, it depends partly on the fact that in the mirror one can see only with a fixed glance which is focused directly on oneself and there is the loss of that very significant play of the eyes and, with it, the loss of what is truly characteristic of one's look. But, apart from this physical impossibility, there seems to be another that is analogous to it though of an ethical quality. One cannot direct his glance toward his own image in the mirror as if it were *another's*, and this is the requirement for the *objectivity* in apprehending that image. Ultimately, the look toward something strange depends on moral egoism with its profound feeling of the *not-self;* and this is indispensable for perceiving all defects in a completely objective and thorough manner so that the image appears in its true and faithful form. Contrary to this, when we see our own person in the mirror, this same egoism whispers a continuous warning that what is seen

is not a not-self, but self, a warning that acts as a "noli me tangere," preventing objective apprehending, which it does not seem possible to obtain without a grain of malice.[2]

All these ambiguities pertain to a kind of reality which, for its distinctness, material consistency, and possibility of external apprehension, would seem to be capable of exact determination. They should serve as anticipation and indication of the difficulties of a self-perception which is directed toward a reality as complex and shifting as psychospiritual reality is.

The problem of self-knowledge moves between distressing contradictions. The first is that this knowledge, which is so imperfect from one point of view, is the most perfect from another. The knowledge of what is external, of what is foreign (including one's own external appearance), comes to us through the so-called external senses, especially sight and touch. The most elementary criticism of knowledge tells us that these senses operate in their own way and provide us with a version of things in which the particular manner of these mediators exerts a powerful influence. Consequently, everything perceived through the external senses is not manifested as it is in reality, whence follows the necessity to formulate scientific and metaphysical hypotheses concerning the true nature of things. On the other hand, what is perceived in one's own inner reality does not suffer from the deformation of the sensory instruments. It is psychism that is grasped directly in its living flow, in a warm immediateness. It is true that Kant and his followers attribute a phenomenal character to this perception, because they maintain that time is not a part of the being that is known, but a mere form of knowledge which is superimposed on the given data, conforming the data to time's own mode. But even if we accept this position, there would always be more truth in these perceptions of one's inner reality because of the great proximity to what is known. They would be distorted only by the imposition of the temporal form whereas the perceptions of what is external are submitted to the dual distortion of space and time. With the interpretation in contemporary philosophy that temporality is not

[2] *Parerga una Paralipomena* (Leipzig: Inselverlag, 1905) ed. Grisebach, II, section 331.

only a characteristic of being, but its mainspring, the Kantian difficulty is eliminated or at least tends to be eliminated, so that what is grasped from within takes on an ultimate or absolute character. In Dilthey, for example, the opposition is complete: every external awareness is of phenomena or of appearance and what is grasped from within is actual reality, "the thing in itself." The vague and confused world of the inner reality, which is so unsusceptible to even moderately strict classification because it is so fleetingly plastic and nebulous, would then, be a world perceived in its true aspect; whereas the external realm, although accessible to reiterated proof and yielding to precise determination, would be little more than a parade of mental images. Provisionally accepting this conclusion, let us note an important consideration. The thesis of the authenticity of self-perception presupposes that we take into consideration only what is actually grasped. However, we have already seen that this apprehending tends to be accompanied by masking, justificatory evaluations, and interpretations which are a part of the apprehending, and which necessarily distort it. Now if this is true for single acts, it is logical that there should be an increase in volume when one attempts to include one's entire personality or the whole course of one's life. These two realities, therefore, are known with great difficulty. If, however, man can know anything as it really is, it is what he finds within himself.

The second contradiction consists in this: the nucleus of the inner reality, that which is radically "self" and cannot be reduced to the category of "what is mine," is a subject. Now, if any definition can be given to a subject, it is this: that which is not an object. But one only knows objects, that is, instances which come before a subject and are known by him. If the subject knows himself, it is through transforming himself in some way into an object for himself, for to know is to apprehend a presence, to recognize the appearance of something. The subject lives his own self directly without objectifying himself, but this living and feeling of his own self cannot be knowledge. Yet, if the subject, in knowing himself, is converted into an object, he gives up his essence to the extent that he is known. The alternative can be stated thus: Either there is only a living and feeling of oneself which lacks actual self-knowledge, or the subject knows himself, is converted into an object for himself, and in his self-knowledge rises above his particular and distinctive characteristic.

These difficulties are undeniably serious. Some philosophers, and not contemporary figures alone, have maintained the privileged condition, the incomparable hierarchy of the knowledge of one's self, as the unique occasion in which being and knowing coincide. What is questionable about this assertion is seen in the difficulties that have been indicated, which, to be sure, are not the only ones. Not only must one take into consideration the transposition which the change from subject to object presupposes but, in addition, the alterations which the observation introduces into what the self observes of itself. Conscious self-perception, the only perception capable of providing a knowledge which is more or less clear, includes the focusing of attention on the inner process which one seeks to know. That is to say, a new element is introduced into the inner process or, to say the least, a witness approaches it which may either stimulate or inhibit through its presence. It is problematical whether an inner process occurs in the same form and is strictly the same when it unfolds in a free and uninhibited manner and when it is subject to a self-observation, which necessarily will be taken as an inspection. It is well known that Comte denied the possibility of psychology as a science because of reasons of this nature, and although the psychologists do not support him in his rejection of introspection, most of them agree that many of the difficulties he raised are valid.

A sound knowledge of something presupposes an awareness of its connections with everything else, not only the connections of actual dependence and influence but those of difference and similarity. For example, it is important to know how an object affects others and to know its situation among those of like kind, and beyond them, in the total picture of reality. Self-knowledge provides little substance for these demands of knowing. The external observer is in a more favorable, and in some instances quite advantageous, situation as when he approaches his object with temporal distance and within broad historical structures. Self-perception is weakened through the pressure of the absolutism with which each human being lives his own life, whereas the perception from the outside makes each individuality comparatively relative. Neither one nor the other is sufficient, because the first lacks a vision in perspective and all differentiating aspects whereas the second disregards, and has no essential access to, the reference which each subject makes to himself; this is an exclusive gift of subjectivity and probably is of a different quality for each individual.

To live one's own self is not to know oneself. Knowing oneself, as we have seen, stumbles upon serious difficulties; some are difficulties in principle whereas others are more or less yielding and circumstantial. Some of these difficulties can be suppressed or minimized in a retrospective vision that associates certain advantages of actual self-perception with others that stem from external perception. When one sees oneself as one was at some time in the past, one is able to think of oneself simultaneously as oneself yet as another. There is a conciliation of the absolutism of self-reference with the possibility of perspective, of evaluation of relations, of comparison with others. However, if, in this manner, one opens a margin for criticism and correction of previous perceptions or interpretations of one's self, it is hardly certain that all real components can be computed and all illusory elements can be eliminated. Assisted by the elements of creative imagination, which are rarely lacking in memory, justifications find new opportunities to embellish the past as well as to darken it. (For example, in the convert who tends to cast deep shadows on that way of life which he understands is being set aside through the conversion.)

As can be seen, the matter seethes with contradictions and abounds in blind alleys, and the only way out is the expedient of jumping over the wall, which is hardly satisfactory. We would never finish if we continued to accumulate the inconveniences and difficulties which arise through merely stating the problem, even though the inspection tour is not very demanding. One of the most fruitful aspects is provided by the difference between two human types, where one is given as expansive, spontaneous, and turned outward and the other as concentrated, reflexive, and prone to probe within. The former reveals a great stream of freely exercised, psychospiritual activity with few inner compulsions, as it flows toward an authentic projection of its purposes. Yet this genuine flow is not an accurate picture of the subject, because there is little inclination to turn toward oneself, to know oneself. The second, who continually exercises the attempt to understand himself, lives in a psychospiritual reality which is often falsified by its very contention, by the violence which occurs in the restraint of spontaneity, and by the tendency to close up which contradicts the constitutive transcendence of subjective activity. If in the one there is a lack of interest in self-knowledge, in the other this interest tends to be falsifying and deforming. There is more, however. Our actual behavior depends above all on two elements—our character and the circumstances or situation—and the relations between them are not simple. The expansive and spontaneous person tends to find himself in situations into which he falls without thinking; they are unexpected. He reveals himself as he is, but the resulting behavior stems in large part from the situation which was little, if at all, foreseen or conditioned by him. The reflective person, who turns toward himself, avoids many circumstances and anticipates or sets up others, so that the situation in any case is more in keeping with his own manner of being than it is for the expansive person. From this stems the greater degree of coherence in his behavior, at least in most instances, but there are also fewer opportunities for his true dimensions to be revealed, because dormant dimensions exist in every personality, even though they may be of a great potential, and they are awakened and discovered only through an abrupt clash with the unexpected. One of the results could be that the personality of a contained and reflective type, which one supposes to be that which most authentically possesses and knows itself, conceals the more enigmatic and profound personality, not only from others, but even from itself.

True self-knowledge can only be achieved through a balanced integration of self-perception, a retrospective vision of oneself, an acceptance of the image of ourselves which others form, and an external, posterior, panoramic inspection which would register all the articulations of the self with respect to what is prior to and contemporary with it. This inspection thus could give some account of all questions concerning origin and interconnection. All of this, of course, would be accompanied by the complete suppression of any masking. It seems unnecessary to say that such an integration is impossible. So we must be content with a limited view, with fragments which are quite variable in size and cognitive value.

In the first place, these considerations go against the thesis that self-knowledge is a basic element in man. We have not examined this question in itself; an adequate study would have required an ordered and exhaustive review of all its aspects as well as a careful evaluation of its results. Neither one nor the other has been attempted here. It has been sufficient for our purposes to have indicated the principal features of the matter, to provide a rough outline, since this seems to be necessary for our theme. What is characteristic of man is not to duplicate himself, to reproduce himself, wholly and in detail through self-knowledge, even though one of his highest aspirations may be to understand himself. What is original in man and inherent is to him to be a subject of partly transcendent acts so far as he is an intentional subject, and of absolutely transcendent acts so far as he is a spiritual subject. Self-knowledge is only one of the projections of universal transcendence, one's cognitive projection toward oneself. Within the nature of the subject, as one of the bases of subjectivity, is the reference toward oneself, the consciousness of oneself and of one's acts; but this reference is fulfilled through knowing and feeling that one is a subject without the necessity of detailed knowledge as to what the subject is in his past, present, and possible being. In principle, we do not hereby deny what we have said on other occasions [3] concerning the *duty of conduct* and *the duty of consciousness*. These concern the dual demand for man which is derived from his being essentially a subject, that is, to work in each case from the depths of his own subjectivity, demanding that it be wholly expressed in each act, and to possess himself reflectively and consciously, to know himself. These requirements, and perhaps primarily the second one, set forth an infinite number of tasks whose fulfillment belongs to the area of the ideal man. For the real man, defined by duality, what is basic in this regard, is the subjective reference which is inseparable from the normal functioning of subjectivity, of the self.

[3] See Romero, *Filosofía de la persona* (2d ed., Buenos Aires: Editorial Losada, 1951) .

X

SOCIABILITY

To be a self, as has been seen, characterizes man. Strictly speaking, this is the necessary and sufficient condition for man to be since intentionality as a normal activity is the new principle which emerges with him and defines him. This condition precedes duality, which, in principle, may not be present in man. Duality is characteristic of the full man, giving shape to what we usually consider to be "human" in man. But man has the prerogative of being man even though he may be described as "inhuman" in the popular sense. This odd situation is explained in terms of what is most characteristic in his nature. An animal is a being that persists and develops in its actuality, a being that is merely what it is. An animal can never cease to be "animal-like." Man is a being of a different kind. Mere intentionality carries with it, as a tendency, as a possibility which seeks to develop according to its internal law, the absolute objective projection of which the spirit consists and which is nothing but the radicalization, the culmination, and the perfection of the original intentionality. Mere intentionality is a halted and a maimed intentionality, something which carries within it a potentiality of a kind whose nonactualization points to a deficiency. Thus, man is seen as what he is and, because of an inner, constitutive demand as what he must become. With these qualifications, we reaffirm what has been stated on other occasions: man is man when he functions as a subject with a world that is perceived objectively in his surroundings.

It is understandable that the broad profile of man's implantation in totality derives from his original structure. The animal is closed off from the world as a world; reality comes to him as stimuli and compulsions, as substance which must be introduced into his organism, as favorable or unfavorable physical conditions, as risks which he must avoid to defend his physical well-being. His psychism is a servant to his corporeality, yet without constituting a center or a self with its own being. It is this corporeality, guided by its psychical servant, which enters into contact with reality. The animal's contact with the world is physical or material. The world as such remains foreign to him, because he considers only the fragment to which he is tangent, and this fragment comes to him only as a positive or negative influence on his organic constitution. Man, however, opens himself to the world; he is not an organism limited to receiving or dodging impacts, but a self who apprehends realities and conducts himself in relation to them on the basis of their objectivity.

We have stated purposely that man "Opens himself to the world," instead of using other words, because objective perception does not consist in turning toward something and then immediately setting it aside; it does not consist in casting a glance at things and then passing them by—man literally "opens himself" to reality. He takes it to himself and is enriched with its substance. In a strict sense, it is the pure subject, the ultimate self who says "I" in its proper meaning, that is, so that this word cannot be replaced by "what is mine." This axis of human individuality is the agent of intentionality, the focus from which all intentional acts project, whether they are cognitive or of any other kind. To say "my self" is to be guilty of an improper expression because there is no thing capable of referring a self to itself. It is the self which refers all to itself. But this pure self cannot subsist in its purity and nakedness, for in essence it is intentional activity, and it is not conceived without the exercise of acts directed to what the self is not, that is, to foreign objects. The true life of the self consists in dealing with objects, to get along with them, to recognize them, to love them, hate them, and want them. Intimate as we may want to imagine the movements of the subjective center to be, they all include something foreign, they necessarily presuppose it. The projection toward the other reaches its limits with the perfection of the self in attitudes that are resolutely spiritual, thereby confirming the constitutive vocation of transcendence, the going out of itself, which the self manifests from its beginning, even if in an imperfect manner. The self, which we might call central or focal, takes on a greater substantivity, acquiring breadth through appropriations which form a part of itself, because they are incorporated into it and henceforth are inseparable from it. In the first place, there are habits which are the consequence of the performance of the acts; then there are the results of the acts as clear or functionalized experience, as impressions of success or failure, as images in the memory. All of this is the result or the repercussion of its intercourse with the other, which is of course conditioned by subjective propensities or characteristics. Around the central selfhood the inner world of "what is mine" is constituted. This is a section of objectivities (perceived, supposed, or imagined), arranged in areas of varying proximity and perceptibility, into which one injects his feelings and desires, which basically are intentional movements, the acts of a self, when they are directed toward objective elements.

Thus it is characteristic of man to be in the world. He is neither a realm closed off from the world, who, through special openings, allows certain elements from the outside, which have been denaturalized previously and accommodated to his specific constitution, barely to filter through. This is what happens to animals. Nor is man a being without an inner principle, without a solid and unique makeup, a being apportioned throughout the external reality, becoming diffused and lost in it. He is in the world, but it is *he* who is in the world. He goes toward the world, yet he brings the world to himself, but it is always he who goes and who brings the world to himself. His special makeup consists precisely in this: to make the world a matter of his concern in many ways; through cognitive appropriation, through practical interaction, through aesthetic elaboration, through moral participation, and so on. The common presupposition of all this is to begin by accepting the world as it is, without prior functionalization, without changing it beforehand into a deposit of elements that are strictly correlated to the demands or repugnancies of organic impulsiveness.

The self-world pair, therefore, takes on a special character. The juxtaposition, and it is well to insist upon it, is quite different from that existing between the organism and its environment. The animal lives his environment, which is already defined by the reference to his biological constitution, but he does not assimilate it as that environment; rather he assimilates it to himself, introducing it into his own organism by transforming it into an organic reality that is like his own: into flesh, fluids, physiological energy, heat, and movement. Aside from all of this, the environment is external to him. For man, however, the world is at the same time both external and internal, but it is external only to the extent that he perceives it and makes it internal. As Goethe said: "As it is outside, so it is inside." The self and the world are not the terms of a duality in which each is self-sufficient and constitutes a realm foreign to the other. The self without a world is an empty possibility, because its life is to tend toward objectivities, toward things other than itself. Undoubtedly, the world exists apart from the self but even the affirmation that it exists can be formulated only by a subject. If we could conceive of the existence of the self apart from its worldly content, we would imagine it as a blind, useless focus, without perspective or activity. The world without the self would lack the one element which knows it, thinks about it, makes enlightened use of it, submitting it to an intelligent colonization and a spiritual sublimation, and in the long run gives meaning to it. The character of the relation between these two terms is given simultaneously in their face-to-face stance, as well as in their interconnection. Self and world are structured through mutually receiving each other in an interpenetration which is never a fusion, because the uniqueness of this encounter stems precisely from the fact that there is an interpenetration which does not distort either element. It is in this unrestrained interconnection that the breadth and fruitfulness of the encounter are to be found.

Something concerning the relation between self and world has already been said, especially concerning natural reality and the connections between man and the community, and between man and culture. Comments on the relationships between human units remain to be added. As for this topic, which is largely a social one and whose thorough study is therefore the responsibility of social psychology as well as sociology, we will consider only those points which seem necessary to the comprehension of man. We have proceeded in the same manner whenever we have been obliged to take into consideration or to touch on matters which seem to be beyond a strict anthropological concern. In addition, of course, we presuppose here what has already been stated concerning the intentional community and culture.

From a certain point of view the self is the absolute unit, because self-consciousness (which must not be confused with adequate self-knowledge) is essential to the self, and self-consciousness is reference to oneself. Only the entity which lives its own self, which is conscious of its existence, and is, strictly speaking, a self for itself can say "I" and be a full self. Pluralizing 'I' [1] into the grammatical 'we' is different from any other pluralizing. We say : the dogs, the houses, the numbers, and in these plurals we add up single entitles which come into the pluralization retaining everything that is or seems to be essential in them. Only in this manner is there a true plural, a collection of objects which answers to the name which designates it. It is inherent to the self to speak for itself, to depend on its selfhood, with its conscious reference to itself.

Let us distinguish the different subjective instances.

The self, as has been stated, is unique in each individual, and it cannot be effectively and fully pluralized. Stated in another fashion, it cannot be pluralized in its essence, since it is a self only for the one who lives it and is conscious of himself.

The expression "the selves" designates an imperfect but indispensable pluralization because we must refer in some manner to the sum which includes the self, who is thinking the plural (the only real self), and the similar selves which he presupposes as the live centers of the other men.

The expression "the selves" includes all selves. This is not true of the word "we," which normally is only a partial sum, except in its less frequent use, as when we say, "we," that is, "mankind." As a rule, the 'we' is either more or less permanent or circumstantial: we Americans, those of our family, those belonging to a given

---

[1] To translate the Spanish word 'yo,' the word 'self' has been used, although, grammatically, the correct translation is 'I.' Given the philosophical context of Romero's work, however, it is appropriate to translate 'yo' as 'self,' unless in specific contexts 'I' seems more appropriate. Where 'I' is used to render 'yo' it is enclosed in single quotation marks.

social class, the adherents to some particular religious communion or political party, the neighbors in this community, those who have liver trouble, the subscribers to this newspaper, and so on. Any human grouping can constitute a 'we' when some point of contact exists, although it may be minimal and even stem from an intense struggle, as when two adversaries say to a meddling mediator, "Don't get into something that is none of your business, because this is our problem and we are going to settle it." The point of contact may vary a great deal in kind. Sometimes, in more or less long periods of time, it comes to be felt so intensely that it practically erases the differences in many types of behavior. Usually the scope of the unifying motive is clearly discernible. The lower limit of the 'we' is found in groups in which the agreement rests on some specific interest, so that the occasion for related contacts, which would encourage human association, barely exists. An example of this is found in the relationships to each other of the stockholders in a large company.

The "other" is one's neighbor, the unique human type as seen by a self. Frequently he has been designated as a "thou," but we feel that it is convenient to reserve this latter term for someone who has entered into a close relationship with the subject for whom he is a 'thou.' This relationship must be personal, though it does not necessarily presuppose physical proximity. A relationship maintained through letters with someone that has never been seen, if it is of this 'personal' kind and not strictly 'official,' professional, or impersonal, provides the impression of the 'thou,' of being face to face with the other person. With the 'thou' thus conceived, it has a more restricted meaning than it is usually given in psychology and sociology, yet it is broader than the grammatical meaning, which restricts the reference of the 'thou' to the person to whom the 'I' is speaking. All remaining human beings are included in the category of 'others,' each of them considered individually as a "he." For this reason 'they' and 'others' are identical.

We do not elaborate on these distinctions because this discussion is sufficient for an anthropological formulation. The distinctions offered can and should be completed with the deepening of what has been affirmed and the addition of aspects that have been omitted. For example, the exploration of the 'we' is of major interest, and it requires much clarification. One need only adduce that every 'thou' composes 'we's' for the 'I', but the 'I' does not accept as 'thou's' all who are included with him in the different kinds of 'we.' A problem of greater significance is that of the totalized complexes, as they might be called, in which the various aspects are important and should be defined. These aspects include the transformation which totalization imposes on the individual, the power and nature of the tie, as well as the function and value of the totalization. As we have stated, we do not think that for the purposes of this work it is necessary to elaborate these topics. These distinctions are not so much along the lines of an anthropological study, such as this one, as they are in keeping with the theory of culture, because they are concerned with the various collective subjects of culture; the attitude and action of each of these subjects are inseparable from special cultural activities and achievements.

In the merely intentional attitude, the self is characterized by being the complete and ultimate frame of actual or practical reference for all its intentional acts. We have referred to this as "subjective return." The 'we's' are conceived as amplifications of this self. The individual, as a component of the 'we,' conducts himself as a member of this group and, practically, acts in benefit of this 'we,' a part of which belongs to him. In some critical and extraordinary cases, the attitude of the individual takes on the character of extreme disinterestedness or even of sacrifice for the benefit of the interest of the group without the presence of the spiritual aspect, as when the 'we' is lived with such intensity, possessing such prestige for the individual, that he surrenders his individuality to it. In such instances the group maintains an attitude which may be referred to as egoistical, even though some individuals may "disinterestedly" sacrifice themselves for the group, that is, for the collective egoistical interest. As for the individual, this attitude may or may not be spiritual. It is spiritual if, erroneously, he recognizes in his group, in his 'we,' an absolute value (as in the deification of the state, or as in the faithfulness to a class because it is held to be the supreme good) . This is not so if the conduct responds merely to a 'we' which is lived as "mine."

In the spiritual attitude we form a 'we' with those who assume spiritual positions similar to our own. The 'we' is a broadening of the spiritual side of the self, whose behavior lacks the subjective return. It is the 'we' who seek the truth or who desire justice. At this point, the difference between the two families of 'we's' is emphasized. The merely intentional 'we' is the point of departure and, also, the ultimate goal of its acts, which redound only to its benefit. The spiritual 'we' is only the point of departure of the acts, since it does not benefit from them. It is the same difference that exists between the correlative single subjects, and from which stems the difference of the bond linking the components of the 'we' in the two instances. In the intentional 'we', the solidarity is established through the unity of goals, acts, benefits, and gains. The concrete character of the attainments, the risk that they may be disputed, the need to conserve and increase them, all strengthen the closeness. In the spiritual 'we,' there is a solidarity in purposes and acts, but the powerful unifying element of practical common interests is absent. There is no gain for the 'we' because spirituality is a giving and not an appropriating, yet the bond is strengthened by participation in an ideal common task and by the mutual esteem that result from it. As a nonspiritual entity, a family, class, or professional 'we' achieves certain goals and distributes the benefits to the group. As a strictly spiritual entity, a 'we' constituted by religious, ethical, scientific, or artistic interests does not take advantage of its achievements, rather it makes them available to all. The former 'we' is closed, turned toward itself because its reason for being resides in itself and tends to be exclusivistic. The latter is open and turned toward its ultimate purposes.

Because of human duality, which sometimes is a superimposing and sometimes an interweaving, the existence of pure 'we's' of one kind or another is rather improbable. Forms that are originally mixed are frequent and those that aspire to be pure never cease to retain, circumstantially, some strain of the element they wish to exclude. A 'we' which is organized to obtain advantages for itself confronts the fact that others, from their point of view, have the same right to similar advantages, and thus it may proclaim that right and even fight for it. A 'we,' which may be a spiritual type because of its form, may tend to close up in order to capitalize on certain gains (which may be economic, or power, or prestige) derived as by-products of its proper function. A 'we' will be predominantly intentional or spiritual depending on whether the subjective return is basic or only accidental. If the constitutive purpose is to obtain benefits for the 'we,' then it will be primarily intentional. If the gain is circumstantial or indirect and the principal projection is spiritual, then the 'we' will be fundamentally spiritual. Every exercise of mere intentionality carries the seeds of, and may develop into, spiritual projection. In the long run, no spiritual activity can maintain itself absolutely pure, because the men who exercise it cannot rid themselves of the conditions of human existence, and these conditions rest, in large measure, on nonspiritual bases.

Every 'we' defines its own boundary, and outside of it are those alien to this 'we,' the 'those' who are scattered or who, together, make up other 'we's,' which are taken as 'you's.' In the light of what was said above, the intentional 'we's' separate themselves from the 'those's' and the 'you's' with whom they maintain relations of indifference, conflict, or some more or less partial solidarity. The spiritual 'we's,' however, do not close themselves off from the 'those's' or the 'you's,' rather they consider themselves to be their instruments, servants, and agents though at times they may feel ignored or rejected. The spiritual function does not require any encouragement from the outside; to act and to be justified on its own belongs to its essence, and, at least in principle, it is as indifferent to adverse criticism as it is to praise.

The intentional 'we' tends indirectly to be an instrument of spiritualization. The coördination of practical interests presupposes human proximity—the experience of the 'thou'—and this experience encourages that of the 'him,' which is an authentic spiritual experience. As we know, there is ethical conduct when the self is projected toward another self and actively accepts him as such, completely setting aside any actual or real bond with that self. The interest in the other self is neither due to his being a member of one's own 'we' nor because one enters with him into a relationship of an 'I' with a 'thou,' but merely because he is a self. If an attitude is to be absolutely ethical, whether toward oneself or toward a 'thou,' it must ideally renounce feeling toward that self as a 'myself' or as a 'thou' and consider it for itself alone and, therefore, as a 'him.' Psychologically, however, the experience of the self in the 'him' requires that of one's own self and of the 'thou.' This is not the place to decide the much-debated question whether the experience of the 'thou' comes before that of one's own self or vice versa. We believe, however, that both precede the attitude which is cleanly projected toward any self as such, and that such a projection can conceive its object only as a 'him,' as a radical 'other.' In keeping with the foregoing exposition, the 'thou,' and the 'I,' always constitute a 'we.' The relation of the 'I' with the 'thou' continuously takes on an intimacy which draws them together, and it is even normal for the self to use the possessive 'my' when referring to the 'thou,' as in my brother, my friend, my neighbor, my correspondent. Everyone whom a self accepts as a 'thou' has entered or enters with him into a special situation which separates the 'thou' from the 'those.' The self establishes with the 'thou' a particular connection, he bestows upon him a privilege which is denied to the 'those's.' It is understandable that the first attitude of the self toward the 'thou' should be intentional, and that later he should turn his attention to the autonomy and the being for itself of the 'thou,' assuming toward him a spiritual attitude. Later the self will come to see that any 'him' is a self with fullness of being and meaning, and he will thus extend the spiritual experience achieved with the 'thou' which was encouraged through the presence and proximity of the 'thou.'

The relationship to the other subjective categories is essential to the self. The self is expansive, transcending. Sometimes it may turn its intentions toward itself, and at other times it may project them disinterestedly toward the other, but its movement is always to go beyond itself. Intentionality is not conceivable in any other way. In going beyond itself, the self achieves an objective vision of external reality, and, in keeping with this, the self regulates its emotional and voluntary behavior. For the self, this external reality is largely social and human even from the first moments. As a general fact, sociability existed before man. It is found in many animal species, and, in those species closest to him in the zoölogical hierarchy, it shows some characteristics which anticipate traces of human relationships. Indeed sociability is probably one of the principal elements in the transition from the inmediately sub-human to what is properly human. The existence of the community is a necessary prerequisite for the formation of an objective language, which, in turn, is the condition for the normal and accumulative functioning of intentionality in each subject. Stimulated by the communal environment, language also bestows upon this environment its exclusive and differentiating character as a human community in converting it to what we have referred to as an intentional community. The first great repercussion of man's social aspect seems to us to consist in the contribution which collectivized intentionality makes to each individual, that is, the constant accumulation and circulation of objective contents. Indeed, if collectivized intentionality presupposes individual intentionality, the former supports, stabilizes, and extends the latter, placing at its disposal a reservoir of incalculable wealth, so that we can hardly imagine what each individual world would be if it were deprived of the collective contribution. One should keep in mind that social participation is not limited to providing materials to the individual but that it also serves in an instructive, stimulative, and corrective capacity. Without being aware of it, each one anticipates or corrects the deviations and arbitrariness in the perception and interpretation of reality through the influence of a subtle and omnipresent social control. The proof of the efficacy of this control is seen in the recluse, the man who habitually avoids others and in whom manias, fixed ideas, imbalance, and wild concepts and evaluations of persons, things, and events are frequent. Any marked unevenness between the individual and his human environment results, in some way, in seclusion and weakens or invalidates the effect of the indispensable collective control which we discussed. History abounds with examples of how the possession and exercise of absolute power lead to situations that are psychically abnormal, that border on insanity or eventually lead to it.

Usually the 'we' is not an event which is external to each one; it is not a whole to which the individual is connected only because he is placed in the group and participates in it as he comes to feel a part of it. If this were so, the relationship would be unsteady and subject to revision at every turn. In many instances the 'we's' which are felt to be such a stimulate to subjective activity because they favor the transcendent attitude within the 'we' itself and because they are concerned with tasks which are inherent in it. The isolated individual may act or may remain more or less empty, but the 'we' in itself is a task either because the group bond has been established with a purpose in mind or because the more passive interests are mobilized when organized into reliable structures. The connecting bond grows in intensity when it involves certain profound human needs and stirs up emotional response. It is constituted then as a vibrant reality within each self, and in some instances and situations it may even displace everything else and relegate it to a secondary level. This does not mean that it is legitimate to presuppose a weakening of the self in such situations. At times these coincide with a vigorous self-affirmation, in which the subject is concerned about the 'we' in the same energetic manner that he is concerned about any purpose, whether this belonged to the natural or spiritual order. If the self maintains its inherent objectifying function, no projection of its own is capable of destroying it, regardless of the extent to which the projection may monopolize the self. However, there is a deterioration or destruction of the self when the objectifying attitude is attenuated or suppressed, as in mob phenomena, which are characterized by the strengthening in the individual of the background of states and a corresponding decrease in the intentional function. Here one might speak of a backsliding to the subhuman or preintentional, with the overflow of obscure, impulsive forces that use intentional vestiges only as pretexts, as designers of targets at which one can shoot. One must distinguish, however, between this basic mob function in which the impulsive overflowing, the setting free of elementary powers, is fundamental—the remainder being only accessory—and the mob function which is rigorously enclosed in the intentional bounds already described. In the latter case, fusion of the multitude and the discharge of emotional and volitional energy occur within a framework which rests on a previous consensus, and it is not achieved through the mob function. Strictly speaking, the mob situations are distinguished from the 'we' in that in the latter each self is important, and even in those instances in which, in large measure, it is subordinated to the group, the self does so conscious of the subordination yet without surrendering its selfhood. However, the evaluation of the individual's adherence to the 'we' depends on the value the 'we' deserves and the type of adherence of the individual. A special and perhaps extreme example of this adherence is interestingly formulated by Royce in his philosophy of loyalty, in which are found

many metaphysical and religious implications as well as the attri
bution of supreme values.[2]

The problem of understanding one's fellowman has been extensively debated in psychology and philosophy, especially since
Dilthey. Regardless of the difficulties of the matter—and they are
many—there seems to be some agreement in considering this
knowledge as much more adequate and certain than that of the
other orders of reality, because it is knowledge of a reality which is
apprehended in its inner reality, in its ultimate and true being.
For the knowing self, the other person is not a "thing," a fragment
of a reality which is radically strange and foreign to him. Neither is
the other individual merely an entity with which one enters into a
relationship of ontological homogeneity, with whom one merely
establishes a continuing and unifying connection of a vital or
emotional nature. Intentionality makes him present to one as an
object who is also a subject, as one who is like oneself, but is yet
another. This duplicity of identity and difference, in that the other
is a self but yet another self, conditions the behavior of the self
toward the 'other.' There is nothing closer to the self than the
'other' when he is accepted as a self; yet from another point of view
there is nothing so strange and foreign, so unsociable and closed
off. This is because no other real structure is so much 'itself' as the
self, none other is so rebellious to being mediate, to being converted into what is properly "mine."

Of all things in reality, the self can have as a friend in the true
sense only another self, yet at the same time the risk of real enmity
is found only with respect to another self. We are indifferent to
things, however; they are neutral, neither friendly nor hostile.
They strike us as useful or harmful, pleasing or displeasing, and
we can put them to use taking direct advantage of their utility,
skillfully managing them so that they take on other uses while we
avoid their obnoxiousness and even turn this to some advantage.
Since there is no center in them which either knows or understands us, they neither assent to our purposes, nor, *ex professo,* do
they oppose them. The friendship which an animal seems to
bestow upon us in some instances is necessarily incomplete and to

[2] Josiah Royce, *The Philosophy of Loyalty* (New York: Macmillan, 1908),
and *The Problem of Christianity* (New York: Macmillan, 1913).

a large extent illusory. Without being aware of it, we provide the animal with a rudiment of humanity. Yet, the only certain thing supporting this rudiment of humanity is the capacity for a blind emotional attachment, which in itself does not go beyond creating a special kind of living contact. We are never neutral toward the self of another, if he enters into a concrete relationship with our own self, because he is another self and we know that he is not indifferent toward us. The relation varies from that of perfect solidarity and fellowship—the only solidarity and fellowship which are real for man [3]—to extreme enmity, the radical hostility that seeks our annihilation—and neither does any other enmity exist for man, any true hostility outside of this one. Man pays for the privilege of being the only entity to which it is given to enjoy the fullness of love and an unreserved fellowship by being also the only entity which can experience a threatening loneliness and on which may fall a deadly hatred. All this stems from the relationship of the self with the 'other,' in which each confronts the other, yet there is also a mutual interpenetration which includes two intentional structures taken as wholes; in their characteristic relationships they have agreements and conflicts infinitely diverse

[3] The theme of loneliness and fellowship is much more complex if it is conceived in terms of kinds of loneliness and degrees of fellowship; that is, if it includes more than the real and authentic loneliness and fellowship which are embodied in the relationships of one self with other selves. If these expressions are made relative, a diversity of levels and qualities emerges. Inorganic entities lack this kind of relation regardless of the sense in which it is taken. Organic beings are related to each other in what can be referred to as some form of fellowship, or, on the other hand, of loneliness. Man feels alone when confronted with the inorganic, but all life is in some sense company to him, including the most lowly plant. Organic nature strikes him at the same time as peaceful and stimulating, because what is life in him communes with that life. From another point of view, there is the desire for a perfect and absolute fellowship with someone who understands us completely, who supports us with incomparable power, who is always present with us. It is a desire for fellowship with God. The same demand that motivates gradual spiritualization and thereby, little by little, perfects conditions for the encounter of each self with the other selves, is raised to the level of this other encounter which is perfect and without restrictions. Christianity not only provides the believer with this fellowship but even improves it by making it much warmer through the maternalism of Mary and the dual nature of Christ. In his human nature, Christ corrects the impression of remoteness which God the Father might produce and he seems to adapt himself to a fellowship that maintains its absolute meaning while adding to it the element of intimate human closeness.

in kind, quality, and intensity. With intentionality, there appeared in the universe the only entities which really *are*, because they are in themselves and for themselves, and in this manner they complete the perfection of being. The spirit also appeared in a budding stage, yet nevertheless real. Through the spirit, being turns and consciously projects itself toward itself with universal intent and thus the whole of reality is completed; it is rounded out, making its final encounter with itself. But these gains are achieved through a genuine suffering, in the face of a fundamental evil and hatred, which are experienced by the self because of the work of another self. With the prerogative of being the only entity who can say "yes" to another self, the prerogative of being the only one who can say "no" is also given to it.

To a considerable degree, the self fulfills itself in its relationship to another. Not only does it receive from the 'other,' as from a mirror, many elements with which it puts together its own image, thus completing itself in possible self-knowledge, but also it receives from the 'other' a multitude of actual influences. On the positive side, one should include the impressions of joy, strength, prestige, and security which are received in the agreeable association with a 'thou' who is in some way favorable to one or over whom one exercises some influence or control, as well as those impressions of opposition or resistance which one is able to overcome. On the negative side, there are the phenomena of depression or deterioration, which stem from an unpleasant or frankly adverse attitude on the part of the other person.

The 'thou's' closest to each other are aware of a root which penetrates more deeply than the intentional structure. In the relationship between parents and children, between the parents, and among the children there is an elementary biological component and a basic affection which depends on the living community and the consequent solidarity of interests which is the consequence of this firm, natural bond. All of this, in itself, is not specifically human but it immediately becomes so through its inevitable inclusion within intentional boundaries, through objectification and understanding on the part of each member of the relationship with another or the others. This takes place in such fashion that, beneath the intentional or objectified organization of the contacts, prior unifying tendencies function which conserve their native energy although they may take on the objective forms that intentionality imposes on them. The transfer or extension of feelings of this kind seems to be a major factor and it cannot be ignored if any intimate relation with the 'thou' is to be adequately understood. All close associations with one's neighbor include an echo of these relations tempered by the situations and the age level. It may be a more or less vague feeling of a paternal or maternal attitude toward younger people, of filial affection and esteem of younger people toward those advanced in years, or a feeling of brotherhood between those who do not consider themselves separated by their ages. Paternalism tends to filter into the attitude of one who has power over others or who has the responsibility of directing or indoctrinating them. Maternalism is evident in many areas of social assistance, a task for which women have felt a special inclination through the ages. In mature marriage relationships it is not rare to find a fraternal attitude structured around a bipolar love which has assumed a paternalistic and maternalistic quality. Fraternity has usually been considered the ideal bond between men, as the form *par excellence* of human relationships. Christianity owes much of its universal appeal and meaning to the religious and ethical transposition of these relationships, which it alone, among all religions, has known to effect. In every man, in moments of loneliness and anguish, there emerges the need to turn to a father who will understand and support him, to a mother who will console and comfort him on her lap. There is a need to return to the fraternal community of one's neighbors. One conceives of an open fraternity, which meets the standards of equality, lively affection, and constant mutual support presupposed by a refined fraternity, as the model for the desirable manner of human association. Although we believe that our interpretation is clear, we must insist that the natural roots of the facts to which we have been referring do not argue against the exclusively human character of these facts themselves. The raw material of his being comes to man from subhuman levels, but that material is completely transformed and becomes a different thing through the work of the intentional constitution and of spiritualization. Perceived objectivity is elaborated with the lived content of sensation. The diffuse emotional state and the impulsive activity are subhuman events, like the tendency to be gregarious, but, through transformation, these became human events when the subject emerges with the objectified world around him. The incomparability of the fact that a self exists, and that it perceives things and other selves, determines the incomparability of all relations between these elements and subhuman situations to which they are likened, even though these serve as antecedents and even as material undergirding.

Although the positive association with the 'thou' may be on a high level and abound in ethical content, the pure ethical relationship in the full spiritual sense is not established with the 'thou' but with the 'him,' as was maintained when we spoke of ethical value. For every subject a 'thou' is always something that belongs to him; it is "his own," and any behavior toward a 'thou' presupposes an element of subjective return. The only fully ethical attitude is projected toward a self because it is a self, and this obligation increases with the increase in transcendence which that self embodies, therefore absolute obligation is direced toward the other so far as he is full transcendence, that is, to the extent that is a spiritual self. If the attitude toward the other is to assume a properly ethical quality, the 'thou' must be ideally deprived of its condition as a 'thou'; it must be deprived of any actual or particular bond with the agent of the intention. Its selfhood must be placed "in brackets," it must be seen in its strict otherness. The self and the 'thou' make up a 'we,' and in every 'we' a separation is at work, a setting apart in favor of the realm which the 'we' isolates. Even though we may not look upon the other selves and 'you's' as adversaries, this separation of the 'we,' in itself, indicates a contrast to the detriment of what remains on the outside. Exception is to be made, however, in the strict spiritual 'we,' for this 'we' is consciously turned toward others, at least with respect to purposes, and thus it prohibits any subjective return. Strictly speaking, the spiritual attitude takes the 'him' into consideration, and it is indifferent to the circumstances in which it confronts him or, better said, it finds him wherever there is a self: in the 'those's,' in the 'thou's,' and in one's own self except that it keeps these latter from being, respectively, 'thou's' and 'my-own-self.' For example, when I, or my 'we,' affirm, respectively, *my* or *our right,* the attitude will be merely intentional if it is affirmed as *mine* or *ours* and spiritual if it is proclaimed and defended because it is *right.*

That is, any self and any 'we' whatever is seen in this self and 'we' and not merely those that may be of special interest.

Although this situation may be altered and complicated in practice, it is not modified in its fundamental aspects. One's own self and the 'you,' in any of its positive connections with the self, do not recognize on their own any advantages stemming from the ultimate spiritual point of view, but they have these advantages for reasons that might be called circumstantial even though the circumstantiality is permanent. Restricted and specialized by the undeniable limitation of each self, the scope of its acts, and the scope and strength of its intentional glance, each subject is circumscribed in its merely intentional as well as its spiritual possibilities, and its accessible environment determines the territory of its effective action, of its peremptory obligation. A vague aspiration for what is far removed may be an expression of an authentic universalism, but it may also disguise an unconscious inclination to escape constraining need, the obligation pressed upon us through the demand of present circumstances. A circumstance in itself is only circumstantial—but frequently it is the best touchstone for what is fundamental. The maxim, so highly recommended by Goethe, that we should prefer the 'duty at hand' works in part as a preventive or corrective of certain flights from immediate responsibility. These flights, which the subject tends to put down to his credit, are interpreted as applied to distant, noble purposes, so that it is no fault of his if they are not attained. This aspect does not exhaust the meaning of the duty at hand. Since each self is its own self, its duty toward its selfhood reverts, in the first place, upon itself as an 'other,' as was stated before. But it must be as an 'other' who is first with respect to order, who must be considered *before the 'others,'* but *not as more or better than the 'others.'* We might say that the preference is formal and not material, one of mere priority and not of a different quality. The same holds, more or less, for the conduct of the self toward the 'others.' Those that are closer have preference, but only in the order, not in the quality, of consideration. Only in this manner is the spiritual attitude converted into actual behavior, into a policy of actual colonization of the world, in which each one has in his charge a specific task, and the spirituality is not lost as it is distributed over the limitless horizons of which it spontaneously takes care. The spirit is universalistic in essence, but its task must not be understood as a total or universal achievement undertaken by each spiritual center, rather each one is to contribute within his own limits to a joint enterprise, which is the enterprise of the human spirit.

In the natural or spontaneous attitude, one's own self is taken as a self by each individual, a 'thou' is taken as an almost-self, and the 'they's' are accepted in varying degrees as almost-thou's and almost-things. Many who would be incapable of causing the least trouble to some 'thou' with whom they maintained some minor social contact, would press, without hesitation, the buzzer whose sound would bring about the death of some distant and unknown mandarin, if thereby they would inherit his fortune, even though the fortune might be quite modest. The experience of the 'thou' is probably indispensable in reaching that of the 'him' as a self. It is easier to come to see a full self in a 'thou' than in a distant 'him,' who, in extreme cases, is conceived as a numerical entity, as an exchangeable unit lacking in content. Yet, once the experience of another's self is achieved in the 'thou,' once the spiritual glance is directed toward that self, one is able to generalize directly with respect to all 'others' because the spiritual attitude toward the 'thou' consists in acknowledging it as an 'other.'

Through this experience of the self in the 'thou' and the correlative inclination or possibility of changing to the spiritual attitude with respect to any 'he,' it so happens that it is not necessary for the 'we' to possess a spiritual character beforehand in order for spiritual seeds or elements to be present in it. Elements of this nature may appear in the inner reality of the 'we' and be independent of the quality of the bond which properly constitutes it. Thus it should be no cause for surprise to discover elements of pure spirituality even in groups whose purposes are decidedly egoistical and even criminal.

A human surrounding is indispensable for constituting the merely intentional self. Other human beings contribute in so many ways to the development of the essence of each self and the fulfillment of its intentions, that a solitary self in the midst of the natural world is unimaginable. More obvious yet is the impossibility of the total isolation of the spiritual self. In the first place, spirituality is constituted upon mere intentionality, which already requires the support of others. Secondly, in its own right, the spirit is a going-out, a total transcendence, an absolute projection toward the other. Objective culture is the creation and legacy of a community in its existence throughout time. Without it the intentional self is inconceivable, and this is still more true of the spiritual self. Not only does this culture presuppose the presence of contemporaries who live, understand, and use it, concurring in their working with it, but, through its own agency, it places each self in a special relationship with past generations, whose most refined substance sustains the self. The ethical projection, which is essential to the spirit, unavoidably requires dependence on others and even consists in this, since it is the seeking of a principle found only in selves. Thus, just as the intentional self needs the 'thou's' and the 'we's' without which it would be a failure, cut short from the beginning, so the spiritual self develops in the ideal community of the spirits, in the final encounter of each with the others. In this manner it shapes a brotherhood which includes not the least trace of a concrete or practical relationship. There is a kind of 'we' which is different from all other actual and limited 'we's' and which associates the self with all the 'they's' and includes the whole body of humanity as a spiritual reality.

XI

HISTORICITY

The problem of historicity is inextricably bound to the problem of time. To deny the reality of time, or to reduce its value so as to conceive it as a neutral roadway that can be traveled as easily in one direction as the other, precludes the possibility of any kind of historicist interpretation. Historicity can be attributed only to realities for which temporality is an actual component. The actuality of time is not adequately accounted for in isolated instants or separate orbits where time sets the pace, for to be truly real a continuous temporal vibration must run through the whole series. Historicity not only demands an actual adherence to time, but it demands a temporal conformation of the entity, that is, that its reality be molded with time. This concrete time in the heart of the entity cannot be conceived as instantaneity, but as something which jells in registering temporalized events and in the living accumulation of the past. There is historicity for each instant of an entity when it can be said truly that for it the past has not transpired in vain.

For the most part, and with the exception of recent developments, Western philosophy has been a rationalism stained with a notorious intellectualism. In its most crude and least critical forms, rationalism sacrifices everything on the altar of strict rational demand; it worships essences and logicality, and relentlessly condemns whatever is opposed to them. The model *par excellence* of ancient rationalism is provided by Eleatic metaphysics with its all-embracing affirmation of identity. Nothing could be further from the historicist outlook. The nontemporalist vocation of the Greek mind is evident in many circumstances: for example, the mobility of being is accepted by chance, at the beginning, but this is immediately sidetracked by the idea of the "eternal return." This notion converts the stages of transformation into a great succession of identical cycles and is thus a roundabout means to restore immobility or stability. Likewise atomism, in need of mobility, restricts the capacity of the atoms to change the situation by adhering to an immobility and a stability within each atom, that is, in the ultimate foundation of reality.

In its most influential phases, modern thought [1] has also sided with nontemporalism. The rationalism of Descartes and Spinoza is nontemporal, as is the new science of nature, which is mathematical in the extreme, for its ideal is to convert the most concrete of its substances—physical mass—into an array of mechanical data. The reduction of matter to space by Descartes is the courageous fulfillment of the latent desire of all rationalism, a desire which is not satisfied until it reaches the total transparency and mathematization of what is real. It is through Hobbes and the materialists of the eighteenth century that this line of thought, stimulated by the rise of physical science, inspired the mechanistic scientism of the nineteenth century. Darwinism, though it carried elements which contributed to a historicist interpretation of nature, served, in its first thrusts, as support to this nontemporal mechanism, because what was strongest and most visible in it was the reduction of biological purposiveness to mechanical causation, with the consequent support of this nontemporal concept. So it happened that the division of living beings into historical series made little impression on a concept which saw the ultimate level of reality— the definitive ontological strata—in the physical masses and their movements, with all other things considered as added phenomena.

In the midst of the rationalism of the seventeenth century the first historicist seeds had already begun to appear in the philosophy of Leibniz, which, in some of its aspects, served as a

---

[1] In referring to modern thought or modern philosophy we mean the period beginning with the Renaissance and concluding with Kant.

precursor to romantic conceptions. As the foundation of reality, the Leibnizian monads are entities which in a sense are historical. These "simple substances which enter into the formation of compounds" undergo a continuous change, and each one of their states "is the natural consequence of its preceding state, so that the present is pregnant with the future." In several aspects of Leibniz's thought, one finds emphasis on an attitude which converts him into the most interesting if not the greatest philosopher of his age. For here is a rationalist who opens up to intuitions whose ultimate consequences are the overcoming of logicist and static rationalism. Thus, for example, his preference for vital, in contrast to mechanical, images; his profound understanding of the continuity which shapes his metaphysics, stimulating the discovery of infinitesimal calculus and, from this approach, bringing him closer to the more pliant view of reason as found in Hegel; and even his conception of philosophical thought as integration throughout time, which also has an important bearing on the interpretation of the history of philosophy as presented by Hegel. One of the various aspects of this last link in the great rationalism of the eighteenth century is turned toward the future. It is the aspect that makes up the revolutionary principles of Romanticism. Like the monads, Leibniz also was laden with the past, teeming with the future.

With the romantics a metaphysical evolutionism emerges, a kind of gradation of being into stages, each of which is prepared by the one that precedes it, and yet each surpasses the earlier stage in dignity. Temporality, however, is an element that romantic idealism did not seek to introduce into being, and this element alone keeps this scheme, as found in Schelling and Hegel, from being properly historicist. Romantic idealism knew, however, how to initiate the recovery of time along another line: that of human history, which for the first time was embraced in a profound and loving comprehension and converted into one of the principal themes of philosophical reflection. The winding, unforeseeable course of human achievements—the nonrepeatable uniqueness of personalities, historical situations, and processes—was not at this time an argument against knowledge of this kind of event. Until this period, knowledge of this kind had been held as much inferior to the knowledge of what was mathematical and physical, of what

could be formulated in the *more geometrico* in keeping with strict
Eleatic or Cartesian rationality. The philosophical achievement of
bringing living temporality into the heart of being, and even
converting being tself into a living temporality, was reserved for
Bergson. Undoubtedly it was his greatest achievement, for here
begins a metaphysical historicism which had already been
sketched, though imperfectly, in the metaphysics of nontemporal
development of Schelling and Hegel. The efforts, trials, and
transitions of this whole process are equivalent to a long struggle
between the rationalism of a rigorous identity, which we might
call Eleaticism, and temporalism. Here, while enjoying the function of its own mechanism, reason regards itself as the unappeal-
able case and, in forging an image of what really is, accepts only
what enters easily into its categories and above all into the category
of identity. Time is belittled for its irrationality and is judged to
be one of the typical aspects of appearance. The continuous
contact with reality, however, shows the insufficiency of Eleatic
reason. Leibniz's formulation of continuity as a cosmic principle is
one of the major corrections imposed on the Eleatic and Cartesian
schemes, and it foretells the acceptance of the temporal flow. In
general terms, the transition from fixedness and identity—the
demands of classical rationalism—to temporalism presupposes an
openness to reality itself, a subduing of the rational demands to data
obtained from reality. In between that fixedness and identity, and
the acceptance of the temporal flow, intermediate conceptions are
inserted, which include those of nontemporal evolutionism. This
intermediary position finds representatives in the metaphysics of
Schelling and Hegel, and parallel to this it appeared in the work
of some biologists, who recognized the arrangement of the species
in a continued sequence, though they did not yet conceive it as a
process developing through time.[2]

The attribution of a metaphysical role to time is not only one of
the principal accomplishments in contemporary philosophy but it
is also, perhaps, its most original contribution. One of the most

---

[2] See Romero, "Temporalismo" in *Filosofía contemporánea* (2d ed., Buenos Aires: Editorial Losada, 1944) and "Sobre los problemas de la razón y la
metafísica" in *Papeles para una filosofía* (Buenos Aires: Editorial Losada,
1945) which discuss some of these issues.

important consequences—not of temporalism alone, to be sure, but of everything that engenders it and empties into it—is the statement of a problem in which satisfactory results are far from being achieved. The problem to which we refer is the necessity of coming to terms between reason and certain ontological aspects that seem to go against it; among these aspects, time is of primary importance. What has been most frequent, because it is a comfortable opposition and a jump from one extreme to another, has been the proclamation of a decided irrationalism. The exposition and defense of this irrationalism are bearers of an inherent contradiction, for they must necessarily be formulated in terms of mental and verbal forms ultimately referable to the logic of identity; and this is but a dependence or an expression of the old Eleatic reason. Be that as it may—the matter is not our concern here—what is important is to acknowledge the temporalist and even the historicist character of the major metaphysical attempts of our day—of the attemps which, with the the greatest justification, seek to offer a satisfactory image of the roots and processes of reality.[3]

Just as the nontemporalist metaphysics of seventeenth-century rationalism corresponded to the scientific conception of the mechanized world, which was alien to the deeper levels of time, so, in like manner, the metaphysics of temporality is akin to the scientific views which depend on time and hold it to be an indispensable element. A historicist interpretation, either implicit or explicit, can be discovered in the contemporary conceptions of the atom and of the physical universe as a whole; that is to say, with respect to the smaller parts as well as with respect to the whole body which these parts form. The world of organisms shows its historical condition with even greater evidence. The surprising fact of the continuous transmission of life, uninterrupted from the first cells, emphasizes the unity of the long chain of forms. The increasing complexity reaches from the most modest beginnings, in which the living being is hardly more than a particle of animated substance, to the prodigious complexity of the superior organisms. The decidedly historical character of the vital series is not manifested solely by means of the bond of generation and inheritance. It is manifested also throughout the series, which seems to become

[3] The metaphysical summary set forth in pp. 174–181 is historicist.

itself by means of trials, experiments, and a constant perfecting, in a task which is consistent in its progressive increase in complexity and unification, in the growing formation of its coördination and of an inner reality, and in a gradual opening up to the surrounding reality. All this provides the organic and psychic foundations on which the human intentional structure is to be implanted.

At this point we stumble upon a problem of major significance. The attribution of historicity to the whole of reality seems to us to be a justified hypothesis. That is, one can say of it the one thing which, according to Jeans, is legitimate to maintain about any generalization on facts, when this generalization seems plausible and when no facts are known to belie it; namely, that it is defensible. Not only do we commit ourselves to the historicity of reality to the extent that it is phenomenon but also to the extent that it is ultimate reality, to the extent that it is the metaphysical foundation of things. For we believe that if there is a possible and valid metaphysical experience, then, according to the philosophical testimony of greatest weight at the present time, this experience confirms such a hypothesis and is juxtaposed to the opposite view. However, we distinguish between the general fact of historicity and the forms which historicity assumes in each of the great segments of reality. In our view, there is a principle which is broader than, and superior to, historicity: the principle of universal transcendence.[4] In real instances, this thrust becomes or is actualized temporally, historically. Yet temporalized transcendence is neither an undivided and chaotic flux, nor a formless current without beds in which to flow. The world is a cosmos with a rigorous order, a reality that is solidly structured and qualified. Were it not so, there would be only a chaos in which the transcending itself would fail. If the world exists and we are able to speak of it, it is because it is a cosmos. Transcendence can change from a blind thrust or conatus to effectiveness with increasing

---

[4] In our view, transcendence is a universal principle in the full sense. Therefore, it governs totality, of which reality is a part (cf. pp. 144–161). In our comments concerning transcendence in general (pp. 174–181), we omitted all reference to transcendence in nonreal spheres. However, some time back, in the first exposition of our thought concerning this matter, we set forth a succinct explanation referring to transcendence in ideality (cf. *Papeles para una filosofía* [Buenos Aires: Editorial Losada, 1945] p. 10).

diversification only because it forms centers from which it functions, foci of a transcending which is ever more perfect and complete. Historicity, which is the consequence of the temporal channeling of transcendence, is neither a uniform process nor does it alter its rhythms and modes directly and of itself; rather, it regulates and diversifies itself according to the nature of the structures in which it occurs, and this is not affected by the fact that these structures themselves are a creation of historicity or of the elementary transcending. Human historicity is thus seen as unique, as irreducible to any other, and as conditioned by the basic structure of man, as we will show later.

Organic historicity, therefore, is not similar to physical historicity. Once life appears, its essential traits impose norms on historical development. With life, a new type of spontaneity and individuation emerges. There is a reference of the entity to itself—a mode of self-possession that is not found in the physical order. The novelties of filial relationships and hereditary transmission appear, and these have incalculable consequences for historicity. Historicity takes on new aspects in the individual, who is subject to a certain vital rhythm from his birth to his death, in the succession of parents and children, and probably in the great number of relationships between individuals and the species, and between the latter and the environment. It is quite feasible that everything that happens leaves some imprint. Every being is a record, a "document," because time inscribes in it a sentence of cosmic history, of the true "universal history." The historical condition of every process presupposes a *mneme,* which many times has been granted as a property of organic substance, and some have conceived it even more extensively as a property of all substance. The historicity of the inorganic has only begun to be discovered; its "tempo" is very slow in relation to the mode and manner of our knowledge and, until recently, human intelligence has shown the same lack of ability to focus upon it as the eye has to see the growth of a plant. Historicity is more easily perceptible in the organic. This is proved by common observation, and the exploration of geological strata has permitted the reconstruction in considerable part of the past of plants and animals, just as the archives and monuments permit reconstruction of the human past. It seems as if reality is becoming increasingly plastic, more receptive of the temporal imprint, richer in the mnemonic record which processes have deposited there, as well as more capable of new projections on the basis of the throbbing depth of this condensed history. Organic substance is then a living, perpetual, unconscious recalling, but also a cumulative recalling, capable of original syntheses, a continuously mobilized deposit upon which the vital creation explodes.

The historicism to which we have been referring deserves to be called ontological to the extent that it proposes a thesis concerning the nature of reality. Beside it, another historicism has been constituted which undoubtedly bears a connection to the one already discussed—to the extent that it is based on the historical conditioning of man—and which, because it upholds the historical relativity of knowledge, should be called gnoseological historicism. This is the last link, in time and maturity, in the chain of the relativist theories of knowledge, and it is well to remember those that have preceded it.[5]

Because of the importance attributed in modern times to knowledge gained from experience and to the establishment and development of science, philosophical skepticism (though decidedly negative in its Greek sources) is gradually and in part becoming affirmative—though not renouncing, to be sure, its basic denials. Thus, in the seventeenth and eighteenth centuries, empiricism places beside its denials a theory of knowledge that rests on empirical grounds, and the Positivism of the nineteenth century, adhering to these denials, organizes philosophy as a system of knowledge acquired through scientific experience. The recent forms of skepticism have this combination of denial and affirmation, and deserve the more adequate name of relativism. They appear as consequences of the strengthening of some scientific disciplines which claim for themselves the examination of cognitive events. When psychology is constituted as an autonomous science, psychologism emerges; when biology is fortified, founding a vast evolutionary doctrine of life, it lays the foundations for a biological explanation of knowledge; when sociology is consoli-

---

[5] Romero, "Escepticismo y relativismo" in *Filosofía de ayer y de hoy* (Buenos Aires: Argos, 1947) should be consulted concerning the kinds and the significance of relativist and skeptical positions.

dated, one of its streams attempts to reduce man to what is social, thus giving first place to a collective psychism to which all the psychical phenomena in man, including knowledge, is referred. As can be seen, psychology, biology, and sociology maintain, respectively, that knowledge is a psychical, vital, or social fact. Much broader, more flexible, and subsequent to these is the historicist form, and, for this relativism, all knowledge is historically conditioned. The reef on which all skepticism finally runs aground—the destruction of the skeptical thesis by skepticism itself—becomes sharply visible here. Spengler, who carried this relativist historicism to its limits, sees the reef before him and, far from executing any maneuvers, sails straight into it, assuming all consequences of the collision. "There are no truths," he says, "except in relation to a specified type of man. My philosophy is itself the expression and reflection of the Western soul, as different, for example, from ancient philosophy and the philosophy of India. And it is so only in the present state of civilization. Hereby are defined its content as world view, its practical importance, and the limits of its validity."

Our present purpose does not include a detailed examination of this kind of historicism. We wish to conclude with a few summary observations. Cognitive historicism derives from what we have called ontological historicism. Thus, just as gnoseological psychologism, biologism, and sociologism maintain that knowledge is subject, respectively, to the psychical, biological, and social structure of man, because they see in them what is basic in human nature, so gnoseological historicism maintains as fundamental the belief that what is decisive for man is his historical condition. However, in affirming the historical relativity of knowledge, the thesis of the constitutive historicity of man, which can only be a thesis formulated by man's knowledge, is itself affected by that historical relativity, and it is converted into a conviction that is characteristic of a certain historical situation and therefore without meaning outside of it; made relative in this manner, its relativism is reflected onto the thesis that all knowledge is historically conditioned. We hasten to point out that this self-invalidation of historicist relativism happens only in its most extreme and radical formulation, in which case, as can easily be seen, this historicism concludes by denying itself. In its more

attenuated forms, the historicity of knowledge is better understood as a process of gradual adjustment, in which the temporal
progression does not consist of merely replacing given situations
by others that are equally partial and relative; rather objectivity
increases through the testing of points of view which, as criticized
and substituted, leave a valid remainder which is incorporated
into the replacing positions. Thus, the recognition of historical
conditioning presupposes an awareness of elements which heretofore were undetected, and it is, by this token, in some way a
surpassing of those conditions.

Our interpretation of gnoseological historicism is included in
our general conception of man. Man is a historical being, but
neither in the sense that everything in him is brought about
through the indeterminate flux of historicity, nor in the sense that
in each instance his being is pure happening and nothing more.
Man is born as such when the intentional structure appears, and in
it is included the spiritual proclivity. Both these events dredge the
channel through which this historicity flows. This channel is
determined in its form and direction, and it imposes on the
temporal flow the general conditions which define and characterize it as human process. There is ample provision, of course, for
variety, for many kinds of novelty, for unexpected occasions, and
even for chance, but all of this occurs within the limits which
decisively separate human historicity from any other existing or
possible kind of historicity. One might say that, in the image we
have used, the channel is like a river, which is subject to notable
changes in its flow; at times the waters stream peacefully through
the regular bed, at others the river is almost dry, though again it
may overflow into supplementary canals; at times it may flood,
converting the whole valley into its bed; or again the surface may
freeze, and the liquid mass may flow silently beneath it. The
possibilites of variation are many but, fundamentally, few things
are as permanent as the course of a river. The same occurs with the
course of human historicity, which is firmly channeled by the
essential structure of man, though at times it may seem to flow of
its own accord. Knowledge, whose primacy or priority was our
concern at the beginning of this book,[6] is a part, and even a

---

[6] Pp. 14–27.

privileged part, of this general ontological situation. The interpretation and evaluation of gnoseological historicism do not present serious difficulties—except those natural and common for the philosophy of knowledge—if we adhere to the structure of what is human as here set forth. This interpretation and evaluation may be derived as a consequence of what has been affirmed earlier and of what we shall state later.

Human historicity depends on intentional structure and spirituality, and on the conjunction of these two moments, which is to say that it depends on duality, which is fundamental for the complete man.

Just as the structure of the inorganic entity and of the living being are linked to special forms of historicity for each of those entities, so the intentional structure impresses its own particular style on historicity. The elementary fact of objective perception is visibly historical; in each instance, to perceive is to organize many earlier experiences around a nucleus, to mold them into this nucleus, and to take the complex thus constituted as the direct result of the perceptive apprehension. This result, in turn, will be incorporated later into the other perceptions of the same type.[7] On his own behalf, the subject not only accumulates these results and thus enriches the circle of "what is his," but he also gains in flexibility, power, operative capacity, and density, because in each instance he is becoming more of a subject to the extent that he acts as one. The strengthening of the subjective focus and the broadening of the area of its objectifications are correlative events of basic significance and of indubitably historical character. There is no reason to repeat here what was stated in the exposition on the intentional community,[8] but it is important to keep in mind that everything stated there redounds to defining human historicity in the broadest terms, and not merely as the advantageous use of the accumulation of past and present achievements by each individual. For, historicity is also indispensable in the transfer of these achievements to others, so that intentionality may become firmly established. This transmission, however, is not to be understood solely as that of discernible content but also as that of tendencies

[7] Pp. 27–44, especially pp. 35–44.
[8] Chapter ii.

and functional activities. This is the manner in which the law of typically human (or intentional) inheritance—the law of the transmission of acquired characteristics—is actualized. For each individual, the most important heritage is the experience of the group, though this heritage of a psychospiritual order does not come to him, as does that of the animal, through the direct lineage of his progenitors. Rather, it comes to him through action which one might say is circular or concentric; it comes through the confluence in him of everything experienced by those who are in some manner present to him, those who, through the succession of the ages, make up a continuous whole with his forebears, so that the community becomes an enormous collective subject reaching back to the most remote human origins. Even though one may accept a certain dose of "tradition" in animals—and we believe that one must accept it, at least in some cases—for example, communication of acquired experience which is passed on to descendents, this dose must necessarily be small, because of the inefficacy of the means of transmission, which are those of somatic imitation and not of the communication of significations. In an animal species or, better said, in a group, each one of its members must execute on its own the same experiences as the others; each generation reiterates an identical life program, except for the insensible change introduced by the evolution of the species. In the sphere proper and exclusive to man, the conquests of the generations accumulate, for the most part, and each heir receives (or in principle may receive) the import of the total heritage. If it is true to say of the organism that acquired characteristics are not inherited, it is also legitimate to say that, typically, human inheritance is inheritance of acquired characteristics. We insist on emphasizing this difference between man and animals, because at the same time that it is indicates a considerable separation between one and the other, it defines the character of the intentional inheritance in contradistinction to the organic inheritance and thereby underlines one of the principal traits characterizing human historicity. As was indicated, the individual is historical in the fundamental activities which provide him with an objectified world and which confirm him in his subjective nature, and he is therefore historical in what constitutes him as man. However, it is primarily in the community where this process of historical accumulation and elaboration functions on a grand scale, with each individual enjoying the benefits of the process, because it is in the community where the actions of coöperation, imitation, mutual encouragement, indoctrination, and correction by one another occur. Obviously we have omitted reference to linguistic communication, an exceptional factor and incomparable instrument which transfers enormous quantities of intentional substance in the degree of condensation and clarification convenient for each opportunity and purpose.

Within man there is an interchange back and forth between perception and memory, a movement which strenthens both of them. The experiences accumulated in the memory, as was affirmed, come to form part of each actual perception, and these, in turn, enrich the memory and provide new materials to complete and perfect new perceptions. The historical movement in these events cannot be doubted. Perhaps it is memory itself which offers one of the most obvious and vibrant instances of the historicity of man, because memory is sediment of the past. The animal *mneme,* even in its most strictly psychical aspect, is unable to reach objective delineation, which is itself inseparable from the intentional function. We do not know for sure what qualities memory assumes in animals, although it is important for much of their behavior, especially for those accepted as "intelligent." But the strict possession of an objectified and separable recollection, of its conscious actualization, are unimaginable outside the intentional mechanism. *Mneme* takes on a completely new nature and a decisive outreach in the construction of what is human, though it is probably parallel to the historicity of everything that is real, with its dark beginnings presupposed in the inorganic and then becoming evident in the functionality of organic substance, whereas it is also an important element in animal psychism. It is in a totally new form, however, that intentionality molds what will later become mnemonic material; this is done as much by objective delineation as by tying the material solidly to a subject who is conscious of it, who organizes it, and who converts it into the foundation of his being and thereby constitutes the vast inner perspective on the basis of which he operates as a subject. The transition from the momentary subject to the permanent self depends on the existence of the mnemonic storehouse, and, because of it, consciousness is not a series of discontinued, uncommunicated instants, each of which passes into oblivion when another appears on the scene. Undoubtedly the differing profiles of each personality are given potentially with the original propensities and qualities of each subject. However, the body of the subjectivity, the dense, throbbing context which converts each individual into a living, psychospiritual reality, when seen from within, is that consciousness which, from the present, extends into the past and makes a single thing of all its essential contents—one tightly interwoven world, the private universe of each individual, the perspective where the self recognizes and encounters itself, because it is its own creation and it is not comparable to that of any other. That world of living and essential recall is the one made of what we have known, loved or hated, built or left unfinished. Everything in it is illuminated or shaded; beside the seductive, joyful, or melancholy images, the spectrum of our omissions, our mistakes, and our failures dwells in it. It is not in any sense a cold, impassive museum, a gallery of frigid forms. It is, rather, a living whole, trembling with the vibration of the affections and judged in the light of its evaluations. When needed, and with effort, we are able to extract pictures of reality or series of thoughts from this complex; we then refer its contents to what is outside of us, by ridding them of their subjective tie, and in this manner we impose on them an impersonal significance. In its spontaneous stratification, however, in its genuine configurations, in the arrangement and corresponding emphasis of its levels, this world is concrete subjectivity, elaboration of the self to the self's own measure; everything outside of it comes to have its echo in the inner vault that is an inseparable accompaniment of the self. What the world is, as organized according to its own principles when the gaze is directed to that outer world, becomes a selective and colored summary when the gaze is directed to the inner world; it becomes a version in keeping with the molds of subjectivity. The world is converted into a biography. Next to the pure self it is what is most intimate and what is unique to each one; it is undecipherable in itself and is manifested to us only through its own intermediacy; it is the history of each individual, at once past and present.

It would be an error to believe that human historicity is written exclusively on any one of the faces of man; every aspect of him participates in it, and each is founded and developed in temporal processes. A history of human feeling, for example, would be exceedingly interesting, and it would not lack those decisive turning points brought on by some collective movements which, later, incorporated some notable mutations into the common heritage, in the sense of deepening and purifying the feelings. Taking some examples at random, one can see that changes of this kind derive from religious revolutions (primitive Christianity, the Franciscan movement), from philosophical or literary schools (Stoicism, Provençal poetry, Petrarquism), and even from more recent movements, such as Romanticism, whose influence in the refining of emotions must be considered a contribution of extraordinary value. The magnitude of this contribution is provided by the first impression gained from the comparison of the emotive attitudes manifested in the literature of the eighteenth century with those manifested in romantic literature. Perhaps a better comparison might be found, however, with later literature in which the exaggeration and fever of the romantic period have subsided and a new delicacy and refinement remain which, as might be imagined, are not mere literary style or conventionalism, but a real purification of what is human, the actual culture of the emotional dimension strengthened by the inclusion of ehtical and aesthetic elements. To be sure, such movements are not the expressions of occasional explosions, of which they themselves are the immediate cause, but they are condensations of scattered aspirations which find in these movements the occasion for adequate expression.

When referring to the community, we have taken into consideration primarily the effect of the communal upon the individual. The community is a uniting of individuals and also has a life of its own which engages yet goes beyond the life of its components, even though every collective event, to the extent that it is an event of consciousness, has no more true reality than is contained in the only consciousness which exists—the individual consciousness. This is not the proper place to elaborate on the complicated phenomena of what might be called communal historicity. It is sufficient to point out in passing that the acceleration of processes seems to be a rule or a law. This acceleration of processes is the gradual increase in rhythm or "tempo" with which the procedures of transformation occur because of the influence of the enriching of intentional accumulation. This necessarily produces a gradual increase in analytical refinement in the perception of things, and consequently makes possible unsuspected syntheses, which sometimes are arranged in graded series and sometimes occasion sudden and revolutionary innovations. Such acceleration is not found in equal measure in all communities, for some give the appearance of stability whereas others show a rapid increase in the readiness for changes and in their speed. More than once this has led to denying historicity to some collectives while attributing a large measure to others. The culture of the West gives evidence of a great acceleration, and, lately, through the prodigious effect of contagion, it has imposed this on most of the Westernized world, which is practically the whole world,[9] though the degree of Westernization differs from place to place. Another rule or law, if such is allowed, would be that of the progressive intensification of collective consciousnesses. This phenomenon is linked to the former by various bonds, and it consists in solidly implanting the communal element in the individual consciousnesses with ever-increasing energy. This communal element is an intimate experience of a common essence, solidarity of interests and ideals—an identity in historical destiny. The principal concern in these collective consciousnesses is for each individual, as a member of the group, to come to feel, not that he is a being who passively lives history, but that he is an agent responsible for historical becoming, an effective subject and protagonist of history. In the present crisis, man's decision to direct history in an active and even in a planned fashion, will probably have an increasingly greater effect, though he has not yet found the manner to channel such purposes into the concordant and harmonious directions demanded by the universal interchange of interests and the unification of the world brought about by technical advance.

The role of generations which Ortega y Gasset has emphasized with great zeal and insight takes on much importance in the

---

[9] Josiah Royce in *The Problem of Christianity* (New York: Macmillan, 1913), Lecture VIII, points out that "this law of constantly accelerating change promises to dominate the most essential interests of civilization in the near future."

collective dynamic.[10] Another important historical factor seems to be that of the rights, lefts, and centers. If the generations are categories with a biological root, these others are more strictly psychological, and undoubtedly they give form to three postures which are so permanent that they give shape to human types. In contemporary struggles, issues have emerged which tend to blur the clear profiles by which the rights and lefts had been previously defined. Authoritarianism, which previously seemed to be a characteristic condition of the right, is now a trait of positions proclaimed as the avantgarde of the left. Yet perhaps this confusion of issues is not as much of our own day as it may seem. What is decisive in these three postures is the tendency, on the right, to conserve and defend the existing situation, on the left, to innovate and change, and in the center, to interweave both in differing situations of compromise or conciliation, which at times lean to the right and at times to the left. This scheme is exceedingly sketchy and rough, and it has an approximation value only. To give a complete account of the matter, one would have to enter into distinctions which are more appropriate elsewhere.[11] One needs to recognize, for example, that frequently the right does not want to preserve the present situation, rather it wants to restore one that lies behind; or it may well seek to impose apparently new situations in which the elements of the past are disguised and mixed with others that are apparently or actually new. It is quite

[10] The excellent work of Julián Marías, *El método histórico de las generaciones* (Madrid: Revista de Occidente, 1949) is concerned with the general problem of generations with particular reference to the thesis of Ortega y Gasset.

[11] That is, in the doctrine of the cultural subject, an aspect of the theory of culture. Right, left, and center are categories whose ideals or pure determination must undoubtedly be attempted, but in practice they become relative, and they are shaded in many ways which should be studied. At times, exaggerated forms of rightism or leftism are properly seen as manifestations of an extreme utopianism, in which the extremism is basic and the content is secondary, which explains the jump from the most violent right to the most daring left and vice versa. The categories of evolution, revolution, restoration, and the like play a decisive role in the above-mentioned categories and in their predominance in any given situation, for they are not exclusively political-social, but hold for every kind of cultural process and, therefore, must be examined also in the theory of culture.

common for every man, on the basis of temperament, character, education, or class to assume, in general, one of these three positions with respect to several or almost all lines of collective and cultural action. However, it is not exceptional that contrary directions should dwell in the same individual, with leanings to the right in some cultural areas (for example, in politics or religion), accompanied by leanings to the left in others (aesthetics, economics). The three postures exercise necessary functions in the regular historical advance. On its own, the right would impose a state of immobility and stagnation (or of regression), which in the long run would bring about the desiccation and eventual death of the realities which it seeks to preserve. The left, without the counterbalance of the right, would convert the process into a never-resting motion, into constant innovation for the sake of innovation, a giddy and destructive course which would deny everything that was gained as soon as it had been obtained. The center lacks content of its own, for it is no more than conciliation, in various proportions, of the other two postures. In each case, however, this tends to count as the positive reality, for it is exceptional that the right or the left should be completely victorious, and even when one of them is triumphant, it tends, in turn, to split into a right, center, and left as it confronts historical responsibility on its own. Thus, in normal situations, the center defends the existing realities, but only partly, without seizing upon them—to do so would convert it into the right—and therefore it shifts toward the direction indicated by the left, though this does not mean that it can be labeled as leftist, for the leftist tendency is one of pure innovation. Neither the right nor the left are ever present in a pure state, that is, as total conservation or total innovation; yet in each historical constellation it is possible to apply these categories in order to under the events, as long as one allows them a convenient elasticity.

What exists, whether good or bad, is ordinarily a more or less solid reality, an "order." Change or innovation, so far as it is desired or in process, is the destruction of the reigning order, though it is not yet another order. It is, therefore, "disorder." What is established and well rooted has a strength of its own, with an "authority" which is in some sense "oppression." The innovating desire contradicts this authority, opposes the oppression and as it sets forth its goals in an autonomous form, is "liberty." What exists appears necessarily as a contradiction of the new demands, either because it draws together and systematizes interests fought by other interests which are gaining strength or because it is seen as standing below the levels reached by the cultural conscience (in the juristic-social, the aesthetic, the cognitive). For example, present conditions will be judged as "unjust" in the light of the demands which social advance esteems to be "just." From here arise the well-known oppositions between order and disorder, between authority and liberty, between cultural realities that are entrenched and mummified and others that seek to replace them (as when standing legislation is felt by many to be "unjust," and when there is a desire to replace it by laws which are "more just"). The right and the left—that is, the conserving and the innovating moments—ascribe a positive value to what is of concern to each and a negative value to what is not. Not only are they in their right in proceeding in this fashion, but the procedure is indispensable for a sane historical life endowed with the tensions capable of shaking or mobilizing it, without which this life would be inconceivable. These oppositions are consequences of the limitation and partiality of men. Because of the human situation and the character of the historical process derived from it, the one great task can be accomplished in depth only if individuals or groups live the partial aspects of the total task in a profound way. To say it another way, they portion out the great, common obligation which is being achieved gradually through the permanent contraposition which is itself a dialectical integration and collaboration. A neutral and dispassionate evaluation discovers that true order requires an element of change, of temporary disorder which serves to perfect it, and that authority needs liberty if it is to continue being legitimate authority, supported by the general consensus—rather than by violence and tyranny—and that what appeared yesterday to be just must now open up to a broader concept of justice. Conceived in simple and comprehensive terms: Leftist tendencies incorporate the necessity to surpass what has been achieved, and they prevent the community and the culture from becoming stagnant, ossified, and dead historically; rightest tendencies prevent the culture and the community from dissolving or from falling over a precipice by insisting on the value of the obtained goods.

The historicity of man, of the community, and of culture, therefore, imply a progression which is related to everything that has been obtained, and it rests on these achievements in order to surpass them and even to deny them. Since conservation as well as innovation are present in full historicity—the former concerned with history that is complete, and the latter with history in the making or yet to be—it is strange that many times it appears that the meaning of history as well as the meaning of what is "traditional" are exclusive attributes of rightist and conservative postures. Nothing could be more erroneous, because these postures grasp only one half of real and true historicity. This, however, can be explained, because the great body of completed history is undoubtedly more visible than the daily forgings of history—to say nothing of future history, which is nonexistent as present reality although it is foreseeable and, fortunately, even inevitable, because of man's constitutive historicity, which necessarily will continue to unfold, until the planet explodes or, rigid with cold, whirls through space, the immense sepulchre of an extinct humanity. Historical meaning is incomplete and even ignores the living and creative actuality in historicity if it has neither an eye for the intensity of each instant nor an imagination to grasp the perspective of future history. As for tradition, the great tradition of man is not that he has achieved these special things on a determinate occasion, but rather that he has done different things at different seasons; and this, therefore, would go against his tradition if he did not continue to do yet other different things on still other different occasions. Historicism and traditionalism of short outreach almost contradict what these names proclaim, and the names actually come to be the disguises of an "ism" that piously sanctifies the past.[12]

This pious, sanctification-of-the-past is antihistorical; it consists in extracting some tendencies or sections from history and attrib-

---

[12] [Romero coins the word "pasatismo" to express the concept thus interpreted.—Trans.]

uting to them an exemplary or absolute meaning which ignores their historical conditioning, their temporal relativism. This emphasis is ordinarily executed with an element of conscious or unconscious deception, illusion, or myth-making: for example, the Greeks were a nation of Platos and Phidiases; all medieval knights were the valiant champions Don Quijote conceived them to be; the conquistadors came to America exclusively to civilize it and proclaim the Christian faith. The counterpart of this pious sanctification-of-the-past—the all but complete rejection of the past which was practiced many times in the eighteenth century—is equally antihistorical. A complete historicism alone is able to understand and accept full historicity, to make privileged exceptions of none of the fragments of the past, present, or future through denial of their historical conditioning. Therefore, it must not only understand and explain, historically, the antihistoricist buds of a "traditionalist" pseudohistoricism but also the condemnation and ridicule of the past. Yet, because of a contradiction which is very much in the nature of man, a clairvoyant historicism and an acting historicity rarely go hand in hand. To see historically is to see according to a temporal *relativization;* to work historically usually presupposes working *absolutely,* without perceiving the historical relativity of one's own action, which in many cases would put a damper on it, depriving it of impetus and conviction as it introduces into the action an element of reserve and even of skepticism. The conciliation of comprehensive historicism and influential participation in the historical process is not impossible, but it is the private possession of only a few people. What is common here, as in most other things, is separation and fragmentation. It is for some to understand history and for others to construct it through their acts.

As a human product, objectified culture has a historicity which largely depends on the objectivity of man himself, but in this historicity special resources from each cultural section also function. Values in themselves are not historical, but their introduction into the human realm through cultural awareness and development is historical. This awareness and development in the area corresponding to each value is historical, as are the inflections which impose on the general course of culture the obvious predominance of a single value or of a determined constellation of values in a given situation. In the following recapitulation it is necessary for us to refer to matters discussed before.

From the beginning, the historicity of the human community and of culture has been seen in such a light that whereas the nonhuman reality has been studied in systematic and nonhistorical sciences, sociocultural phenomena usually have been recorded scientifically in historiographical terms. The great attempts in the nonhistoriographical study of societies and cultures appear in Positivism with the development of sociology, which in that day was extended until it constituted a more or less complete theory of culture. Since that time, and in various ways, a spreading opinion has been that it is legitimate and even necessary for each branch of culture to create a systematic science alongside the corresponding historiographical discipline. As yet, however, little progress has been made in this direction. Not only is there a continued preponderance of historical examination bound to the concrete succession of events, with each segment of culture taken separately, but also these segments seem to take on their true meaning only when they are referred to the total becoming of human culture, whose fundamental framework is described in what is commonly known as "history."

Each order of cultural reality has a historical succession which is exclusive to it. Not only is there a difference in the human interests and ideals to which each of these orders correspond, but there is also a difference in the barriers which must be overcome and the matter which must be domesticated.

The appearance of persons gifted with powerful intelligence is decisive on the level of philosophical knowledge, where the free play of ideas predominates. Not everything, however, is linked to the chance that exceptional minds may emerge, because certain intellectual experiences must be completed in order to provide for the possibility of others. On the other hand, if the contribution of the genius finds acceptance it is widely spread, and if not it remains paralyzed and circumscribed. This depends on whether the contemporaries are in a condition to understand and take advantage of this contribution. Let us take, as an example, the thesis of the flux and mobility of being, that was premature with Heraclitus and therefore condemned, in its own day, to remain a solitary episode, hemmed in by the dominating concepts of the stability and solidity of being. Much later, in the Romanticism of the nineteenth century, it gathered strength and acceptance, and in the thought of our day it is gaining increasing predominance and authority. Many issues, which cannot be listed here, influence the rhythm and orientation of philosophical processes. It is sufficient to point to the bonds that philosophy has with religion, science, and politics, each of which introduces special modes in the formation of philosophical theories and in the constitution of "schools" —the element that crystallizes and dogmatizes, because of the stabilizing power which everything that is institutionally organized tends to develop. The extreme case occurs when a great social body embraces a philosophy (Scholasticism, Marxism) as canonical doctrine. Scientific knowledge of reality obeys another set of conditions, which ascribes a different historical procedure to it through the application of the effective examination of things. This requires many concurrent efforts as well as the use of technical resources, whose existence is at the same time the result of scientific progress. These resources are immediately directed back into science, causing further advance, so that the special historicity of technology coincides partly with that of science. A significant factor in the development of cognitive processes is the contrast and struggle of its theses with others which may dominate in the same area or in a similar or tangent territory (conflicts between religion, philosophy, and science). This occurs in such a way that the modes of historicity and the development of these different lines are complicated in many instances by intromissions, difficulties, stimulations or predominant factors, which lead to exceedingly diverse situations.

A general trait of the cognitive is a constant enriching with a gradual correction and accumulation. Knowledge is set forth as an unlimited task, with a progressive proliferation of problems. For, at the same time that man stores up learning, he becomes more aware of his ignorance. In sharp contrast, cultural activity on the level of the arts seems to reach an insuperable perfection in many instances in the course of history, and the passing of time neither affects the dignity of its most eminent creations nor imposes on them those corrections which are inevitable on the level of knowledge. Yet this cultural activity is capable of placing, successively, alongside these works others of equal perfection, in its permanent attempt to achieve all aesthetic possibilities, that is, to colonize completely the whole of reality in an aesthetic fashion. In knowledge, man has totality before him, and though it is invisible in many sections, he struggles to transcribe it in conceptual expressions. Genius does not suffice to subdue this infinite matter, which in part is foreign to it. In addition the task is a progressive conquest without rest and without end. The artist elaborates an element that is within himself and then attempts to implant it, as a form, in matter that is external to him, but this matter is no more than the small part of reality he needs to give full objectivity to his inner purposes. This divergence in respective natures justifies why art, other than the obvious historicity of knowledge manifest in its progressive accumulation and constant corrections, should enjoy an apparent autonomy with respect to history and time, since it offers perfect achievements in almost every age. But in many aspects art also lives submerged in history. The will-to-give-form makes infinite attempts before attaining the great creations, and many attempts are lost without leaving a trace; generally, this advantage is in its favor—the will-to-give-form is much more primitive and common than is the desire for critical and reflexive knowledge. From the beginning this will is identified with the differentiated and organized constitution of the inner reality of man, with the recognition of and emphasis on what is perceived or imagined—that is, it is identified with the struggle to introduce order and clarity into the primeval mists of consciousness. The great artist is not an anomalous being who is an incomprehensible exception. On the contrary, for, among all the great developers of culture he is the one who has the most ancient heritage, since he is the natural heir of that universal artist who was and continues to be man, indeed every man, to the extent that he takes the formless material of the preintentional psyche and constructs his own world as a harmonious order of forms. In this task, the conscious and lucid distinction between the true and the false—subtle and difficult in many instances—will come later and is even obscured by the propensity of the spontaneous creations of the will-to-give-form to assert themselves, to appear as referring to realities, as in fables and myths. The same will-to-give-form and expression—a consequence or manifestation of intentionality—is found in the roots of language, which, because of its sources, is itself close to artistic expressiveness and to myth. The historicity of language arises from elements of a quite different kind and, to a large degree, it is parallel to the historicity of human psychism. The growing mass of objectifications enlarges it; modes of community polish it and make it more flexible; physiological and psychological factors intervene, respectively, in phonetic and semantic changes; there is a continual decantation into everyday talk of the refinements achieved in reflective knowledge. Great writers also contribute their genius for language, which little by little leaves a residue in everyone's language. One should not exclude from this historicity some modification and disturbance caused by the appearance of new factors, capable of influences previously unknown. For example, the practice of reading, which is becoming ever more common, may in the long run greatly detract from the plasticity and continuous change of a language—conditions which stem primarily from a spoken and heard language—because written expression, always more rigid and conventional than oral expression, is continuously before the speaker as a model or a standard. Language is a most complex and many-faceted event, the conveyor of all individual and collective life, and the promoter of that life, and it becomes a universal and elastic environment surrounding man. All human becoming is reflected in it, shaping the language in keeping with its own needs and according to its demands.

Primarily as examples, these comments should suffice to recall the obvious fact of the historicity of culture, because no manifestation of culture eludes it. In its relationship with value, culture implies the progressive embodiment of values in creations which seek to incorporate them to a degree that is ever more inclusive and refined. Many times the apprehension of values is collective or social, and at other times it occurs through the native brilliance of unique individuals. Even in the latter instances, however, the community has the final word, because its approval permits the personal accomplishment in which the value is given to take on a truly cultural existence, whereas indifference of the community relegates the accomplishment to be little more than an episode without effect or efficacy in the life of the discoverer. It frequently happened that magnificent discoveries have had to bide their time patiently, ignored and practically nonexistent until social consciousness on its own, with developing maturity, or perhaps stimulated by a group of watchful spirits, was in a condition to understand them and add them to the collective treasure.

As an unperceived mediator of immeasurable power between man and culture, there occurs the formation of what is referred to as a "world view." This is a vision and evaluation of life and of the world, interwoven with every kind of psychical and spiritual element, which accompanies and enfolds every man—individually, with his own characteristics and with nuances which depend on his originality, as well as collectively, including the major groups of mankind and the minor groups on many different levels. Although world views tend to assume elements of relative fixedness, taken together they have a temporal character. If we speak of great historical periods, it is primarily because we detect certain temporal alterations in the world view and in life also. Undoubtedly these alterations occur in unperceived variations, yet they can be reduced to more or less definite paths in the same sense that the continuity of the course of the individual life does not prevent one from identifying in it the periods of infancy, adolescence, youth, and adulthood. The world view, with its historicity, is one of the elements in the general historicity of culture. Sometimes it forcefully demands that culture adapt itself to the world view; at others it introduces new meanings into certain cultural realities which are apparently intact, or it decrees the actual end of others, which seem to continue to live though they may be no more than empty shells. It is like a historical atmosphere which, from the outside, imposes its special seal on all culture, conferring upon it a unity of style and in many cases a unanimous meaning. One might consider, as an example, the universality of the religious element in medieval culture.

In the historical process of culture, three great topics can be distinguished: the reflection of the historicity of man upon his cultural activity, the specific historicity of culture itself, and the repercussion of this cultural historicity upon that of man. These are themes that cannot be excluded from an anthropological framework, but their thorough examination is more properly located in the theory of culture. Concerning the first two, we have already said in the preceding pages what is necessary. As to the third, a few words need to be added, though almost everything we have to say has already been expressed in earlier passages of this book or can be derived directly from them.[13]

As we have seen, the historicity of culture takes on a character that differs with each branch of culture considered. There are various kinds of relationships between man—as a creator—and what he creates. In some instances the creative action is literally collective (for example, language) ; in others it is collective in a secondary or metaphorical sense, as when the product takes on cultural significance more from communal acceptance or adoption than through creation (refrains, strictly "popular" songs) ; in still others it is personal, as in great philosophical, artistic, and technical achievements. Even in these matters, one can generally see that if objective culture and the individual are taken separately, the former is of considerably greater import than the latter. In effect, great as the linguistic genius of any individual may be, the body of language which is at his disposal and which is the creation of countless generations, infinitely surpasses his genius. Outstanding as one's philosophical, scientific, artistic, and technical ability may be, the treasure already contained in these various areas surpasses it, even though his ability may be capable of extraordinary outreach and revolutionary novelty. This ability could never completely annul what had been achieved, nor would it have been feasible without the corresponding tradition. Recapitulated in culture, we find, on the one hand, the common attainments of all and, on the other, the exceptional attainments of outstanding people. This condition brings about the superiority of the level of the former over the latter. The individual's contact and association with culture serves as a stimulation; he becomes attuned to an objective reality which, in each of its aspects, surpasses his corresponding psychospiritual ability, though one may need to allow for exceptions whose import would need to be examined in each case. The result is an acceleration of the historical rhythm of the individual, an ascent from his private historicity to the cultural complex. Individual processes are multiplied and made more pliable through stimulation, through the appearance of new elements, and even through the strong pressure of the existing culture. This has been referred to in speaking of the influence of

[13] Chapter ii and pp. 117–121.

the community and of culture on man,[14] but we must insist upon it now in order to emphasize the manner in which individual historicity increases its "tempo," sometimes gradually and sometimes in leaps and bounds, through the influence of culture. By way of summary it can be stated that the historicity of the individual is accelerated continuously through his bond with objective culture, with benefit for each individuality taken separately. Nonetheless this does not contradict the fact that the cultural advance occurs through the contribution of the whole group: on the part of some—the majority—through the mere act of living culturally, thereby renewing the common good, and on the part of others—the minority, the creators, discoverers, or innovators—the unique conquests which are gradually incorporated into culture.

Let us turn now to an important and difficult matter. Duality is characteristic of the total or complete man and is the indwelling in him of mere intentionality and spirituality, two principles or structures of opposing traits. The tensions between these two principles exercise a powerful influence on the historicity of the individual and of groups and constitute, perhaps, the principal factor in the total historicity of the species, in the vast process which one has in mind when one speaks of "history."

For the individual, the functioning of mere intentionality is already decidedly historical. As we attempted to show,[15] each stratum of reality reveals an increase in its processes compared with the processes in the stratum which precedes it and upon which it is implanted. Intentionality presupposes a decided increase in the rhythm of history—not only because of the acceleration of the processes, but also because of the intensification of the awareness of what has happened, that is, the awareness of the presence of the past in the present, which is the condition of all historicity. The appearance of the spirit brings with it a new growth in historicity in the two respects that have been indicated: the processes themselves and the constant, living actuality of what has transpired. Spiritual acts, because of their intensity and their expansive or radiating character, confirm the subject in his being, contribute to his own organization, and broaden his field of action.

[14] Chapters ii and iii.
[15] Pp. 59–70.

Through its activity, the self is linked to a great number of objects, many of which are distant, and in this manner it is in communication with extensive areas of totality. The triumph of the spiritual principle would not be, properly speaking, a historical task—a process subject to certain temporal rhythms with a progressive accumulation of the results—if it did not bring about the colonization of the nonspiritual by the spirit. In the individual, the conflicts between the two moments are not rare, and they would be manifest with a greater frequency if the level achieved by the community in each instant did not resolve many of them for him beforehand. In effect, every community, in each of its stages, imposes upon its members a line of conduct which obliges them to observe a typical manner of reconciling the nonspiritual with the spiritual in such a way that the major part of the actual, felt conflicts occur in the following two ways: One may either turn one's back on the community, that is, one may ignore its regulations, withdrawing from its consensus, usually covertly or deceptively; this usually happens when the conflict is one that has already been overcome by the communal average. Or, if the conflict is above the communal average, then the spiritual principle affirms a norm which the community has not as yet made its own, but which some individuals accept imperatively as necessary and right. Individual demands of this last kind are those that gradually raise the level of the community when, little by little, they are accepted by the majority, thus constituting ever higher levels. Then, again from these, additional important demands emerge which, in turn, tend to promote a higher average level. Generally speaking, the conflict between the nonspiritual and the spiritual is often resolved beforehand for the individual, and for all practical purposes it is nonexistent; but this is because before this time the throbbing conflict, the difficult contradiction, found a solution which was expressed later in a tacit norm of the general consensus which came to be accepted regularly without resistance. In other instances it may be a rebellion of the nonspiritual element, which rejects the accepted solution in the community, whereas in others it is the requirement of spiritual demands which are more pure and exacting than those ordinarily admitted by the group at this particular stage. It is primarily the latter which "make history," thrusting reality forward in a procession which was already being obscurely structured, when life first emerged above inert matter or perhaps when the processes in the physical order began to diversify and structure material reality, preparing the conditions which eventually made life possible.

The appearance of each form of reality results in an act of colonization.[16] The inferior level is used by the superior level, which obliges the former to yield to its ways and to accept its goals. With intentionality, the colonizing aspect becomes conscious and capable of clear, intelligent, and planned action. All colonization presupposes conflict, because it is never accomplished without resistance from the colonized level. In the colonization of the intentional by the spiritual, this conflict takes on special characteristics. In the first place, both terms are conscious and, as principles, they are opposed as if though fencing with their reason and their respective justifications. Above the spontaneous and contradicting impetus of one and the other rides the struggle of arguments which duplicates, or at least complicates, the clash. In the second place, it is not, as in previous situations, a matter of one particularism which attempts to subject to itself another particularism of a lower hierarchy, rather it is a universalist rule which seeks to establish itself and to predominate above the most elevated form of particularism, that is, intentionality. The first of these two conditions adds risks and difficulties to spiritual colonization; the supremacy of the spirit is opposed by the native energy of the nonspiritual, as well as by its justifications, arguments that are more or less true, and the confused tangle of its maskings. The second condition confers on the spirit its specific strength, the conviction of its absolute worth, the security of establishing an instance that is definitive and beyond appeal, yet which is also destined to set forth and protect the legitimate rights of the nonspiritual. In the order of events, the spirit embodies a historicity of the highest level because it bears within itself the duty of making reality spiritual, of pressing its molds upon reality. It aspires to linguistic perfection—that everything might be said; to aesthetic perfection—that all possibilities in the realm of the arts might be achieved; to cognitive and ethical perfection and all others. These aspirations, however, involve tasks and operations in

---

[16] Pp. 59–70.

time; they are not achieved in instantaneous acts, in trances or ecstasies, in reverent and passive submission to supreme values, but through a hard-working zeal which manipulates an indifferent or hostile reality, molding it, exalting it, converting it into the dwelling place of meaning. The impression of the interminability of the task accompanies the task itself, which is necessarily historical and is identified with the life of the spirit. The struggle with the nonspiritual is not an unfortunate situation for the spirit or a state that we should lament or which might be some other way, even though many times this would appear so, rather it is something which stems from the nature of the real and from the specific nature of the spirit. The most magnificent conception of the inevitability of this situation is found in the metaphysics of Fichte, in which the absolute self, the highest reality, produces and separates from itself the non-self so that the self, which is pure activity and ethic, can actualize its essence. This essence would be annulled if the self were deprived of the resistances which provide the occasion to act, to develop the ethical aspect of the self, to be in actuality what it is in essence and possibility. And it does not cease thereby to be closely linked with the moving phrase of Lessing: "If God had the whole truth in his right hand, and in the left hand the ever-living desire to pursue it, even though this condemned us to perpetual error, and He would say to me, 'Choose one,' I would humbly reach out for the left hand, exclaiming, 'This one, Oh Father; for pure truth is for Thee alone.' "

Undoubtedly the historicity of the spirit has dimensions that are internal to it and concern it alone—for example, that which pertains to its modes of appearance. But its most effective historicity is unfolded in the process of the spiritualization of the remainder of reality, which is its own, unrenounceable mission. We know the spirit only as it emerges and dwells in man, as it is situated in a vast complex of a nonspiritual reality, as it is also closely linked to a special part of this reality, which constitutes the other half of man. If there are other species of spirits, free from all contact with a reality foreign to them as they placidly enjoy their sovereign perfection, they have little to do with the human spirit, an event limited to our planet and a being who fulfills his destiny upon it. Work, colonizing activity, is innate to this spiritual terrain; each one of its phases or faculties points to an aspect of reality which can and should be spiritually elaborated and possessed. As long as there is an enigma to clarify, an aesthetic possibility to be actualized, an evil to suppress, the spirit will find no rest except by denying itself. And it is obvious from the nature of reality that these tasks will never end. As the spirit becomes aware of its role and significance, it understands itself as having the leading role in human history. The mere functioning and the conflict of natural motives in the history of man leaves a trail of little significance, whereas the achievements and strivings of the spirit are retained and accumulated. Those thunderous events, whose spiritual content was little or nothing, pass on and are all but effaced, whereas the events sealed by the spirit, which in their own time seemed insignificant when compared with the volume and tumult of the others, are added to one another and come to form a consolidated whole which is the historical foundation for successive events. The historicity of the spirit is not blind like that of the other forms of reality; it is the vocation to and consciousness of being history, it is the very will to make history. And as there is no full, future historicity without the latent presence of the whole past in the present and the projection of the present into the future, the spirit, from its present, is continually concerned with the future and the past. It is concerned with the future in order to impose its own standard upon it effectively and with the past in order to become reacquainted with itself and to reëncounter itself therein. However, it is concerned not only with its own past reality but with every kind of reality, since the whole of reality is its predecessor as well as the setting for its drama.

XII

MEANING

Every voluntary act is necessarily endowed with mean-
ing for the one who performs the act or, at least, to the extent that
he acts. A voluntary act presupposes the perception or conception
of a goal or objective, the resolution of the will, and the selection
of the means or resources for reaching the goal or objective.
Meaning is not identified with any of these three elements; it
hovers above the act and comes to be the justification of the act for
the agent. Our will is neither resolved solely on the basis of
attention to the mere convenience or desirability of the goal or
objective, nor solely on the basis of the consciousness of its
accessibility—that is, to have at hand the means and resources to
achieve it—rather the resolution comes through the conjunction of
both elements. One decides to act when the achievement of the act
becomes desirable and possible, or, better said, when it is seen as
provided with both of these requirements, which work together in
order to confer meaning on the act. In other words, an act of a
hardly desirable purpose may have meaning, at some time, if there
is a great possibility of its achievement, and, inversely, an act with
a minimum of possibility for achievement may appear to be
meaningful if the desirability of the objective is maximum. Desirability is a necessary supposition for the will to resolve to act, but
this is also true of possibility, for the act conceived beforehand as
impossible would be a nonact. The awareness of impossibility, of
inevitable and accepted frustration, inhibits the will. We may

fervently desire to go to the moon, but, at present,[1] under the actual circumstances, we cannot imagine that the corresponding act has any meaning because it is manifestly nonrealizable since we cannot imagine it as a real act. We can visit our neighbor with the greatest ease, but we do not conceive of the act as endowed with meaning if we do not have the least interest in seeing him. The decision to act presupposes the attribution of meaning, which means that the combined magnitude of the desirability and possibility of the object is greater than that conceived for any other object which may appear on our horizon at that moment. The meaning to which we are referring is that which is associated with the voluntary actions of man. Naturally, it demands the existence of the act, whether actual and completed, or truncated and unsuccessful, yet always affirmed by the will and imagined before as possible. Basic to the act, if it is to take on meaning, is that its purpose must be presented with sufficient incentive to bring about decision, and that its possibility must be admitted. Error in either or both of these evaluations does not suppress the meaning of the act, though later it may show up as erroneous or ineffective. If someone passionately desires to go to the moon and believes that it is possible to reach it in a rocket or a plane, it may be that he will attempt the act and continue to consider it as endowed with meaning even after his failure, if he is still in a condition to be able to judge it. If a neighbor, whom we have rarely seen and who ordinarily is no bother, should burst forth with shouts in the midst of the night, we might rush over to his house to see if we could provide help in the face of imminent danger. And we would continue to believe that our action had meaning, even if it was distasteful and inopportune, because the neighbor was dreaming or entertaining friends.

The actual, true meaning belongs to the act that has been decided upon and undertaken (or decided upon and not undertaken because of some material hindrance), and not upon those false decisions which remain paralyzed and intended, because here the meaning falls upon the paralyzing decision. It might seem that several acts could have meaning simultaneously for a subject; but this is not so except in rare cases of chance selection between two

---

[1] [Written in 1951.]

or more acts which make a parallel appeal, and even here the meaning is arbitrarily attributed to the act which we decide upon, to which we give a real consistency, because we recognize that there is meaning in concretely deciding for one act and that constant shifting among various acts lacks meaning. In the other instances, when a specific motivation predominates and the corresponding act is decided upon, in that moment the others are eliminated from the actual meaning, though until that time the fulfillment of these other instances could be meaningfully foreseen. In effect, to carry through on one act in place of another whose motivation is more satisfactory and demanding would imply a negation of meaning, and, naturally, this never happens. The act that is decided upon and deferred constitutes a special kind of meaning which includes postponement; its motivation is actually split into that of the act itself and that of its postponement, and the same is true of its meaning.

Every act decided upon by the will necessarily has meaning; the meaning provides the justification of the act, and the act that is not justified for the agent cannot be conceived by him as an act of his own. It is obvious that this is just as valid for acts that take place in the inner reality of the subject as it is for those that are channeled into the external reality through expressions or other kinds of bodily action. The act for which we decide may be to think about some given matter, the resolution of a mathematical problem, or the correction of a bad habit. When we do not find meaning in a psychical operation, it is because it occurs causally and not purposefully. Examples are to be found in a vague dreaming, an arbitrary linking of ideas with no purpose, motivated only by association or by occasional stimuli.[2]

Let us examine some aspects of the relationship between the possibility of the act and its meaning in order to avoid any misunderstanding about what has been stated above. If the act is conceived as impossible, we will not decide to carry it out, for to undertake it strikes us as lacking in meaning. The act may be impossible in itself, but not appear as such to us because of an

[2] It is evident that acts of this kind, such as dreams, can have a particular "meaning," that is, a special significance, a special background, which is more or less hidden but decipherable. This kind of meaning, however, has nothing to do with that with which we are concerned.

error of evaluation; although the act may remain an unproductive intention, its achievement will appear to us as endowed with meaning. The situation is similar to what occurs when an unexpected hindrance brings an act to nought, although normally the act is possible. The meaning is not affected in either of the two situations because it is implanted in the act in keeping with the way the subject sees it and decides upon it, and it does not depend upon the real act, as it is frequently shaped through the intervention of circumstances or elements not taken into condideration. The attainment of the goal or objective may be extremely difficult, almost impossible; but at times, and for special reasons, because of the magnitude and importance of the achievement, the goal dazzles us and impresses itself upon us with such prestige that we are hindered from focusing on the remoteness of its attainment. Generally a balance exists between the degree of desirability and that of possibility, which in each instance makes up a single situation. Thus, an objective which is highly desirable but whose attainment is problematic has as much (or more) significance for the motivation of the act and its meaning as one that is easily attainable but less desirable. It is not essential that a difficult objective should deceive us about the probability of its attainment. A remote possibility, which is coolly understood and evaluated, justifies the act and gives meaning to it when the nature and scope of the goal tends to shrink and almost annul everything else, as when someone sentenced to life imprisonment decides to escape from a well-guarded jail. The clear perception of the inattainability of the goal, of the real impossibility of the act, prevents the act by showing that it lacks meaning. In all those cases in which acts are undertaken whose impossibility is obvious to the subject, either factors are at work which are causal in nature rather than final, or another parasitic goal, which is the one that actually confers meaning upon it, is added to the normal purpose of the act. Examples of this are to be found in extreme cases which have serious consequences for the agent, such as the demand to uphold and protect one's honor, the purpose of serving as an example, the desire for glory, or a disguised desire to commit suicide. Many times the actual purpose pursued is to find some way out of an unbearable situation. The meaning constitutes the inner justification of the act; the act which is decided upon and undertaken is, without exception, the one whose attainment has meaning for the agent in the instant in which he decides to do it.

It therefore becomes impossible for man, voluntarily, to perform acts without meaning. For him, meaningless acts are limited to those whose origin is merely causal, that is, without motivation, whether the causation is psychic or organic or whether it stems from external factors. External coercion leads to meaningless acts only when it is materially and directly causal in relation to us, as when someone voluntarily pushes us or makes us fall. Here, the act evidently has meaning for the one who gave the shove, but not for the one who received it and fell to the ground. It is a different matter if the coercion is directed against the will, because the will, even when it is constrained, cannot decide apart from meaning. If someone is forced by threats to perform an act which is repugnant to him and lacks meaning for him, the act nevertheless takes on a sharply defined meaning for him: to perform the act in order to avoid the injury that would come upon him if he did not do so. This justification of the act is sufficient—were it not so, the act would not be performed—but the impression of the meaninglessness of the imposed act subsists. Anyone forced to perform acts of this kind suffers in so doing; often it is this suffering which is sought when the acts are enforced, and it gives meaning to the act for the one who enforces it.

We never escape meaning in an action decided upon by the will, not even when it is compelled and forced, as has just been seen. Let us imagine the most unusual and absurd action, in sharp contradiction to the accepted mores, to our own particular interests, and to the values we respect—if we decide to perform that action it will be because we attribute meaning to it. There is no escape from this conclusion. The extreme case is that we should plan expressly to perform an action without meaning, but that purpose is in itself contradictory, because if we decide to undertake such action it will be because at that instant, to attempt a meaningless act takes on meaning for us. The practical joker who, with exaggerated gestures of affection, embraces the unknown person he bumps into upon turning a corner; someone who intentionally provides erroneous information to a lost traveler; a mischievous boy who drops a banana peeling on the sidewalk to cause some passer-by to slip; a person who throws rocks at a passing train or shoots at it with his shotgun—all these perform acts that are meaningful, acts which, to their own inner satisfaction, are fully justified, incomprehensible though they may appear to others when these acts are seen from the outside. The insane person, to the extent that his conscious life is not a completely disjointed obedience of blind impulses, performs acts with meaning. He finds himself secluded in his own particular world forged by his mental imbalance and out of adjustment with the normal world; his world is a realm of *sui generis* images and evaluations, whose black walls present occasional cracks and crevices through which we can observe and discover the inner connection and the key to demented acts, so we can find out what confers meaning upon them.

Generally speaking, although allowing for a few exceptions, we are capable of perceiving the meaning of any human act. The fundamental structure of the human psyche is one, and it is permanent. In the vast realm of that structure, each man marks out an area in which he ordinarily lives, the area of his most frequent and intense experiences, his interests, and his habitual evaluations. In addition, within the common human nature— which, more than a normal nature, is the whole of all possibilities given to man—habit shapes a special nature for each man. Everything we do not consider legitimate, convenient, proper, or acceptable for us, if it belongs in any way to the realm of the human, throbs within us at a greater or lesser distance from that psychical realm which our own particular manner of being, education, example, and habit have cut out and strengthened, thus shaping our everyday soul, our normal being. The landscapes of the psyche which we do not frequent surround those that we ordinarily inhabit, though we sometimes walk through the former when a powerful motive breaks down our normal inhibitions and thrusts us into this new territory. An excessive ambition, terror, a sudden passion can shift the center of a clean, ordered life into dark recesses of meanness and disgrace. Yet, certain stirrings can uncover bright horizons of ideals and values for someone who never suspected them. Even those regions of the psyche which we are radically prohibited from entering to establish our everyday activities are accessible to us for understanding their corresponding meanings. If the great pages of history are more than the recording of physical events or of the succession of movements of human bodies, it is because we are capable of grasping the meaning of historical events, different as they may be from the events of our own existence and of the meaning which is embodied in them. The novel and the theater have elaborated a prodigious gallery of human portraits, from the most abject to the most lofty, relentlessly exploring even the remote boundaries of human nature, showing it in every imaginable situation. The purpose behind this certainly has not been to benefit a reduced circle of readers or spectators, who are interested only in counterparts shaped by poetic imagination and who limit their horizon to successes and destinies which accord with their own. Rather, they have depended on the universal capacity for the comprehension of meaning which is to be found in every man. What tends to appear as the incomprehension of meaning, which we express when we say that "we do not understand" some given behavior or that some person's act "has no meaning," is, rather, the rejection of the value positions assumed by the respective agents. It is as if we affirmed that under similar circumstances we would have decided to act in a different manner. Therefore it is not a matter of mere comprehension, but of confrontation with conduct which is alien to what we would have chosen in the same case. In addition, the position of each individual with respect to the acts of others is quite different, once we set aside apprehension of meaning in the strict sense, which is universal, though it may fall short of this. We do not always reject or minimize the act of another individual which at present we would not perform under similar circumstances or which might be frankly impossible. On the contrary, frequently we judge the act of another individual to be of much greater value than our own act performed under equivalent circumstances. This problem would not be brought up here were it not closely linked to another, that of the meaning of life—a meaning which does not depend on each act having its own separate meaning, which is inevitable. When, compared to a similar act of our own, we have a high regard for the act of someone else, it is usually because we have referred to the other individual's act to an elevated level, to behavior that implies a value superior to that on which our own act rests. We have such an example in a self-denying or courageous act which we do not feel capable of performing. There might seem to be exceptions as when someone attributes more courage to a brutal and unmerciful act of another individual than he does to his own more moderate and restrained act. But in such instances, what is depreciated is timidity, formal obedience to conventions, or cowardice in the light of an act performed immediately and daringly.

Rickert probably belongs to those philosophers who have given most attention to the notion of meaning, assigning to it an important role in their philosophy. From one point of view, Rickert's philosophy is primarily a doctrine of values and meaning; or, seen from another point of view, a theory of world views elaborated on the basis of the inseparable notions of meaning and value. Rickert distinguishes three realms or sections in totality: sensible and temporal reality, values, and meaning. The realm of meaning—the "third realm"—is the intermediary member between the other two, the bond that unites them in a unique fashion, yet neither destroys the autonomy of one or the other, nor fuses them into one. The two subsist in their own particular nature while the third remains only the bond that unites them. The resulting synthesis is as much a joining together as it is a separation of the temporally real from the valuable, which is nonreal and alien to time. To understand totality to be one, it is necessary to have a bond uniting temporal existence and value. This uniting element, however, does not subsist on its own as is true of real objects and processes and nonreal value. It is only the moment connecting one realm to the other. Although lacking the autonomy of the orders it links, the realm of meaning is more of an inner experience, closer to us, and more habitual than the others; we live it in a manner that is more intimate and warm. In Rickert's opinion, the function of philosophy is to provide clarifications of the meaning of life. Therefore, philosophy is obliged to investigate meaning in general, and meaning can neither be found in mere real being nor in pure values, when these are considered separately. It is therefore the joining of these two orders which must be investigated because it is here that meaning resides. In itself, life is a complex of real acts—taken as a whole, it is something real. Meaning, however, refers to value, is determined according to it, and can only be thought of as related to value; and undoubtedly it is something nonreal, just as value is. Values are apprehended primarily as they are implanted in realities, as qualities of valuable realities, and there are two kinds of these—goods and evaluations, or attributions of value. An object in which value resides is called a good; to understand how value is added to the object and converts it into a good we must go back to the act by which value is incorporated. The meaning of life undoubtedly consists in the "achievement" of values; but one must neither interpret this from a subjectivist point of view nor from the point of view of the psychology of valuing. In order to avoid this difficulty or misunderstanding one must keep in mind that psychology is a descriptive science addressed to the real, to processes that are given exclusively in time, and therefore, does neither deal with value in itself, nor with valuations so far as they refer to pure value. Because of their nonreality and their nontemporality, these cases remain beyond the scope of this science. The inquiry into meaning is foreign to psychological considerations because meaning is connected with both the realm of the real and that of value, and psychology does not have access to that kind of consideration. Meaning is the signification of the act to the extent that it is the affirmation of a position concerning a value, and it is therefore as different from the real act, the actual fiber of the act, as it is from the value to which it points. Let us take as an example a cognitive good—a true judgment. In the first place, judgment is the real act of judging, an act which the subject does in time. In the second place, we also refer to something quite different as a judgment; this is the nontemporal structure, transcending the subject, which stands independently of the actual acts of thinking or judging— that which is thought in the corresponding acts of judgment. The first belongs to the sphere of real being, the second to that of nonreal value. The immanent meaning is neither the real act nor the nonreal value; it is not a psychical event nor a transcendent ideality. It is, rather, the conjunction of the two, a conjunction which relates the two without adding them together, without fusing them. The meaning is internal to the act, a part of the third realm that is in it. Thus emerges a third meaning to the word judgment, in which the two earlier meanings are associated. For our present purposes these comments on Rickert's position are enough for keeping in mind his explanation of meaning and of the significance he assigns to it when he makes of it a third realm in which the order of the temporally real and of values are harmonized and woven together. We should point out that our conception of meaning is very broad and allows for reference to what is valuable in itself—and to what each subject holds to be valuable in each case—in terms of a scale which we will attempt to define and order in terms of a hierarchy.

In the consciousness of the acting individual the meaning of an act and its spontaneous justification are the same. If the act was decided upon and undertaken, it was because it was clothed with meaning for the subject when it was singled out along with the things adjacent to it—which are quite varied in their extension and complexity—within the field of his consciousness. When self-consciousness exerts a strong influence, the attribution of meaning is complicated because something is added to the primitive or original meaning of the act itself. For, in the act that is lived spontaneously, without clear reference of the subject to himself, the determinative elements are desirability and possibility, that which concerns the act itself and only the act with its goal or objective and the means for its achievement. The subject, as it were, remains in the background for, although he produces the act and lives its meaning, he does not clearly apprehend himself as the agent, and he tends to be momentarily absorbed by his act. In the act that is reflective or accompanied by self-consciousness, an element that is new and of major significance appears: the subject, who sees himself as the agent and who must find meaning in the act—not in the act itself, but in it as *his* act, as the act of a self who recognizes himself as prior to, contemporary with, and successive to the act. In general, the breadth and height of the meaning depend on the extension of the horizon of the existences and values perceived and lived by the subject. They depend on the magnitude of the realm in which he resides and in which his own individuality moves, not only as the area of his action, but as the territory populated by many manifestations of being and valuing which he must take into consideration in diverse ways. Among the entities which at times do not emerge on this horizon and thus pass on as undetected and as nonexistent, and others which are emphasized and implanted upon it in different degrees of intensity and relief, there is the very subject of the act. At this point we will not discuss the psychological problem of whether the intensity of self-consciousness coincides with the degree of involvement and organization of the conscious realm in general. It is probable that they coincide in part but not absolutely, since there is a psychological type which is continually turned toward itself, observing, analyzing, and watching over itself with an unhealthy preoccupation. This attitude should not be confused with that of the vain megalomaniac who puts himself in the first place, sees himself as immeasurably great, and holds himself to be the most important thing in the world. This is an attitude which can be coupled with a small degree of self-perception.[3] What is important to emphasize here is this essential difference: in the spontaneous and direct act, with little or no self-consciousness, the meaning is rooted exclusively in the act; in the act with more or less clear self-perception, when the subject is aware of himself as the agent of the act, the meaning of the act is consciously manifest as the meaning of an act belonging to such a subject. The self-perceived subject and his act constitute the entity upon which the meaning falls. This does not establish a difference in the degree of the value to which this meaning may refer. Spontaneous and direct acts as well as those accompanied by self-consciousness can be good or bad, generous or stingy.

The problem we now confront does not demand that we decide if there actually are acts without self-consciousness or if, when there seems to be no self-consciousness, the consciousness of the act predominates to the extent that it obscures the perception of the self, reducing it to a minimum. One need only admit that, practically, the subject does not clearly apprehend himself as the agent of his act, whereas in other instances he knows himself to be present and takes himself into consideration. In the first kind of instance, as was stated, the act is justified through the meaning. In the second kind of instance, the act must have meaning for the subject as an act of his own, not only as an activity but also as a responsibility. It is as if the agent recognized that the act is neither something he performs and leaves behind without making an impression nor is it something that he turns loose when he finishes it. It is rather, for others and for himself, something that hence-

---

[3] As shown indirectly by inferiority complexes found in individuals who are strong introverts.

forth is an act performed by him, something that is irrevocably added to his own being, which will constitute a part of the accumulation of his past life condensed under the label of his name. For everyone, this past life is the most obvious reality of his being, the only reality which is his own which he can unequivocally display, since the pure present is only an instantaneous and ungraspable throbbing and the future is only hope and design. Having said this much, it is clear that self-consciousness in conceiving the act as one's own tends, at the same time, to conceive it as an act perceptible by others that will be judged by them although the real presence of others is not indispensable. An act which would have meaning when performed spontaneously, may appear to us as lacking meaning when we think that from now on it will be an act performed by us, something inseparable from our lives. An act which may have meaning in this second situation because we assent to it personally and justify it in our inner conscience, may be shown as lacking in meaning if it must brave public scrutiny, or if we imagine it as examined and judged by persons whom we love or greatly admire. For purposes of simplification we include all these situations in the act of self-consciousness, even though such a simplification annuls the nuances whose differentiation would be more in keeping with a special study of meaning.

When the act occurs in the vivid awareness that it is our act, its meaning serves concomitantly as justification of the act and as justification to the subject who performs it. In such an instance the subject is aware of his own partial development in his performance of the act. He is reflected and actualized in it and he feels it as an extension of himself. The simple, spontaneous act rests on its own inherent meaning, but, at times, when the subject thinks upon it, the meaning is insufficient. Everyone has an idea of himself, a conception of his being and of his significance. It would be too lengthy and complicated to identify the elements that compose the personality which each one attributes to himself, living it and "being it" in some cases, while in others he carries it as a secondary and superimposed reality, but not therefore lacking in effectiveness. For it is affirmed in rather diverse ways, ranging from the naïve belief that this is what one really is to a partial awareness of its falsity, although this carries with it the conviction that one must be thus or at least it is the way that one should conduct oneself in public. The component elements may depend on one's personal attitude toward life, of his own values, of everything that is his own, genuine background; but it may also depend on education, on examples and pressures of the family, class, or professional circles. When one acts with self-consciousness and—it might be said—in the presence of the idea that one has of oneself, the subject hesitates, though in a direct attitude he may have been drawn into committing a determined act. He stops and says "I cannot do that" (that is: "Such an act, performed by a subject, such as myself, lacks meaning") ; or "A man who has my name cannot perform such an act"; or he acts in accord with the pressure of his professional dignity, when exercised as an aspect of his person, or he acts in keeping with his racial, national, or class pride. In these situations it is the subject who looks on himself as the agent of the possible act. In other situations, according to what has been stated, he adheres to the idea that others have of him or that he wishes they had of him. The consideration of others is either taken indifferently or in levels or groups, from occasional acquaintances to those who deserve his love and respect, though they need not be spectators of the act or even know about it. Rather there is, on his part, a secret admission, as it were, of the idea that they have formed of him, which he values not only for its quality but because it provides the support of a favorable opinion. Yet, in other situations, it is a matter of the actual publicity of the action, the judgment concerning it expressed by those who really know the situation. In these situations one usually is a more severe judge of the behavior of others than of his own. For each one feels his own individual interests intensely; he lives his egoistical motives, and in his own fashion joins them with ultraindividual demands, either of a communal order or of a purely ethical order. Others, however, without the keen aliveness which the agent has in his private motives, detect to a greater degree the motives of an extraindividual nature when they judge his conduct. For this reason, all publicity is moralizing. Not only does it deprive certain acts of meaning by presenting them to the possible agent as elements of the situation which includes reprobation, but, in anticipation of imagined or expected publicity, it stimulates the highest motives, so that the subject's appreciation of them is enhanced through the belief that others will have comparable appreciation for these motives. However, in conditions of social dispersion, because of actual isolation of the individuals or reduced evidence of the idea of community in each of them, the great preponderance of narrow, individual motives is probable. Frequently these motives are weighed down with egoism, and they are contrary to common custom and to ethical imperatives. That interpretation which seeks to avoid vulgarity through rejection or depreciation of the "what will they say," is oversimplified at the least. Certainly, the "what will they say" is the opinion that will be voiced concerning our conduct by many spectators whose judgment is of little or no value or of a reverse value, where censure becomes praise and vice versa. But, to a large extent it is also what will be said by those in a position to appraise the conduct in the light of the highest and most extensive demands, for they do not feel as acutely what each subject takes as necessity, private convenience, and concrete interest. And it is well for each subject to look at himself in that mirror, to tame his egoistic impulses, and to strengthen those that lead to the common good or to the support of universal principles.

When considering meaning from the point of view of the agent, we can say, in keeping with what has been stated that in some cases the subject spontaneously lives his act alone, and the meaning of the act at that moment comes to be meaning for him, since his consciousness coincides at that instant with that of the act itself. In other cases, however, in the attempt to give meaning to the act as an act of his own, the subject takes himself into consideration, either in an honest manner, by achieving in his work the values to which he personally adheres, or through the intrigues of masking. In addition, the subject justifies himself in many other ways. If some act of the past appears to him at a later date to lack meaning, he will attribute it to lack of experience, insufficient education, bad examples, or pressure. He may reject it and put it away from himself, repenting of having done it, doing all he can to erase it from his present being. Whence comes this necessity of the subject to justify himself in the court of his own conscience? To what does it respond? Why must he find meaning in himself? Of all realities, one alone is complete and effective for each individual, one alone is absolute reality directly for him, and this is the reality which he is. Entities and values do not exist for him except as they are given to him; even divinity itself, which he may worship, exists tor him only to the extent that he believes in it. This absolute reality that each consciousness is to itself is over and above the distinction between the natural and the spiritual attitudes, or, better said, it includes them both. For within this absolute reality occurs the most outrageous affirmation of the concrete individual with his particular interests, as well as the purest attitudes of sacrifice and self-denial, of the denial of one's own impulses and the adherence to universal values, because these values come into the individual's realm only when he apprehends them and actively adheres to them. Paul Hoffmann maintains that philosophy must be renewed on the basis of this verification, which is not foreign to the reasons that were used by Husserl to found phenomenology. For Hoffmann, "to be" and "to be an object" have meaning only in their relation to the subject. That is, the subject experiences or perceives the world of what is and at the same time he perceives himself as an exceptional and incomparable instance, as a being with an intrinsic fullness of meaning which is juxtaposed to everything else. But the meaning itself is manifest to him as meaning only in the relation of his self with the world of objects, a relation which consists in knowing them and wanting them. Properly speaking, meaning is the living subjectivity of the self; everything outside of him is given at a distance from the self, a distance which is precisely the objective meaning through which all this is thought of as what "is." One must distinguish between the self-object (the object designated as a self) and the act of saying "I," which is what gives meaning to that object-self. In Hoffmann this interpretation of living intimacy as meaning leads to a conception of the meaning of life.

We agree with Hoffmann that the subject necessarily conceives himself as endowed with meaning and that he is the only and the universal bestower of meaning. The discrepancy between his view and that of Rickert is clear enough, but we do not believe that it is important for our purpose, which makes no attempt to exhaust the discussion of the problem, but selects from it what is indispensable for our anthropological scheme. Hoffmann emphatically centers the problem of meaning in the subject, whereas Rickert makes it depend on values. Yet, for Rickert, meaning is the connection between the reality of the act, which is the immediate product of the subject, and the values which the subject takes into consideration. Now if the act has an obviously subjective source, the values are given to the subject only through subjective grasp or appreciation. With this in mind, the difference between these two points of view is at least somewhat attenuated even if it is not completely erased. Rickert's proposal is of interest primarily for the absolute and final meaning of acts and of life.

Every act necessarily has meaning for the subject who performs it, at least when he decides upon it. Every subject aspires to meaning and, if he is aware that his meaning is not obvious to himself or to others, he attempts to heighten and emphasize it through justification, through propounding his own worth, through the search for power and prestige. Many times these are nothing more than ways of asserting one's own meaning. However, if all this can be verified without much difficulty, why is the problem of the meaning of life so serious and confused? Why have so many different answers been proposed, even by a single student of the matter, for example Nietzsche, who has successively set forth, as the supreme meaning of human life: creation, aesthetic enjoyment, cognitive investigation, and the will to power?

The reason for this is that, for man, the problem of meaning is not one; it is not the same for acts taken separately and for the subject or for human life as a whole. Meaning in itself is one and the same, and it implies the fullness and justification of the event or being upon which it falls. But the level or the platform from which meaning is apprehended and judged is different for the three instances we have mentioned. To appreciate the difference one must keep in mind that acts are temporally arranged; we might say, in the words of Ortega y Gasset, that they are conditioned by "man and his circumstance," and the most cursory observation reveals that these acts do not accord with one another, that they do not have the same unity of meaning for each subject. Just as every act, as an actual event, has meaning, so the subject feels and accepts its actual meaning, that of the instant which he is living, in keeping with the act which is performed in that instant, though perhaps it may not be in accord with the meaning of the act performed a few days or even a few moments before, and it may be in sharp disagreement with more remote acts. Regardless of the identity assigned to character and to the permanence allowed in the basic foundations of each subject, the fact of functioning introduces a change in the subject, because after each act he is not the same being as before. He is the self who performed the act, who feels compelled, because of the completed act and the new situation which it creates around him, to perform another. However, he may disown the act performed and find himself in the curious situation of harboring the traits of an act which he rejects and which he would like to cast away from himself. Every instant the subject is growing in vital and reflective experience because of the completed acts, assenting to some, dissenting from others, in a simultaneous solidarity with and struggle against his past. In order to grasp any meaning in the center of his own self—in the only way in which this is possible, that is to say, actually related to each act—one must disregard the meaning of much of one's past behavior. That is, one must perform the act—with actual meaning for oneself—of denying the meaning of certain previous proceedings of one's own, for one's present meaning depends in no small part on the denial or rejection of past meanings. Sufficient for distinguishing the meaning of the self from that of its acts, taken as a whole, is the awareness that, apart from its usual acts, the meaning of the self includes, in each instance—actually or possibly—the acceptance or the rejection of the meaning of acts that have already transpired. The self, therefore, achieves a unity of meaning through its present behavior and the position it assumes concerning its own past.

Just as the meaning of a subject's many acts and the meaning of the subject do not always coincide, neither do either of these coincide with the meaning of life.

For each individual, the meaning of life refers to his life as a single whole; it depends on the whole line of the parabola of life, appearing as endowed with a meaning. This includes life in its decisive experiences, in its general direction, and, above all, at its height and culmination. This culmination may be conceived as simultaneous with the actual end of existence, or it may be felt as occurring before death (the impression of a "completed life," of "having completed one's mission") . The difference between the meaning of life and that of acts—the mere sum of the acts—immediately becomes evident. Each act inevitably has meaning when it is performed, as was shown at the beginning of this chapter. But

the subject may view his whole life, at its conclusion, as either endowed with meaning or as lacking it. On occasions, a conscious and
decisive rejection of a part of one's past is an essential part of the
meaning of life, even when this part is very extensive, for example,
in conversions and repentances. Even in ordinary cases, many acts
are rejected whose meaning was obvious and perhaps central for
the agent when he performed them. This rejection occurs through
forgetting, through a simple separation, or perhaps through judging these events to be irrelevant to the meaning of life. The
meaning of life is also different from the meaning of the subject,
and in this regard we might repeat what was asserted above: the
subject cannot be conceived as lacking in meaning, but his life can
be conceived as lacking it, in an act of judgment or verdict which,
like every other act, is an act with meaning. That is to say that the
subject, who is the source of meaning, cannot decide that his life
does not have meaning except as he functions in his customary
form—as the source and performer of acts in which meaning is
inevitable.

Whereas the meaning of acts and of the subject are never absent,
the problem of the meaning of life may or may not be confronted.
The meaning of each act, and the meaning that for each individual
is rooted in his own being, are enough for man to live. However,
the fact that the problem of the meaning of life as a whole can be
stated, and that it is actually stated with frequency and with
varying degrees of clarity, derives from the fact that constitutes
man, namely, to be a subject in a world of objectivities. This
problem can be stated in terms of the meaning of human life in
general and in terms of the satisfaction, or lack of it, of one's own
life in particular, in its relation to the world seen as a closed series
of acts. That is, when life is reduced to a single complex act, and
the debits referred to have been subtracted, does life appear as
endowed with meaning or not? For beings in whom rather base
interests predominate, life can manifest meaning even in its last
stages if they find that in the final balance the goals they have
habitually persued are not found wanting—granting, of course,
that their values have not been other than wealth, pleasure, power,
or flattering vanity. This exception should be mentioned: one can
feel that there is meaning, though it may be imperfect and not
completely satisfactory. Taking all things into consideration, those

who live on this level and are content with what appears on it, are usually in a better situation to attribute final meaning to their lives than many who are keenly sensitive to spiritual demands, and who find the balance unfavorable to them because of the imbalance between what they achieved and what they feel they should have achieved. Naturally, the fullness of the meaning of life stems from the intimate link of the value of the goals pursued and the awareness of having devoted to them the best of one's energies—and in all probability the impression of success or effectiveness is included also.

Now we see how one assents to meaning and how, at times, it is disvalued on the basis of other meanings. The self, conscious of itself, can disvalue acts in which it failed to take itself into consideration; it may back away from them. In contemplating one's existence as a whole, one can deny meaning to many of one's acts performed without reference to the meaning attributed to the self. Meaning can also be denied to acts originally based on the meaning of one's self, if the image one has of oneself does not satisfy when evaluated on the basis of a completed life, which, henceforth, must be justified in itself, with no possibility for correction or change. At times one may attempt to attribute meaning to one's life by denying what one's accustomed self was, by lifting oneself above it with a dissatisfaction and scorn, which, in a special sense are ways of recovering and proclaiming a final meaning, which is built on a kind of self-condemnation. Complete satisfaction occurs only when the whole life is conceived, definitively, as bound to a reality or a constellation of values capable of conferring upon it a full, total, and unconditioned meaning.

Actually, in its highest form, the awareness of the meaning of life presupposes a component other than the mere fact that the final account, when taken as a closed book, is satisfactory. Considered in this way, each life would be a system immanent within itself and closed off from the rest. Man, however, as we have seen, is already an accelerated transcendence on his natural side, and he becomes an absolute transcendence on his spiritual side. The true meaning of life can only be found in transcending, that is, by seeing life as yielded to something higher, going beyond itself in order to affirm itself as something greater than itself. Not every man can conceive this problem clearly and confront it on his own.

But the problem is never lacking in cultures which are extensively objectified, collective structures; and, undoubtedly, one of the functions of such cultures is to satisfy the demand for meaning in human existence.

If we examine the three major cultures of which we have some knowledge—that of India, China and the West—we see that they have a certain dignity and universality which others do not have. It is because they have known how to find the formulae—perhaps the only three possible formulae—by means of which man has a destiny and feels that his life is endowed with meaning. Probably what has molded these cultures in their unequaled grandeur, is the obscure, collective desire to confer spiritual and transcendent meaning on human life. And what has afforded their long duration, their cohesive and cementing power, their amazing capacity to assimilate vast human masses has been that spontaneously and, we might say, automatically they provide in their midst what is indispensable if men are to feel that their existence is endowed with meaning. In all three cases, a reality of an extraordinary magnitude and dignity has been presented to the collective desire, a reality toward which each individual life could transcend, becoming inserted in it, and even spilling over into it. For the traditional culture of India, that reality is the great undivided whole, the common foundation from which all things and beings are born and in the presence of which each particular existence is a passing instance, without meaning in itself, and attaining meaning only as it becomes a part of the universal one. In the classical culture of China, the supreme reality is the social complex, conceived as a family governed by its ancestors, which carry it back to an infinite past and sanctify it by serving as the nexus with the supernatural order. For the culture of the West, the supreme reality is the marching spirit, in its personal form, which colonizes nature and develops in a manner ever more inclusive and perfect. Merely from the point of view of the meaning of life, each of these three cultures provides a purpose adequate for the individual to feel that his destiny has been fulfilled through his implicit or explicit adherence to that purpose. But of these three magnificent schemes only that of the West includes an element that, in keeping with what we have been saying, is fundamental to man: historicity. The Indian culture is nontemporalist, it disvalues and denies

time. The Chinese culture is "eternalist," it detains time and
paralyzes it when it places every present in the shadow of the past
as it subjects all living men to their ancestors. The culture of the
West, however, rests on time as a throbbing consecutiveness,
maintaining it as an indispensable ally in its purpose of historically achieving the demands of the spirit. Undoubtedly, our
culture has much to learn from the others; but it alone offers men
a way—a way which is none other than a broadening of the way
which, from the beginning, passes through every man. If the
citizens of the other cultures abandon them in order to join ours, it
is neither through caprice or passing fashion, nor because of an
exclusively materialistic outlook. It is because the culture of the
West—with all its stains, errors, and crimes—is the only one that
has known how to be at one with what is innermost and genuine in
the being of man. The two great and illustrious Asiatic cultures,
the only ones in which, outside of that of the West, we are able to
recognize a background of spirituality and universality,[4] undoubtedly confront transcendence with admirable goals. The individual
finds in them a satisfactory destiny when he is united to and even
dissolved in realities which infinitely surpass him and which he
imagines overflow with meaning. Yet, as has been said, both deny
not only the constitutive historicity of man, but also his condition
of being essentially a subject who is strengthened and purified in a
self, in a being who gradually universalizes himself and struggles
to implement the supremacy of the spirit. Both of them depreciate
and finally annul the human privilege of judging. Man is born
when he emerges as a subject, when he confers objectivity upon
the world through judgment. And upon assuming the spiritual
attitude, which is the supreme consequence, as we have seen, of
the objectifying attitude, he adds to the judgments of objectification and to those of intentional evaluation other evaluating judgments as a function of the spirit. The West has chosen a more difficult destiny, but it is also more worthy, acceptable, and satisfactory
than that chosen by the men of the great cultures of the East. It has
chosen not to give up judgment. It has made this principle

[4] We understand that the universal elements of the other great Asiatic culture—the Jewish—have been embodied in Western culture and that they form
an inseparable part of it.

intimately its own, for it is at the root and in the source of what is human, and, unconquered in its countless defeats, it embraces this principle and strives toward the far-flung goals of the future.

INDEX

INDEX